The Oberammergau
Passion Play

ALSO BY KEVIN J. WETMORE, JR.
AND FROM MCFARLAND

The Theology of Battlestar Galactica: *American Christianity in the 2004–2009 Television Series* (2012)

Back from the Dead: Remakes of the Romero Zombie Films as Markers of Their Times (2011)

The Empire Triumphant: Race, Religion and Rebellion in the Star Wars *Films* (2005)

Black Dionysus: Greek Tragedy and African American Theatre (2003)

The Athenian Sun in an African Sky: Modern African Adaptations of Classical Greek Tragedy (2002)

EDITED BY KEVIN J. WETMORE, JR.

Catholic Theatre and Drama: Critical Essays (2010)

Portrayals of Americans on the World Stage: Critical Essays (2009)

The Oberammergau Passion Play

*Essays on the 2010 Performance
and the Centuries-Long Tradition*

EDITED BY
KEVIN J. WETMORE, JR.

McFarland & Company, Inc., Publishers
Jefferson, North Carolina

ISBN (print) 978-0-7864-9603-7
ISBN (ebook) 978-1-4766-2794-6

LIBRARY OF CONGRESS CATALOGUING DATA ARE AVAILABLE

British Library cataloguing data are available

© 2017 Kevin J. Wetmore, Jr. All rights reserved

No part of this book may be reproduced or transmitted in any form or by any means, electronic or mechanical, including photocopying or recording, or by any information storage and retrieval system, without permission in writing from the publisher.

On the cover: "The Last Supper" (Passion Play Oberammergau 2010, photograph by Brigitte Maria Mayer)

Manufactured in the United States of America

*McFarland & Company, Inc., Publishers
Box 611, Jefferson, North Carolina 28640
www.mcfarlandpub.com*

To the memory of Claire Sponsler

Claire was a generous colleague and mentor whose scholarship made exceptional contributions to medieval studies and theatre studies. Her work on the American fascination with Oberammergau inspired many of the authors in this volume, and she moderated the conference panel from which this collection originally emerged. Claire passed away unexpectedly on July 29, 2016, as this volume was nearing completion.

Acknowledgments

I would like to thank a number of individuals without whom the volume would not exist:

First and foremost Jill Stevenson and the Religion and Theatre Focus Group of the Association for Theatre in Higher Education. Professor Stevenson organized the original panel out of which this project emerged and much of its success belongs to her. Her own scholarship has also strongly shaped mine, and I am duly grateful and want to express admiration and respect for her work in the field.

The contributors, especially Glenn, Jutta, David and Jill who have been with the project from the beginning, who have been patient with the process and with me, and whose scholarship inspired my own.

The College of Communication and Fine Arts and Loyola Marymount University, which have provided support, both for my research in Germany and for the volume itself, and its leadership, Dean Barbara Busse and Dean Bryant Keith Alexander.

Colleagues and friends who have been willing to discuss theatre and theology at length, including but not limited to Father Grant Garinger, S.J., and the Rev. Jeff Siker as well as David Sanchez and Cecilia Gonzalez-Andrieu. Thanks to Rob Hillig for his technical assistance with the images.

My family: Kevin Sr., Eleanor, Lisa, John, Sean, Tom, Eileen and Toni, and especially my wife, Lacy Wetmore, who put up with the long absences during research, and our son, Kevin III, and daughter, Cordelia, both born after my seeing the Passion Play but before the publication of this volume, who put up with long absences during writing.

And lastly the village of Oberammergau. All of the contributors to this volume traveled to Bavaria in 2010 to stay in the village, see the play and speak to the people who make it. Their kindness, generosity and artistry are greatly appreciated. We thank them for what they do, and encourage those who have not seen the play to travel to Oberammergau the next time it is performed. It is indeed an amazing experience.

Table of Contents

Acknowledgments	vi
Introduction: Forty-First in the Twenty-First	
KEVIN J. WETMORE, JR.	1

Part 1. Oberammergau 2010: Responses

The Role of Their Lives, or Jesus on a Bike: Oberammergau on Stage and Off	
GLENN EHRSTINE	16
"What's a nice Jewish boy like you doing in a Catholic play like this?": Oberammergau 2010 and Religious Identity	
KEVIN J. WETMORE, JR.	32
Dialectical Aesthetics of Change and Continuity in the 2010 Oberammergau Passion Play	
SHARON ARONSON-LEHAVI	53

Part 2. Comparative Oberammergaus

Spiritual Voyeurism and Cultural Nostalgia: Anglophone Visitors to the Oberammergau Passion Play, 1870–1925 and 2010	
JOSHUA EDELMAN	66
Atemporality in the Heidelberg Passion Play, the Passion Play of Oberammergau and Sarah Ruhl's *Passion Play: A Cycle*	
JUTTA EMING	88
Tableaus and Selves in Vrindavan and Oberammergau	
DAVID MASON	108
Oberammergau in America/America in Oberammergau	
KEVIN J. WETMORE, JR.	130

Part 3. Interviews

An Interview with Frederik Mayet (Actor, Christ)
   DAVID MASON 160

Passion Playing: An Interview with Sarah Ruhl on the Shaping Influence of Oberammergau
   JILL STEVENSON 168

Conclusion: Forty-Second in the Twenty-First: Oberammergau 2020 176

Works Cited 183

About the Contributors 191

Index 193

Introduction
Forty-First in the Twenty-First

KEVIN J. WETMORE, JR.

The Oberammergau Passion Play has been staged forty-one times since the initial vow was made in 1633. Once a decade the small Bavarian village mounts this huge production, with over half the local population taking part directly in the production. In 2010, 102 performances of the play were offered between May 15 and October 3. In that time, half a million people, over half from North America, descended on Oberammergau to see the play and its related epiphenomena as well as to experience the village itself. It is, for many, "a religious experience and not simply a day in the theatre."[1] Yet the production is part of a larger history of religion, civic identity, anti–Semitism, theatre and a tension between international perception and the actual activities of the villagers in performing the play.

Oberammergau is a small village on the Ammergau River, on the crossroads from Venice to southern Germany in very Catholic Bavaria, about an hour southwest from Munich. There is a monastery in nearby Ettal, and shrines to Mary everywhere. During the religious wars of the sixteenth and seventeenth centuries, the Ammer Valley was more Catholic than the pope. The Oberammergau Passion Play represented an embodiment of the village's faith.

History of the Passion Play

According to *Das Grosse Versöhnungsopfer auf Golgotha oder die Liedens- und Todes Geschichte Jesu [...] aufgeführt zu Oberammergau* (The Great Redemptive Sacrifice at Golgotha, or the Story of the Passion and Death of Jesus [...] Performed at Oberammergau), published in 1830 in Munich in conjunction with the performance of the Passion Play that year, the origins of the play were thus:

> In the year 1633 there raged in the neighboring districts [...] such an infectious disease that only a few people remained alive. Although the Ammer Valley is separated from those districts by mountains and all precautionary measures and steps were taken to protect people from this terrible scourge, it yet arrived here unexpectedly when a local labourer ... crept into his house having crossed the mountain by secret paths from Eschenlohe where he had been working in the fields during the summer, and brought the plague with him. Only two days later he had died, and within three weeks 84 people with him. In this universal distress the local community sought help from the Almighty—with a solemn vow publicly to present the story of the passion of Jesus, the world's Saviour, for grateful adoration and edifying contemplation. The power of faith won out—not another person died of the plague, although many had been struck down by the infection. In the following year, 1634, the story of Jesus' passion was performed for the first time in fulfilment of the vow.[2]

The village itself is in a sleepy little valley where the locals like to claim they have lived relatively unchanged for centuries. The official history of Oberammergau expands on the account above. As it notes, during the 30 Years War plague decimated the village. It was estimated that 21 percent of the village died. "Six and twelve" members of the village council deliberated and the solution they arrived at was The Vow. On October 27, 1633, the village council promised to perform Christ's passion and death every ten years if God delivered Oberammergau from the plague.

According to the official history of the village, the plague deaths ended immediately. The first Passionspiele performance was held a year later, in 1634, in a field outside of town. The tradition began and the number of performances began to grow. In 1680 the village changed the performance tradition from years that end in 4 to years that end in 0. There was no performance in 1770, as all passion plays were banned. There was no performance in 1920, because of World War I, although after the war, in 1922, a scaled-down version was presented. In 1934, for the three hundredth anniversary, the village celebrated a huge production, attended by Chancellor Hitler. There was, however, no performance in 1940, because of World War II. Production resumed again under the auspices of the American occupation in 1950. Other than an additional season of performances in 1984 for the sesquicentennial, the Oberammergau Passion Play has been presented every decade since 1950, uninterrupted.

The problem, as James Shapiro has outlined in his definitive book *Oberammergau: The Troubling Story of the World's Most Famous Passion Play*, is that the village's official history is not supported by the facts. According to Shapiro, the plague had more or less slowed down the previous July. The dying did not abruptly stop in October after the vow; there were at least two or three deaths per month after that. In fact, many scholars think the play predates the vow and represents a sixteenth-century village tradition given an official backstory in the late seventeenth century.

Interestingly, the local historians point out the inconsistencies, it's visitors from other nations and Catholic Germans from outside Oberammergau who perpetuate the myth.[3] This idea will be a recurring theme in this volume, especially "Oberammergau in America/America in Oberammergau": it is the visitors who need Oberammergau to be an unchanging, simple, pious village, who need the myth of Oberammergau. The villagers themselves are rather realistic about who they are and what they do, and have developed strategies, as discussed in "The Role of Their Lives, or Jesus on a Bike: Oberammergau on Stage and Off," to keep the frames of reference separate, both for themselves and for visitors.

The script has also undergone a process of evolution. Originally, for much of the seventeenth and early eighteenth centuries different texts had been used, but in 1750 Father Ferdinand Rosner, a Benedictine monk, wrote a baroque text for the Passion Play that remained in use until the nineteenth century. In 1811, Father Othmar Weis wrote a new version of the text. Weis's pupil, Father Alois Daisenberger, crafted yet another new version based on Weis's for the 1850 production. Almost all subsequent passion plays have been rooted in this version. As a result, for much of the twentieth century, even after the Second World War, the traditional script of Oberammergau was the product of mid–nineteenth-century thinking and theology. The most recent version has been developed over the past few cycles by Otto Huber; it is based on Daisenberger's play but responds to global criticism of the text, especially regarding anti–Semitism and the depiction of the Jews as Christ killers.

Though the present-day village is still small, and many of the traditions in regard to the Passion Play are still preserved, the community has also changed with the times. The current director, Christian Stückl, was born in Oberammergau, which allows him to serve as director, but he spends much of his professional life away from the village as a professional director in Munich, Salzberg and throughout much of German-speaking Europe. The village is neither isolated nor disconnected from contemporary Germany, although the tourist industry does benefit from the international identity of Oberammergau as an Alpine village that mounts the world's most famous passion play as a communal theatre project going back centuries. On the one hand, the Passion Play defines the village identity to this day (simple, wood-carving people who love Jesus, His Holy Church and the village of Oberammergau), on the other hand, it has become a huge tourist event attracting half a million visitors in performance years and still a regular but much smaller flow of tourists in off years.

Oberammergau's play is very Catholic—the original text was composed by priests, the theology of the text is Catholic, the theological advisor to the

Figure 1. Oberammergau, a "simple village" (photograph by the author).

play is also the theological advisor to the archbishop of Munich, and until recently only Catholics in good standing could participate; indeed the very identity of the play is rooted in German Catholicism, as is argued in "'What's a nice Jewish boy like you doing in a Catholic play like this?': Oberammergau 2010 and Religious Identity." Indeed, James Shapiro identifies the very existence of the play as good Catholic theology—the vow is an object lesson "in the efficacy of good works."[4] In more recent years the specific denominational aspects of the play have been downplayed by the village, partly in response to a changing German church but just as much to appeal to non–Catholic Christian tourists, who find in Oberammergau a story that reflects their perception of the historical reality of the events at the start of the Christian faith. "Protestants who praised the Oberammergau Passion Play often described it as a journey back in time."[5] There is a narrative here that continues into the twenty-first century—especially given that American Protestants, who do not believe in the efficacy of good works, form a large contingent of attendees—that the power of the story of Christ is still relevant today. And yet, the whole experience of the play is pure nostalgia.

Furthermore, according to Gordon R. Mork, the post-war attendance by English-speaking audiences tended to be dominated by Protestants instead of Catholics, who "looked upon the trip to Oberammergau as a deeply religious experience."[6] My own experience at Oberammergau confirmed this. I had several meals with a Baptist couple from North Carolina who were in the same hotel as I who were deeply moved by the play and not at all troubled by the Catholic origins of it, despite their own belief that Catholics were "wrong." At dinner after the play ended the husband told me the play got everything right: "It was exactly how it happened." There is a sense of Oberammergau as time machine, not just back to medieval pilgrimage passion tradition but also back to first-century Judea, in which audiences catch a glimpse of how it must have been, reinforced by the idea that these are not movie stars or professional actors (although the director, designer, music director and several of the actors are, in fact, professionals) but simple, rural people fulfilling their ancestors' vow to pay honor to God and Christ. The sensation of being there is a powerful one. The power is rooted in nostalgia for a simpler time that most if not all in the audience have never known, but imagine regularly.

When we perform medieval theatre, we are doing theology and we are engaging theological texts that make statements about the relationship between the human and the divine. What strikes me as particularly challenging about modern stagings of premodern plays, including the Oberammergau Passionspiele, is that the theology of the plays is frequently not the theology of the audience. The Oberammergau Passion Play to this day still evinces a medieval Catholic theology that the audience, especially the Protestant audience members, seems to ignore in favor of this nostalgic view of both play and Biblical event.

And yet, locally and in advertisements for the play in 2010 there was a tension between the religious/faith aspects of the show and the idea that the play represented civic tradition as much as if not more than the religious aspect. Already by the mid-twentieth century, the Passion Play evinced a de-emphasis on religion and the promotion of tradition and history, partly to reinforce the above-discussed erasure of doctrinal differences and partly because religion itself was under fire, at the turn of the century, in the wake of the Holocaust and in postmodern Europe, especially in Germany. The village's play, therefore, was presented as much an aspect of Germany history and the civic identity of Oberammergau as religious identity. The play also served as a counter not only to postmodernity but could also serve as an erasure of modernity. As will be argued in "Oberammergau in America/America in Oberammergau," Americans especially needed Oberammergau to be the image of Oberammergau presented in the United States, as it served as a model of a more simple, more Christian time, in contrast to the conflicts created by technology, immigration and modernization. In that sense, is

Oberammergau that different in the early twenty-first century from how it was in the early twentieth? The 2010 production took place during debates in both the European Union and the United States in regards to immigration and the fear that the religion and culture of the immigrants would prevent assimilation. Likewise, the production came at a time of increased awareness of technological and global changes. (My hotel, like all others, advertised its free wi-fi!)

Indeed, the common narratives in popular media show the paradoxical nature of Oberammergau: the people are "simple villagers" (that phrase appears a good deal)—common folks, not professional artists (except, of course, for all the ones who are, but we won't count that as they were born in Oberammergau and cannot help that they are not wood carvers but professional theatre artists outside of the Passion Play), and the village is also a multicultural enclave fully in the digital era (many of the articles in the build-up to the 2010 production cited non–Germans who were born and live in the village, especially the significant Turkish population, and also made sure to mention the actors' use of cell phones and email). They are a simple, mountain people who live in twenty-first-century Germany. The paradox of the narrative is how different Oberammergau is and yet how not.

The next great narrative of Oberammergau is that the village performs the play out of piety, not out of commercialism (except it does and by 2010 many participants claim to no longer be Christian and are deeply troubled by the Church, all the reviews focus on how much the village relies on the Passionspiele for income to survive the next ten years and also mention the many souvenirs for sale throughout the village). The village is admittedly a place of pilgrimage that is also a tourist destination. (Jill Stevenson referred to her trip in 2010 as "probably as close to understanding a medieval pilgrimage as I'll ever get."⁷) As noted above, many do have genuine religious experiences there, and yet the village can also be viewed as a place of tremendous commercialization of religion. Every shop carried the same souvenirs and tchotchkes: mousepads, t-shirts, jackets, hats, compact discs of the music, postcards, mugs, etc. In fairness, pace Stevenson, medieval pilgrimages and pageant plays were also tremendous commercial events, with large numbers of merchants offering all kinds of wares. In that sense, there is continuity in contemporary Oberammergau of the medieval experience of a Passion Play.

The twenty-first-century incarnation of Oberammergau was a product of the cumulative developments of the past hundred and twenty years. By the end of the nineteenth century, the play had become a tourist destination. Three primary reasons were the cause of this. First, improved transportation made it easier to reach the village: a rail line finally extended from Munich into Oberammergau. Second, at the end of the nineteenth century, after long centuries of religious wars and conflict, Europe saw a diminishing antagonism between Catholics and Protestants. Lastly, there was an increase in public awareness of the play through presentations by those who had been and even those who had not. Oberammergau was presented in travel literature and lectures as a sort of real Brigadoon—an inaccessible mountain village that opens once every ten years to show modern Westerners how people lived centuries ago. This marked the beginning of the Oberammergau myth. While villagers, as noted above, do not perpetuate it, it is used by travel companies to promote the Passion Play.

The play was problematized for many by the rise of the Nazis. Hitler attended the play in 1930 and again to great fanfare in 1934 for the tercentennial production as chancellor, a short time before that office was merged with the presidency to make Hitler "führer" in August. His visit to the play was a major event for both him and the village, and is detailed in Helena Waddy's book *Oberammergau in the Nazi Era: The Fate of a Catholic Village in Hitler's Germany*.[8] In a speech to the community after he witnessed the performance, Hitler said:

> One of our most important tasks will be ... to remain forever watchful in the knowledge of the menace of Jewry. For this reason alone it is vital that the Passion Play be continued at Oberammergau; for never has the menace of Jewry been so convincingly portrayed as in the presentation of what happened in the times of the Romans. There one sees in Pontius Pilate a Roman racially and intellectually so superior, that he stands out like a firm, clean rock in the middle of the whole muck and mire of Jewry.[9]

The Nazis adored Oberammergau as it fit their narrative in regard to the Jews. This adoration would make the play problematic in the postwar period, as outlined by Waddy and Shapiro. The play was not performed in 1940 because of the war, and a changed Oberammergau performed again in 1950, where, as will be discussed in "Oberammergau in America/America in Oberammergau," the United States military allowed it to be performed as part of the recuperation of Germany. Alois Lang was not allowed to play Christ since he had been a Nazi party member, but he was allowed to perform the prologue.

In the wake of the Second World War, criticism of anti–Jewish elements in the Passion Play increased, most notably from American sources, especially Jewish ones and groups dedicated to Jewish/Christian relations. Although Oberammergau resisted change, by the 2000 production, substantial changes were being made in response to criticism, although the changes failed to blunt the criticism or meet the requirements of those demanding change.[10] The changes were put into place by the artistic team that was also responsible for the 2010 production, which saw the most substantial changes yet.

The men most responsible for Oberammergau in 2000 and 2010 are the previously mentioned Christian Stückl and Otto Huber, who for all practical purposes wrote a new text for 2010. These two men have worked on the production in 1990 (when Stückl was only twenty-eight years old), 2000, and 2010. These are the two who have had far more influence in reshaping and changing the Passion Play for the twenty-first century. They and their work are well represented in this volume. See especially "The Role of Their Lives, or Jesus on a Bike: Oberammergau on Stage and Off," "Dialectical Aesthetics of Change and Continuity in the 2010 Oberammergau Passion Play" and "Atemporality in the Heidelberg Passion Play, the Passion Play of Oberammergau and in Sarah Ruhl's *Passion Play: A Cycle*."

They are not the only ones responsible for the changes, as they are appointed by the Passion Play committee, which is a civic organization within the village. Furthermore, the majority of the village must support the desired changes, as the play involves much of the village of approximately five thousand. Twenty-five hundred individuals applied to be considered for roles in the play, including a ninety-year-old man and an as-then-unborn infant, whose parents applied to have the child on stage, since he would be born before the performances began in May 2010.[11]

In addition to textual changes, the village moved to further modernize the experience by changing the start time in 2010. The production now begins at 14:30 with a dinner break before the second half in the evening, instead of nine or ten in the morning with a lunch break before the second half in the afternoon. This means the crucifixion now takes place at night, and the audience exits the play under the stars, rather than in the late afternoon sun and heat. The change has been transformative.

Also of significance in 2010 are the epiphenomena of the production: a light show set to music in the village church, a lecture series in the Kleine Theatre, ecumenical services, artistic displays, a museum, the environment of the theatre itself, with a series of displays around the building, not to mention dozens if not a hundred shops filled with wood carvings, Passionspiel memorabilia (I am wearing my Oberammergau 2010 baseball cap as I write this), and other souvenirs. One does not go to Oberammergau simply to attend a play. It has become like attending any festival or, to the cynic, a theme park—there are multiple events, performances and activities. Most packages to the village are three days, two nights, so one arrives, has time to see the other events and shop, have a day dedicated to the Passion Play, and then a day to finish up and depart. Furthermore, the experience is shaped by the fact that the cast also all work and live in the village. Thus one might watch the apostles question Jesus at the Last Supper, and then return to one's hotel to be served dinner by one of those same apostles. Glenn Ehrstine explores this phenomenon much more in his essay. The commerce and the epiphenomena also shape the village's identity both in and of themselves and in terms of the literal messages in the lectures, museum displays, church services and municipal tablets and signs.

Lastly, 2010 was further problematized by the global financial crisis. Visitors to the village were reduced by 20 percent, but ticket prices were doubled and hotels charged more at a time when the United States dollar and British pound were weak against the Euro.[12] Many reviews and previews of the 2010 performance discussed at length how the global economy affected Oberammergau. One thing to note is that the increase in prices also makes the event aimed more at those who can afford the expensive production, and while the village might still be perceived as simple and poor, the audience grows ever more elite.

The volume you hold in your hands concerns the 2010 production, while also looking toward 2020 and the next performance of the Oberammergau Passion Play. The 2010 production was seen by scholars from the United States, United Kingdom, Germany and Israel, all of whom attended the play individually. Each was then invited to write an essay engaging the 2010 production. Some compared the performance with other texts and performances, others examined specific aspects of the 2010 show that marked the changes and continuity of the event. All of us look to cite and site our experiences of the play in 2010 to give a sense of what this unique and remarkable event is and means. There is some overlap, especially about anti–Semitism and 2010's attempts to combat that charge. By nature, projects of this sort can be repetitive, especially since many of the scholars involved wrestle with the same issues. All of the essays engage in some way with James Shapiro's seminal *Oberammergau: The Troubling Story of the World's Most Famous Passion Play* (2000), now a decade and a half out of date, yet still the dominant study of the cultural phenomenon. Despite any repetition or overlap, however, it is my hope that when put in conversation with one another, the nine essays of this book form an intertextual discussion that creates a much more complex portrait of the village and its play than any one essay could. I think it fair to say that all contributors greatly enjoyed their experience of Oberammergau and its Passion Play, and even those of us who critique it do so from a place of sincere admiration and respect for the village, the villagers and the production.

The volume is divided into three parts. The first part consists of three essays that are responses to the 2010 production. The *Los Angeles Times* travel section for June 6, 2010, featured an extensive narrative by Susan Spano who went to the village and saw the Passion Play in its opening weeks. Delighted by the rural, small village charm, her hotel and Oberammergau's restaurants, she noted, "I'm pretty sure I saw this season's Mary Magdalene riding a bike across the square."[13] In an interview for this volume, Frederik Mayet, one of two actors who played Jesus, admits he would frequently ride his bicycle around town during intermission on the days he was performing. Seeing Biblical figures on bicycles (the preferred mode of transport in the village in the summer, which allows the cast to move quickly to and from the theatre through the small, crowded streets) became a recurring theme in the press. In "The Role of Their Lives, or Jesus on a Bike: Oberammergau on Stage and Off" Glenn Ehrstine argues that extra-theatrical appearances of the cast are equally performative, as the actors are identified with their roles. The village itself is a set, the extra-theatrical framing of the play—the media, the actual physical village of Oberammergau with its painted walls, the deliberate cultivation of medieval imagery in the architecture and streets, and the performers seen in public all contribute to the larger experience and meaning of Oberammergau. Ehrstine also looks at the borders and how porous they are: between villager and outsider, between performer and role, between performer and spectator. He argues the above-discussed influx of tourists from Europe and North America since the late nineteenth century is what has developed the extra-theatrical apparatus that actually maintains the medieval experience of the play: "its continuing function as devotional theater, one based in ritual, piety, and the belief in efficacious performance." Or to put it glibly, Oberammergau works because we feel it working. The audience is allowed a vicarious experience of community and devotional theatre. Ehrstine also makes very valid and interesting observations about the reinvention of the self for the performers, since they are "always on," so to speak.

The next two essays explore the Jewish influence and identity present in the 2010 Oberammergau Passion Play. In "What's a nice Jewish boy like you doing in a Catholic play like this?" I analyze the Catholic history and nature of the play before considering how the 2010 production represents Jesus and his followers as Jewish. The play remains very Catholic, but the Jewishness of Jesus is emphasized. A close reading of the script and of reviewers' constructions of the play are the tools by which I evaluate the shift in both Jesus's identity as more Jewish and the village's identity as less Catholic, while still maintaining a very devotional, pious, medieval Catholic narrative within the play.

Conversely, Sharon Aronson-Lehavi considers the Oberammergau Passion Play through the lenses of Jewish artists in "Dialectical Aesthetics of Change and Continuity in the 2010 Oberammergau Passion Play," offering a unique perspective on Christian iconography. She explores the use of design (color, shape, texture, other visual elements, etc.) to generate meaning in the production that veers away from the traditional anti–Semitic, anti–Jewish tropes and instead engages a Jewish Jesus through Jewish artists. As her title suggests, the play paradoxically is both changed and the same, yet can be understood differently in 2010.

The second part, "Comparative Oberammergaus," offers another four essays comparing and contrasting the 2010 Passion Play with other experiences of religious drama, from Oberammergau's own past, from other Passion Plays from Europe and America and from Indian pilgrimage drama, as well as an exploration of the historic shaping influence of Oberammergau on Passion Plays in the United States and the shaping influence on Oberammergau of American audience members, particularly in 2010.

In "Spiritual Voyeurism and Cultural Nostalgia: Anglophone Visitors to the Oberammergau Passion Play, 1870–1925 and 2010," Joshua Edelman explores the hybridity of the Oberammergau experience, both in 2010 and a century ago. Relying on accounts of the Oberammergau Passion Play from late nineteenth- and early twentieth-century British and American tourists' narratives as well as his own experience at the 2010 production, Edelman explores in much greater depth than this introduction the idea of cultural nostalgia—that Oberammergau allows visitors to experience a replica of something that never existed.

Oberammergau can be "read" in a variety of conflicting ways: spiritual pilgrimage versus "tourist trap," nostalgic religion versus capitalist modernity, devotional art versus cynical commerce and monetized tradition. In Edelman's telling example, on the reverse side of the Oberammergau Passion Play tickets was an advertisement for BMW. Edelman, considers how critics "treat Oberammergau anthropologically, not theologically."

In his survey of tourist narratives from the turn of the nineteenth century to the twentieth, Edelman observes the construction of the world-weary urbane sophisticate who finds simple beauty and charm in the artless, rustic, rural performance, itself valued more for its simple pious devotion rather than any artistic achievement. While 2010 brought about a shrunken "global village," Oberammergau still consciously projects and presents itself as a "simple Alpine village, whose humble and pious citizens embrace and continue this centuries old tradition." Edelman also discusses the double coding of the 2010 Oberammergau script. Moving beyond what I do in my essay, he argues that the use of the Shema and unattributed quotations from the poetry of Hannah Senesh represent a signal to Jewish audience members that is not likely recognizable to Christians.

Jutta Eming compares Oberammergau 2010 not with its past incarnations, but with another historical German Passion Play and a contemporary American theatrical exploration of Passion Plays. "Atemporality in the Heidelberg Passion Play, the Passion Play of Oberammergau and Sarah Ruhl's *Passion Play: A Cycle*" proposes to examine three passion play "traditions": the late medieval Heidelberg Passion Play, the Oberammergau Passion Play and Sarah Ruhl's remarkable *Passion Play*. The larger concerns Eming brings to the fore are the Tableau Vivant and Jewish identity as well as the relationship between past and present in Passion Plays. She engages the visual aspects of the tableau, noting their "atemporality—the visual images of the production are non-chronological and are presented out of order." These images therefore form a matrix of interpretation for atemporality in Passion Plays. Eming reminds us that traditional Passion Plays begin as "contemporary" events that represent the past. Like the Heidelberg Passion Play and the Oberammergau Passion Play, American playwright Sarah Ruhl offers a "modern play" (for its time) about the past. Eming is concerned with "what it means to put on a passion play and where its points of contact with the present lie." In 1634, a fairly homogenous society created a Passion Play. In 2010, a fairly heterogeneous society creates one based on that original. Thus Oberammergau 2010 presents three levels of time: the present, Oberammergau's historic past and Biblical time, which in and of itself consists of both the events in first-century Palestine and the Hebrew Bible. The role of the players in Oberammergau is to link all three (or four) periods together, which creates its own set of complications.

The tableau are also of concern to David Mason, who, in "Tableaus and Selves in Vrindavan and Oberammergau," opens with a discussion of the philosophical underpinnings of naturalism and mimetic performance, noting the tableaus are non-naturalistic in contrast to the more mimetic scenes from the play proper. Relying on role theory and reader response theory, Mason proposes understanding the non-mimetic nature of the Oberammergau Passion Play through Indian devotional theatre. Just as Oberammergau dramatizes the story of Jesus, Vrindavan dramatizes the story of Krishna through the use of *râs lila* puppets. Mason argues that Oberammergau is implicitly non-mimetic, especially in the tableau moments, even as it is explicitly mimetic in dramatizing scenes from the gospels, literally transforming the selves of the audience, who are also playing a role as spectators to the event.

Also concerning transformation is my essay "Oberammergau in America/America in Oberammergau." Beginning with a survey of the construction of Oberammergau in the American popular imagination from 1880 to 1950, I offer the 1897 Edison Manufacturing Company film *The Oberammergau Passion Play* as a model for understanding American perception of Oberammergau. The film, despite its title, was actually made in New York City, on a rooftop, with American actors. Numerous other public lectures and presentations would also offer to the public images of Oberammergau that were not actually of the village or its play but constructions based on travel photos and other Passion Plays, all in the service of a narrative of a village in Germany that showed a simple, pious village holding onto medieval Christianity in the face of modernity. American productions attempted to create the same mythos for themselves by either being dubbed or dubbing themselves "America's Oberammergau." Many of these productions frame themselves as similar but superior to the German play, overlaying the piety of Oberammergau with American nationalism.

Using this idea as a base, I go on to consider the shaping influence of American groups that either work with or publicly critique the village for the anti-Semitism supposedly still in the script for 2010. I argue that in the United States the 2010 Passion Play was also framed by the controversies surrounding Mel Gibson's *The Passion of the Christ*, which was also accused of anti-Jewish content and distorting the gospels. I close with a survey of American critical reviews of the 2010 production which focused more on the civic identity of the village in a multicultural, digital era, instead of the religious content.

As Jeremy Cohen observes, the challenge of analyzing Oberammergau is a complex one, as to criticize the play is to criticize the village and its citizens as well, for the village's entire identity is invested in, shaped by, and rooted in the Passion Play.[14] "The play has steered the course of critical life decisions, from negotiating family matters and choosing a vocation to planning for the years ahead, from one performance to the next."[15] Performers and technicians, all involved in the production, come from the same families for generations, going back to the vow. It is our hope that we have met the challenge of respectful critique and analysis.

The third part of the volume consists of a pair of interviews with individuals related to Oberammergau. David Mason interviewed Frederik Mayet, one of the two actors who plays Christ and who also works in the publicity office for the production as well a press liaison by the Müchner Volkstheater. Mayet offers insights and information about the process of rehearsing and performing the play, as well as his own perspective on Oberammergau 2010 and also looking forward to the 2020 production. Jill Stevenson interviews American playwright Sarah Ruhl, the subject of Eming's essay in this volume, on the influence of the Oberammergau Passion on Ruhl's own drama, *Passion Play*. Ruhl was inspired to write her play by the German Passion, which was the result of a commission to write, in Ruhl's words quoted by Stevenson, "a play about America, and I figured there's nothing more American than the nexus of religion, politics, and the theater." Stevenson, who has also written elsewhere about Oberammergau and Passion Plays, cannily explores with Ruhl how Oberammergau continues to shape and influence American understandings of religious theatre.

The volume closes with a conclusion looking toward 2020. Obviously this project began with the 2010 Oberammergau Passion Play, but as it developed and took shape, we also began to look at how the forces that shaped 2010 would begin to affect the next production. As this book is completed just past halfway through the decade, we stand in between performances of the passion. It is our hope that this book might shine a light on what happened in 2010 and look forward to what might happen in 2020, allowing those who attend that production to have greater insight into the experience.

Notes

1. Council of Centers on Jewish-Christian Relations. *Ad Hoc Committee Report on the 2010 Oberammergau Passion Play Script.* May 14, 2010. http://www.ccjr.us/images/stories/CCJR_Oberammergau_Report_2010May14.pdf. Accessed March 23, 2014. 5.
2. Quoted in George W. Brandt and Wiebe Hogendoorn, eds., *German and Dutch Theatre, 1600–1848* (Cambridge: Cambridge University Press, 1993) 64.
3. James Shapiro, *Oberammergau: The Troubling Story of the World's Most Famous Passion Play* (New York: Vintage, 2000) 108.
4. Shapiro 108.
5. Sonja E. Spear, "Claiming the Passion: American Fantasies of the Oberammergau Passion Play, 1923–1947." *Church History* 80.4 (December 2011): 842.6.
6. Gordon R. Mork, "Christ's Passion on Stage—The Traditional Melodrama of Deicide." *Journal of Religion and Film* 8.1 (2004): http://www.unomaha.edu/jrf/2004Symposium/Mork.htm.
7. Jill Stevenson, "Oberammergau's Passion Play 2010: Performance and Context." *Material Religion* 7.2 (2011): 304.
8. See Helena Waddy, *Oberammergau in the Nazi Era: The Fate of a Catholic Village in Hitler's Germany* (Oxford: Oxford University Press, 2010).
9. Jeremy Cohen, *Christ Killers: The Jews and the Passion from the Bible to the Big Screen* (Oxford: Oxford University Press, 2007) 215.
10. See Shapiro.
11. Don Heimburger, "Behind the Passion: Backstage at Oberammergau's Forty-First Passion Play." *German Life* (February/March 2010): 21.
12. Oana Lungescu, "Bavarian Passion Plays to Global Crowds." BBC News Europe. 31 May 2010. www.bbc.co.uk/news/10198502. Accessed April 25, 2012.
13. Susan Spano, "In the Alps, a Saving Grace." *Los Angeles Times* (June 6, 2010): L4.
14. Cohen 216.
15. Cohen 216.

Part 1

Oberammergau 2010: Responses

The Role of Their Lives, or Jesus on a Bike
Oberammergau on Stage and Off
Glenn Ehrstine

Although it is heir to the theatrical traditions of the late Middle Ages, little about the contemporary Oberammergau Passion Play is in fact medieval. First performed in 1634 on the cemetery grounds of the local village church of St. Peter and Paul, the play now takes place in the capacious 4,700-seat *Passionsspielhaus* (Passion Play House), constructed at the end of the nineteenth century. The music for the 2010 performance was not even two hundred years old, originally composed by local schoolteacher Rochus Dedler in 1811 and adapted with new additions by current musical director Markus Zwink. Indeed, the one truly medieval foundation of the Oberammergau performance tradition—the late fifteenth-century Augsburg Passion Play,[1] one of two texts that underlie the oldest surviving Oberammergau play manuscript of 1662—has had no lasting influence: revised as early as 1674, the text of 1662 ceased to serve as a basis for local performances by 1750, when Ferdinand Rosner, a monk from the nearby Benedictine Monastery of Ettal, composed his *Passio Nova*, a complete reworking of the text, itself more recently superseded by the 1860 script of village priest Joseph Daisenberger.[2] While there has been discussion of returning to earlier roots—Hans Schwaighofer directed a 1977 revival of the Rosner play, one which he had hoped to mount as the official 1970 Oberammergau production before villagers voted against the plan[3]—no one talks of returning to the text of 1662, much less to one from the late 1400s, so that a revised version of the Daisenberger text remains the basis of current performances.

To judge by sheer audience size, contemporary Oberammergau performances certainly seem more reminiscent of modern mass spectacle than medieval theatrical practice. An estimated 515,000 spectators attended the one hundred and nine performances that made up the 2010 season[4]; indeed, the play has attracted on average roughly a half-million visitors every ten years since the early twentieth century. The obvious touristic aspects of recent tradition have not redounded to Oberammergau's reputation, at least not among scholars of medieval theater. Alexandra Johnston contrasts Oberammergau, for example, with the *Assumption of the Virgin* as performed every August in Elche, a town of over 200,000 in Spanish Catalonia; Elche represents the more authentically medieval performance tradition because this Catalonian community performs its play for itself, i.e., for an audience composed primarily of area residents and dignitaries, whereas Oberammergauers perform primarily for visitors.[5] Seen from the perspective of fostering community, the focus of Johnston's analysis, there is no denying that the Bavarian village maintains a strict boundary between locals and outsiders, not only for spectators, but particularly for performers: if one is not a native, one can act in the play only after having lived for twenty years in the village, although a shortened, ten-year waiting period is permitted for those who marry a local resident. Yet Elche similarly limits participation in the *Assumption* to the native-born.[6] Perhaps the deciding factor that has preserved the communal focus of the Elche tradition, the intertwined identities of performing and viewing communities, is that it is calendar specific. Performed only once a year on the Feast of the Assumption (August 15), it cannot be extended over a whole playing season without losing its ties to the liturgical calendar. Still, should the Oberammergau tradition be less authentic simply because it attracts a far larger audience, one in which performers and spectators are strangers to each other?

As I argue in the following, the influx of foreign spectators over the past one hundred and fifty years in Oberammergau has promoted the development of a modern, extra-theatrical apparatus that paradoxically helps to maintain what is arguably the play's medieval core: its continuing function as devotional theater, one based in ritual, piety, and the belief in efficacious performance. For while audience members cannot experience the play as a member of the Oberammergau community, they can join that community vicariously. In the following, I would like to examine Oberammergau's current array of extra-theatrical measures, those aspects of the Oberammergau experience that do not belong to the play proper, but nonetheless frame the primary performance and shape audience reception by making the role play engaged in by locals transparent. Some, such as the off-stage appearance by local actors, are performative, while others, like the play text with foreword made available to all visitors, are medial, but all such measures are designed to activate a twofold viewing of the passion by the audience, inviting them to see not just the story presented, but also the act of piety or community engagement inherent therein. As I hope to demonstrate, such extra-theatrical play components are indispensable for any type of ritual theater that has become dislodged from its original cultural context if it is to maintain its claim to efficacy.

Ritual Performance and Two-Fold Viewing

In two-fold audience reception, the spectator is conscious of the role play engaged in by performers, perceiving it as "restored" or "twice-behaved behavior" as defined by Richard Schechner.[7] In Schechner's model, which considers theater in a broad sense as both entertainment and ritual, all performance is twice-behaved, i.e., an actor's actions reproduce and cite from a variety of social behaviors found in everyday life. In the illusionistic/realistic tradition familiar to Western audiences, however, the essential "twiceness" of performance is customarily hidden. A successful performance is judged primarily on an actor's ability to disappear behind the character portrayed, and audience knowledge of the actor's personal circumstances is not essential. Star performers might attract interest in their private life, but in most cases performers assume roles independent of biographical background or group affiliation. The rewards for a successful performance are clear: professional actors are paid for their time, in addition to whatever social capital may accrue to them, whereas amateur performers make do with social capital alone.

In contrast, ritual performance, whether a medieval passion play or an ostensibly primitive fertility rite, derives its efficacy from the overlapping, yet distinct identities of participants as both role player and community member. Here, actors and audience are united in a mutual social or religious community; except in some cases of masking,[8] a performer's everyday identity remains known to observing spectators or co-participants. Performance by and for a contained community thus guarantees a two-fold perception of performance activity, with the viewer reflecting not only on the role presented, but also on the personal circumstances of the performer, including social status and motivation for assuming the part. Pecuniary motives are secondary, if not wholly anathema to the purpose of such ritual enactments. The performers' rewards accrue, in Schechner's terms, in relation to "an absent Other,"[9] i.e., some type of deity, and they hope to secure other types of benefits: a good harvest, the curing of illness, or some other efficacious result. The performances are thus often propitiatory in nature, seeking the deity's support for a particular undertaking. Accordingly, the personal circumstances of performers must be acceptable to the powers that be, divine or otherwise: whereas a Hollywood actor might parlay misbehavior into increased marketability, a ritual actor must lead a life beyond reproach as measured by community standards. The expectation of exemplary conduct in the private lives of performers is perhaps best illustrative of the inseparability of on- and off-stage realities in a ritual performance context.

The simultaneous perception of role player and role played occurs naturally when audience members are co-participants. Two-fold viewing as a basis for efficacious performance continues to function for community members even when outsiders are present, provided they represent a minority of spectators. Once strangers outnumber locals, however, the essential intertwining of on- and off-stage perception breaks down. The results can be "touristic" in the pejorative sense, such as the Asaro mudmen dance in New Guinea, in which the original community-affirming function of the dance—commemorating a mythic moment in the history of the village, when attackers took the mud-smeared bodies of locals who had been hiding along the local riverbank to be ancestral spirits and fled—has been supplanted by the commercial interests of tourist agencies, who bus in spectators looking for exotic entertainment rather than cultural understanding.[10] Since there is little shared cultural context between audience and performers, whose everyday lives remain invisible to their guests, two-fold viewing remains elusive here, even for those who may seek some type of cultural understanding.

However, it is possible to promote a doubled awareness of performer as well as performed persona through other means. The most familiar approach in a non-ritual context is Bertolt Brecht's *Verfremdungseffekt* (alienation or distancing effect): through direct addressing of the audience, acting style (*Gestus*), and other techniques, Brecht sought to make actors' role play visible, distancing the audience from the characters on stage so that they might reflect on the circumstances of the performance.[11] However, given Oberammergau's tendency to attract a culturally conservative audience, one that would be discomfited by a non-realistic performance,[12] the village has developed other, less alienating means of doubling spectators' perception of local stage illusion. After an initial examination of the Oberammergau passion play tradition in the context of ritual performance, my essay focuses on the extra-theatrical, secondary reception frame established for visitors via media, village material culture, and public encounters with actors, particularly an out-of-costume Christ. These medial and live interactions draw back the veil on village life for out-of-town guests, so that, come performance time, they are fully aware of the play as role play engaged in by the entire community.

Devotional Performance in Oberammergau

There is little dispute that the Oberammergau Passion Play originated in a ritual performance context, i.e., one in which the play's performers expected their efforts to effect change in the temporal world through divine intervention.

A local chronicle of 1733 first recorded the legend of the play's founding: when a deadly plague sweeping the Bavarian countryside in 1633 entered Oberammergau in late September and left 84 villagers dead within three weeks, local elders responded by swearing a solemn oath on the eve of the feast of Saints Simon and Jude (28 October) to perform a passion play every ten years in honor of the bitter suffering and death of Jesus Christ.[13] The oath produced immediate results: all deaths ceased, and villagers fulfilled their vow by performing the first Oberammergau *passions-Tragedi* the following year. From a contemporary perspective, the historical veracity of this account seems questionable: the archival record gives no evidence of a sudden end to the plague in October 1633, and it seems likely that the villagers fulfilled their vow by continuing an existing local tradition rather than beginning a new one.[14] Yet the possible rewriting or re-remembering of the play's original circumstances makes an even stronger case for the power of local belief in efficacious performance. Indeed, the community continues to renew its vow before every ten-year performance season, in which young actors relate the 1733 chronicle account and the miraculous banishment of death from the village through the power of the play.[15]

Other aspects of the Oberammergau tradition clearly fulfill the ritual performance criteria outlined above. The play has long derived its theological legitimacy from its close ties to local Catholic institutions. For nearly 200 years, the performance site alone testified to the play's close ties to the local Catholic cult, with the grounds of the local parish church accommodating both stage and spectators until 1830. The play's authors have also traditionally been Catholic clergymen, alongside Joseph Daisenberger and Ferdinand Rosner, for example, other Ettal Benedictines such as Magnus Knipfelberger (1747–1825) and Othmar Weiß (1769–1843). Local actors performed not for monetary gain, but for the greater glory of God: Anton Lang, who gained fame for his portrayal of Christ in the productions of 1900, 1910, and 1922, considered his portrayal of the Lord to be a form of worship.[16] Spiritual benefits accrued to the audience as well, as explained by Daisenberger in his sermon cycle *Früchte der Passionsbetrachtung*, written for the performances of 1871.[17] And the expectation for exemplary conduct in the private lives of performers was very much in place in Oberammergau, at least for women. Until 1990, female actors were expected to be unmarried and under the age of 35. When her affair with a male villager was discovered in 1880, Josepha Flunger, slated to play Mary Magdalene, was banned from the production. However, no such action was taken for the popular Joseph Meyer, who played Christ in the same 1880 production, when it was discovered that he had fathered a child out of wedlock.[18]

What remains of Oberammergau's ritual context today? Among villagers, the play's close ties to the Catholic church have loosened somewhat, with the

2010 performance representing the latest effort by director Christian Stückl to reposition the play in an ecumenical age, which has not always met with full village approval.[19] Since 1990, Stückl and his deputy director Otto Huber have struggled to eliminate the anti-Jewish elements of Daisenberger's text while creating a more historically accurate portrayal of the Jewish faith practiced by Jesus and the disciples.[20] For the last two productions, Protestant clergy have joined their Catholic counterparts at the ceremony in which villagers renew their vow to perform the passion,[21] and a local Muslim actor has also taken part alongside Protestant performers.[22]

The inclusion of non–Catholic performers raises the question as to whether contemporary Oberammergau actors view their performance as "worship" as did Anton Lang. Frederik Mayet, one of the two actors portraying Christ in 2010, has stated that one need not be very religious to play the role, provided one has an interest in the character,[23] and the village suffers from the low church attendance rates that affect other areas of Germany.[24] At the same time, Andreas Richter, the second Christ of 2010, has emphasized the personal growth that all Oberammergau actors undergo while contemplating Christ's mission.[25] And while the village as a whole has benefitted financially from play, personal gain is not a motivating factor; actors are reimbursed for their time, but it is a maintenance wage intended as compensation for income lost from their regular employment. Berlin's daily *Tagesspiegel* summarizes current performers' motivations as follows: "first team spirit, tradition, and theater, then religion and money."[26] Some actors may still perform as an act of faith, but participation in the play is now primarily a service to the community, forging group identity while honoring local tradition and the belief in the play's transforming power.

Nonetheless, Oberammergauers understand that the play's efficacy, whether religious or financial, is dependent on the indivisibility between the performance and its place of origin. The village has thus long declined to take the play on the road or to film the performance, lest it destroy its nimbus of authenticity.[27] This has not only helped to preserve local control of audience reception, but also allowed the village to benefit from another lingering vestige of medieval ritual, that of religious pilgrimage. Even before international audiences discovered the bucolic mountain hamlet, the passion play enjoyed a regional fame that attracted spectators ca. 1770 from Bavarian and Austrian towns such as Munich, Innsbruck, and Augsburg,[28] at the time more than a day's journey from the alpine Ammer valley. By the end of the nineteenth century, the English travel firm of Thomas Cook openly advertised its package tours to the village as "pilgrimages."[29] Today, "pilgrims' guides" direct devout spectators on their spiritual journey to the Bavarian Alps. Michael Counsell's *Every Pilgrim's Guide to Oberammergau and Its Passion Play*, written for British travelers, nicely illustrates the devotional reception many such spectators strive for: nearly half of the book is devoted to an appendix with Bible readings, prayers, and "Your Passion Play Hymn Book," all interspersed with photographs from the 2000 production.[30] This pilgrimage aspect distinguishes Oberammergau from the "tourist shows" considered by Schechner: one seeks out the village not to experience a cultural Other, but, for most spectators, to experience a lingering reminder of one's own cultural heritage.[31] The only non–Western, non-majority-Christian country that is well represented among visitors at Oberammergau is Japan; otherwise, the majority of foreign spectators come from the United States, Great Britain, South Africa, Australia, and New Zealand.[32]

Not all spectators come to Oberammergau for a devotional experience, of course. Some are looking for entertainment, some are dragged along by relatives, and some are simply curious. Nor is performance reception ever single-valent. Nonetheless, the village offers several pre-performance frameworks that make two-fold viewing accessible to those audience members who seek a devotional mode of reception. Drawing upon my personal impressions while attending the play in 2010, the remaining sections of my essay examine three areas: the village's medial presence, encountered by visitors before they arrive; devotional frescoes, woodcarvings, and other components of village material culture; and the encounters with village actors outside the passion play house.

Extra-Theatrical Framing 1: Media

Oberammergau has long depended on popular media to attract visitors. In the nineteenth century, travel accounts in popular magazines such as *The Ladies' Home Companion* or *Harper's* propagated the village's image as bucolic, pious mountain hamlet.[33] Once circulated, such accounts served to attract visitors to subsequent performances and helped to create a sense of familiarity with the rhythms of local life. Many featured their authors' interactions with local performers, giving readers the vicarious experience of having met the play's actors.

Even at this time, however, the village sought to regulate the information that circulated regarding the play, forbidding notetaking and photography during performances.[34] Today, the town continues its efforts to shape audience perceptions by influencing the media portrayal of inhabitants and local tradition. Reporters register with the village press office, which provides them with a press kit whose English-language version contained the following information[35]:

1. The Adaptation of the Passion Play text for the 2010 season
2. Working on the Living Pictures for the 2010 Passion Play

3. The Stage Sets of the 2010 Passion Play
4. The Music accompanying the Passion Play
5. The 2010 Passion Play at a Glance: Dates and Facts
6. Chronicle 1633–2010
7. Biographies of the Production Team
8. The Cast
9. Brief Biographies of Players and Soloists

The kit initially focuses on new directions in the play's production, with the directors, stage designer, and musical director discussing their reasons for minor or major alterations in local tradition. The second half of the kit, however, is devoted to the play's performers. There are no life narratives here; biographical information is presented in tabular format. Nonetheless, the information provided—age, occupation, past roles—does a remarkable job conveying in shorthand the ordinary lives of local actors and the extent to which their lives are measured in play years. One learns that Anton Zwink, one of two actors to play Simon of Bethany in the 2010 production, is 71 years old, a wood carver by profession, and has acted in the play since 1950, portraying Longinus and Joseph of Arimathea, among other roles. While such information is insufficient for coverage of the play by major newspapers, the kit's biographical details nonetheless form the building blocks for articles in smaller publication venues. Note, however, that the play's commercial aspects are not part of the press packet: beyond ticket prices and the capacity of the Passion Play house, the kit offers no information on the plays' finances.

Even for major press outlets with independent reporting, however, the "story" of Oberammergau clearly is that of the performers: How does it feel to bear the burden of an over 350-year-old tradition? Press coverage thus takes a predominantly human interest approach. Nearly every article concerning the 2010 performances includes at least one local interview, and actors clearly make themselves available to reporters. In addition to the obligatory account of the play's origins and recent history, articles strive to offer an insider's perspective on current village life. Readers learn about the narrowly won plebiscite that allowed director Stückl to stage the second half of the performance, i.e., the crucifixion scenes, in the gathering dusk of evening,[36] or the crisis of faith prompted by revelations of sexual abuse of young boys at the nearby Ettal monastery school.[37] Actors' commitment to their parts is also a frequent topic, illustrated by their willingness to endure sub-zero temperatures during wintertime rehearsals in the unheated Passion Play House, or by the *Sündenkatalog* (Catalog of Sins), i.e., self-imposed fines for infractions on stage, such as inappropriate laughter or missing one's entry.[38] Interviews probing the inner motivation of Frederik Mayet or Andreas Richter, the two actors portraying Christ, are of course particularly popular,[39] but one also learns that

Judas is for some the more challenging, and thus more desired role.[40] Even before embarking on one's journey to the village, one could, with little effort, draw upon a vast array of print and online sources regarding local life, allowing one to indulge in a sense of recognition while encountering local residents.

Surprisingly, the photographs accompanying such articles do little to lift the veil on performers' lives. Pictures occasionally show the actors in street clothes, but all images from the production itself are controlled by the village and are not released until the play's premier in May. Any publication that appeared before the May premier could thus show photos only from the 2000 production. However, large, coffee-table-format photo albums are available for purchase in the village once one arrives. The function of such photographs is thus distinct from that of news coverage: they are intended to draw spectators into the visual experience of the play itself rather than elide the boundaries between stage performance and village life.

Perhaps the most effective media for prospective audience members to meet Oberammergau performers vicariously are television and film. On 13 May 2010, two days before opening day, Bavarian State Broadcasting (*Bayerischer Rundfunk*) broadcast a documentary by filmmaker Jörg Adolph on the making of the 2010 production entitled *Die Oberammergauer Leidenschaft* ("Passionate Oberammergau").[41] The film mixes historic footage with behind-the-scenes glimpses of rehearsals, stage and costume design, and village politics, offering a unique glimpse into the village's creative process. It was clearly intended as part of the play's marketing, with DVD copies available for purchase at any village souvenir shop during the 2010 season, and Adolph has since recycled footage from "Passionate Oberammergau" in a lengthier work, *Die große Passion* ("The Great Passion") of 2011. Both documentaries weave complex narratives; however, they begin *in medias res* and lack all exposition via voice-overs or "expert" interviews. In other words, viewers must possess some pre-knowledge of the Oberammergau tradition in order to contextualize the scenes portrayed. Despite the availability of English subtitles, moreover, the film's dialogue—often conducted in the local Bavarian dialect—is not easily comprehensible for non–German speakers, i.e., the majority of the Oberammergau audience.

In an effort to generate interest among potential North American spectators, play organizers thus turned to a more accessible television format: the talk show interview. Frederik Mayet and Eva-Maria Reiser—Christ and Mary Magdalene, respectively—toured the United States and Canada, giving ten interviews over the course of a week.[42] These included talk show appearances on Christian-oriented media outlets, in particular Crossroads Television System and Trinity Broadcasting Network, the world's largest network focused on religious programming. On the TBN show *First to Know*, Reiser and Mayet spoke with host Paul Crouch, Jr., on personal faith as well as the Oberammergau tradition. As Mayet noted afterwards, such questions would be difficult for him to answer in German, much less in a foreign language.[43] Nonetheless, both actors came across as quite competent in English, and any lack of idiomatic fluency simply added to their authenticity as amateur performers. This was not a glossy promotional tour; rather, they appeared modest and sincere, appealing to prospective passion play attendees in a wholesome small town manner. Crouch ended the interview on a "family-values" note, asking if Reiser and Mayet hope that their children can act in the play (the answer is "yes") and suggesting that the next "baby Jesus" may already be among the villagers.

Reproduced without commentary by Jörg Adolph in *Die große Passion*, the close of the TBN interview serves to highlight the self-imposed limits of the Oberammergau media presence.[44] Crouch notes that if viewers cannot make it to Oberammergau, they can still visit the passion play performed at TBN's own Holy Land Experience theme park in Orlando, Florida. Immediately afterwards, a commercial for the Holy Land Experience fills the screen, inviting viewers through a series of images of Christ to "Experience Love— Experience Peace—Experience Joy—Experience Jesus." The unstated contrast between interview and commercial advertisement speaks volumes: the organizers of the Oberammergau Passion Play, the documentary suggests, would never stoop to such crass commercialism. And indeed, the village shuns traditional means of advertising: no television commercials or magazine advertisements, in English or in German, appeal to visitors to attend the play. Clearly, Oberammergau authorities understand that any direct association with commerce would rob the play of its aura of devotional ritual, undertaken for spiritual, not for earthly gain. Indeed, in all aspects of the play's media presence, the village strives to emphasize its obligation to tradition, one based on a promise to higher authority.

Extra-Theatrical Framing 2: Physical Environment and Material Culture

The physical environment and objects of daily life that greet visitors to Oberammergau offer yet another extra-theatrical framework for audience reception of the play. When asked by the Munich daily *Süddeutsche Zeitung* how it felt to live in "idyllic postcard-perfect surroundings,"[45] Korbinian Freier, who played the apostle Philip in 2010, assured reporters that the village was not built of papier-mâché: locals experience it as genuine. Nonetheless, the sensory impressions encountered by spectators during a typical two-night stay in the village easily lend themselves to the stereotype of an isolated mountain hamlet where handicraft and religious traditions hark back to an earlier time. For those arriving by train, Oberammergau is literally the end of the line, the last stop on a rail spur from nearby Murnau. Following a short walk into town across the Ammer River, travelers find themselves among traditional timbered houses with plaster facades, many of which feature colorful frescoes, often with scenes from the life of Christ. Typical among these is the *Pilatushaus*, named for the house's garden-side fresco that depicts Christ before Pilate. Another fresco depicts the resurrected Christ in his glory. Combined with the ubiquitous crucifixes that stand alongside roads and hiking paths, such open-air frescoes give visitors the sense that Christ is omnipresent in Oberammergau.

The town museum in particular offers passion play attendees an opportunity to gather tactile impressions of living village traditions. All visitors who purchased the standard Oberammergau accommodations package in 2010 received a free pass to the museum, which covers the history of both the village and play. The first floor is devoted to wood carving, a crucial component of the local economy since the eighteenth century, with display case after display case filled with children's toys as well as religious figurines. The second floor meanwhile covers the play. On our visit, a brief 10- to 15-minute loop of historic play footage played on a small video screen in an alcove, but there was surprisingly little explanatory text to place these images or other items in context. Instead, the focus on both floors was on material culture: costumes, props, and other tangible objects that no amount of media coverage could adequately convey. The items, such as an angel costume from one of the tableaux vivants of the 2000 play, conjure stage presence, allowing an imagined proximity to the biblical events portrayed. This applies particularly to the passion itself: the column at which Christ is scourged is prominently featured, together with the crown of thorns. Similarly, the woodcarving display culminates in a reconstructed workshop from the nineteenth century. Frozen in time, the workshop offers up a near-life size figure of Christ as it is prepared for a crucifix, inviting visitors to imagine the woodcarver physically interacting with the sculpture, caressing it while inflicting the very wounds that mark humanity's complicity in the death of the savior. Such intimacy with the battered body of Christ, the museum suggests, particularly qualifies the villagers to reenact his death in another medium. At the same time, the display allows viewers to share in that same intimacy, fostering devotional encounters with, if not consumption of, the religious carvings available for purchase in the numerous woodcarving shops throughout town.

Extra-Theatrical Framing 3: Performers in Public

Personal encounters of course provide the most intimate form of drawing back the veil on local performers' lives. The village itself promoted such encounters through a free behind-the-scenes introduction to the play in the passion playhouse, held in the morning before the afternoon performance. Expecting village functionaries as our guides, we discovered upon arrival that we were to receive true apostolic treatment. While Maximilian Stöger, the actor playing Peter in that night's performance, whisked off the English speakers for a separate tour, none other than Christian Stückl, the play's director since 1990, greeted the remaining guests in Bavarian-tinged German. I cannot say whether Stückl personally directed this tour before every performance, but the effect upon our group was striking: we immediately felt privileged, as if we had become part of the ensemble, and Stückl proceeded to honor us with intimate behind-the-scenes anecdotes from rehearsals and insights into the local politics behind the play. Stückl was 29 years old when he first directed the play, part of a younger generation determined to shake up a conservative tradition, and could speak from personal experience regarding efforts to make the play more inclusive, eliminating anti–Jewish elements and allowing Protestants, Muslims, and even divorced women to join the cast, as discussed above. Stückl's turn as gracious host was more than just good PR: it invited guests into the heart of the community's dedication to perform the play, a commitment rife with its own conflicts and rewards. In so many words, Stückl communicated that "we are just like you," inviting audience identification not with the characters within the play, but with the actors as subjects. That evening, the members of Stückl's tour could all the more easily imagine themselves upon the Oberammergau stage, sharing in the community project.

Other actors are conspicuously visible as they go about their preparations prior to performance. Situated at the right rear of the playhouse just one doorway past the audience access for the foremost seats, the stage entrance invites attention, and as playtime approaches, villagers of all ages stream through the doorway. Some actors loiter in costume, providing a foretaste of things to come. Others offer studied portraits of pre-performance casualness as they enjoy their last cigarette before the play begins. The appeal of the portal becomes all the greater during intermission, since one now recognizes the most prominent players as they emerge from the doorway. The stage entrance thus becomes an integral component of the Oberammergau viewing experience, highlighting the transformation undergone by villagers every time they step into the playhouse.

The power of such personal encounters became particularly apparent when our five-person entourage encountered Frederik Mayet by chance outside the playhouse during the play's intermission. Mayet, who was half-way through his portrayal of Christ that evening, appeared on a bike in casual clothing alongside director Christian Stückl after most spectators had already sought out their appointed restaurants for dinner. Moving quietly down the mostly empty street, Mayet did not invite attention, but he did not deflect it either, pausing willingly to converse with a group of admiring audience members. While it had been intriguing to see actors with smaller roles emerge from the stage, the encounter with Mayet was of a whole other magnitude. We had not expected to see the star of the evening make a public appearance, particularly one out of character.

Mayet's presence on the street with mere mortals begged the question: Was he simply on his way home to dine and rest before the second half of the performance, one that would require a high degree of physical stamina from him, or was this a calculated appearance, undertaken as part of the larger Oberammergau performance? Given that Stückl was by his side, his appearance in public apparently did not violate the director's wishes; indeed, to judge from the documentary "Passionate Oberammergau," in which Stückl, on foot, and Mayet, on his bike, share a quiet discussion on their way to the passion playhouse, the director and actor were indulging here in a familiar habit.[46] Still, Mayet's appearance seemed anything but Christ-like. Riding a stunt bike with a low seat, in shorts and an untucked shirt, he seemed instead to symbolize secular youth culture.

The break between Mayet's on- and off-stage persona thus represents a radical moment of two-fold viewing, undermining any tendency on the part of more devout playgoers to equate him with the role he played. Past portrayers of Christ, such as Tobias Flunger in 1850 or Joseph Mair in 1870, had been known to do just the opposite, moving through the village during the play season dressed for their part and exuding piety.[47] Regardless of Mayet's own religious disposition—we know from his comments above that he did not considered a deep religiosity a prerequisite for the role of Christ, but he also chose to remain a member of the Catholic church following child abuse scandals at the nearby Ettal Monastery school[48]—his public appearance in street attire strongly suggests that he did not wish his personal identity to be subsumed by the larger community project. In his case, Oberammergau's extra-theatrical performance frame thus contrasts as well as reinforces the play proper, allowing actors to escape a simple one-to-one identification with their role.[49]

Yet the difficulty in isolating Mayet's motivations based solely on surface analysis ultimately points to the inevitable blurring of boundaries between the two performance frames. In an earlier time, the performers who won praise for their portrayal of Christ were precisely those who elided the boundaries between personal identity and stage role. This suggests in turn the most significant distinction between the ritual context of religious theater and the secular stage: No one advises living one's actual life on the model of Willy Lomax, Blanche DuBois, or Hamlet, while the emulation of Christ remains, for some, devoutly to be wished. The fascination of Oberammergau, in terms of performance theory, lies in the complex interactions between personal lives and stage persona. As Korbinian Freier suggests, the village's actors have a more difficult time than their professional counterparts in distinguishing between stage role and personal identity.[50] The Passion Play, as lay theater, ultimately confronts audience members with the continual performance of identity that individuals engage in on a daily basis, and the play can attract a half million spectators from around the world every ten years precisely because visitors intuit the inherent elision between play and reality in the villagers' willingness to mold their own personal lives on some level more closely around a religious ideal. In an unstable world, the play offers the optimistic reassurance that the reinvention of a better self is still possible.

NOTES

1. *Das Oberammergauer Passionsspiel in seiner ältesten Gestalt*, ed. August Hartmann (Leipzig: Breitkopf & Härtel, 1880). See also Rolf Bergmann, *Katalog der deutschsprachigen geistlichen Spiele und Marienklagen des Mittelalters* (Munich: Beck, 1986), 260–262, no. 116.

2. James Shapiro, *Oberammergau: The Troubling Story of the World's Most Famous Passion Play* (New York: Pantheon, 2000), 58–65. The official website for the 2010 Oberammergau production offers a chronicle of the play's development: http://www.passionplay-oberammergau.com/index.php?id=126, accessed 29 June 2012.

3. Shapiro, 62–63.

4. "Das war die Passion," Bayerischer Rundfunk, November 9, 2011, accessed 12 June 2012, http://www.br.de/themen/bayern/inhalt/kult-und-brauch/passionsspiele-2010-bilanz100.html.

5. Alexandra F. Johnston, "The Communities of the York Plays," in *The York Mystery Plays: Performance in the City*, ed. Margaret Rogerson (York: York Medieval Press, 2011), 162–163.

6. Pamela M. King and Asunción Salvador-Rabaza, "La Festa d'Elx: The Festival of the Assumption of the Virgin, Elche (Alicante)," *Medieval English Theatre* 8 (1986): 21–50.

7. Richard Schechner, "Restoration of Behavior," in *Between Theater and Anthropology* (Philadelphia: University of Pennsylvania Press, 1985), 35–116.

8. See "Playing and Masking: Observations on Masked Performance in Papua New Guinea and Beyond," in John Emigh, *Masked Performance: The Play of Self and Other in Ritual and Theatre* (Philadelphia: University of Pennsylvania Press, 1996), 1–34.

9. Richard Schechner, *Performance Theory*, 2nd revised ed. (New York: Routledge, 2003), 130.

10. See the section on "Theater for Tourists" in Schechner, *Performance Theory*, 136–152. The development of the Asaro tradition as a cultural commodity is explored by Ton Otto and Robert J. Verloop, "The Asaro Mudmen: Local Property, Public Culture?" *The Contemporary Pacific* 8 (1996): 349–386. On the disputed origins of the mudmen dance, see Otto and Verloop, 353–355, and Emigh, 11–13.

11. John Willett, *Brecht in Context: Comparative Approaches* (London: Methuen, 1984), 218–221.

12. Compare the hostile reactions to Brechtian staging techniques during the

production of the York cycle in 1960: Claire Sponsler, *Ritual Imports: Performing Medieval Drama in America* (Ithaca: Cornell University Press, 2004), 180.

13. The original chronicle account of the oath is reproduced in *Leiden schafft Passionen: Oberammergau und sein Spiel*, ed. Holzheimer, Tworek, Woyke (Munich: A1 Verlag, 2000), 63. While the chronicle text list 84 deaths, Shapiro gives a figure of 81: Shapiro, 103–106.

14. Shapiro, 103–109.

15. Shapiro, 102–103.

16. "Für mich, den jungen Menschen, war die Darstellung meiner Rolle Gottesdienst." Excerpted from Lang's 1930 autobiography *Aus meinem Leben* in *Leiden schafft Passionen*, 213.

17. Joseph Alois Daisenberger, *Die Früchte der Passionsbetrachtung, vorgestellt in fünf Predigten, welche zu Oberammergau in der heiligen Fastenzeit des Passionsjahres gehalten wurden von Joseph Alois Daisenberger: Ein Gedenkbüchlein für die Darsteller und Besucher des Ammergauer Passionsspieles* (Regensburg: Manz, 1872).

18. Shapiro, 124.

19. Regarding the controversies over Stückl's revisions to the play, see Shapiro, 187–223. For the 2010 production, see Katja Thimm, "Bavarian Village Divided over Updates to World-Famous Passion Play," *SpiegelOnline*, May 15, 2010, accessed 29 June 2012, http://www.spiegel.de/international/zeitgeist/modernity-vs-tradition-in-oberammergau-bavarian-village-divided-over-updates-to-world-famous-passion-play-a-694970-druck.html.

20. See Kevin Wetmore's essay "What's a nice Jewish boy…" in this volume.

21. Shapiro, 101.

22. "Bavarian Village Divided."

23. Daniel Scheschkewitz, "On Being Jesus: Interview with Frederik Mayet," *Deutsche Welle*, 4 April 2010, accessed 13 July 2012, http://www.dw.de/dw/article/0,,5391027,00.html.

24. Julie L. Rattey, "Behind the Scenes at the Passion Play of Oberammergau," *Catholic Digest*, January 2010, http://www.catholicdigest.com/articles/travel/no_sub_ministry/2010/05-04/behind-the-scenes—at-the-passion-play—of-oberammergau.

25. A. Hagelüken, K. Riedel, and H. Wilhelm, "Als Jesus verdiene ich horrend viel: Interview with Korbinian Freier and Andreas Richter," *Süddeutsche Zeitung*, September 17, 2010, accessed July 19, 2012, http://www.sueddeutsche.de/geld/reden-wir-ueber-geld-passions-darsteller-als-jesus-verdiene-ich-horrend-viel-1.1001121.

26. "Erst Team, Tradition, Theater, dann die Religion und das Geld." G. Bartels, "Oberammergau: Der Deal mit Gott," *Der Tagesspiegel*, 7 March 2010, accessed 19 July 2012, http://www.tagesspiegel.de/kultur/buehne-alt/oberammergau-der-deal-mit-gott/1714438.html.

27. In 1900, for example, Oberammergau's leading performers rejected an American offer to perform the passion in New York. Sponsler, 133. Villagers similarly rebuffed a Hollywood studio that in 1922 was willing to pay handsomely for the right to film the performance. Shapiro, 126.

28. As mentioned in the village's official protest to the play's suppression in 1770 by Bavarian authorities: *Leiden schafft Passionen*, 83; Shapiro, 122.

29. Shapiro, 119.

30. Michael Counsell, *Every Pilgrim's Guide to Oberammergau and Its Passion Play: The Definitive Companion and Guide*, 2nd ed. (Norwich: Canterbury Press, 2008), 47–89.

31. Cf. Schechner, *Performance Theory*, 144.

32. "Das war die Passion 2010."
33. Shapiro, 116; Sponsler, 129–131.
34. Shapiro, 125.
35. "Press Kit," Passion Play 2010, Oberammergau.
36. "Oberammergau: Der Deal mit Gott."
37. Nicholas Kulish, "Church Crisis Shakes Faith of German Town," *New York Times*, May 14, 2010.
38. "Als Jesus verdiene ich horrend viel." See also Lissy Kaufmann, "Passionsspiele: Strafe für die Apostel," *Der Tagesspiegel*, September 17, 2010, accessed July 20, 2012, http://www.tagesspiegel.de/weltspiegel/passionsspiele-strafe-fuer-die-apostel/1936334.html.
39. Tom Chesshyre, "Oberammergau Passion Play: The Day I Met the 2010 Jesus and His Bearded Bavarian Twin," *Mail Online*, October 5, 2009, accessed July 6, 2012, http://www.dailymail.co.uk/travel/article-1218098/Oberammergau-Passion-Play-The-day-I-met-2010-Jesus-bearded-Bavarian-twin.html. Scheschkewitz, "On Being Jesus: Interview with Frederik Mayet"; Hagelüken, Riedel, Wilhelm, "Als Jesus verdiene ich horrend viel," *SZ*, September 17, 2010.
40. Rattey, "Behind the Scenes at the Passion Play of Oberammergau."
41. "Dokumentation: Die Oberammergauer Leidenschaft," *Bayerischer Rundfunk*, May 13, 2010, http://www.br.de/pressestelle/inhalt/pressemappen/Oberammergau102.html. *Die Oberammergauer Leidenschaft/Passionate Oberammergau*, dir. Jörg Adolph, 90 min., if... Productions, 2010, DVD.
42. Ludwig Hutter, "Passions-Darsteller zu Talk-Shows im U.S.-Fernsehen eingeladen," *Merkur-Online*, November 5, 2009, accessed July 6, 2012, http://www.merkur-online.de/lokales/landkreis-garmisch-partenkirchen/passions-darsteller-talk-shows-us-fernsehen-eingeladen-516422.html.
43. Christine Dössel, "Oberammergau (1): Jesus in Amerika," *süddeutsche.de*, November 27, 2009, accessed 22 July 2012, http://blogs.sueddeutsche.de/gehtsnoch/2009/11/27/oberammergau-1-jesus-in-amerika/.
44. *Die große Passion: Hinter den Kulissen von Oberammergau*, dir. Jörg Adolph, 144 min., if... Productions, 2012, DVD. The interview begins at 51:14 in the film.
45. "Als Jesus verdiene ich horrend viel."
46. *Die Oberammergauer Leidenschaft / Passionate Oberammergau*. The scene begins at 6:21.
47. On Flunger, see Shapiro, 116–117. On Mair, see Sponsler, 128.
48. "Church Crisis Shakes Faith of German Town."
49. Indeed, Mayet himself notes during his interview with David Mason in this volume that most audience members could distinguish between his role and his person. Not all could, however.
50. "Als Jesus verdiene ich horrend viel." http://www.sueddeutsche.de/geld/reden-wir-ueber-geld-passions-darsteller-als-jesus-verdiene-ich-horrend-viel-1.1001121-3.

"What's a nice Jewish boy like you doing in a Catholic play like this?"
Oberammergau 2010 and Religious Identity

Kevin J. Wetmore, Jr.

Catholic Place and Catholic Play

Oberammergau and its Passion Play are firmly rooted in the Catholicity of Bavaria. Helena Waddy calls the village "a bedrock of Catholic culture."[1] Partly that is due to demographics: in 1900 the population of Oberammergau consisted of 1542 Catholics and seventeen Protestants; no other religious groups were represented.[2] A century later the village is far more diverse in terms of religion an ethnicity, but it is still dominated by Catholics. Gordon R. Mork reports, "The people of Oberammergau saw themselves as expressing a mainstream religious tradition in Catholic Bavaria."[3] We must remember the play began life as a devotional act of Catholic people who performed the play as a result of a vow to God, a vow the village renews every time they perform the play. One might note, however, Waddy refers not to Catholicism in and of itself but to *culture*. The Oberammergau Passion Play is as much responsible for the Catholicity of Oberammergau as the Church is, and perhaps even more responsible for Oberammergau's reputation for Catholic piety, even as the Catholic identity of the village fades in the twenty-first century.

Crosses dominate the village and the landscape that surround Oberammergau. One may climb the Kofel and find a crucifix at the peak. The Crucifixion Group monument, featuring Jesus on the Cross, John and Mary at his feet, donated by King Ludwig II and carved by Professor Halbig of Munich, sits on a hillside outside the village, one of many devotional spots visitors are encouraged to see. There are also numerous Catholic epiphenomena that surround performances: The Church of Saint Peter and Paul (local Catholic Church) stages *Son et Lumière: Making Faith Shine*, a light show set to music in the sanctuary of the church. Prayer services and singing of hymns are offered throughout the Passion Play performance season. In short, when attending the play, one is surrounded by Catholic culture, both material and performative.

The text of the play is rooted in religious Catholicism as well. In 1750 Father Ferdinand Rosner, a Benedictine monk, wrote a baroque text for the Passion Play, which was used several times. In verse, it doubled the length of the previous script and added what James Shapiro refers to as "particularly 'Catholic' elements," including the laments of the Virgin Mary.[4] Shapiro also calls this text "Jesuit-influenced" for its theology and baroque elements that emerged out of the Jesuit Theatre of the Holy Roman Empire in which it was written and produced.[5] In 1811, Father Othmar Weis wrote a new version of the text. Weis's pupil, Father Alois Daisenberger crafted a new version based on Weis's for the 1850 Passion Play. Almost all subsequent Passion Plays have been rooted in this version. Otto Huber in 1990 became the first writer/adapter of the play not a Catholic priest.

Historically, the play was perceived as Catholic. Catholic intellectuals of the nineteenth century promoted the play and numerous Catholic aristocrats, royalty and ecclesiastical figures made the Pilgrimage to Bavaria to see this most Catholic play.[6] In the twentieth century, popes and future popes came to see the production. While Apostolic Nuncio to Munich, Cardinal Ambrogio Damiano Achille Ratti, the future Pope Pius XI attended the Oberammergau Passion Play. Prior to becoming Pius XII, Cardinal Eugenio Maria Giuseppe Giovanni Pacelli, also while Apostolic Nuncio to Germany, was a prominent guest at the Oberammergau Passion Play in 1922 (the 1920 production proving impossible in the immediate wake of the First World War). Similarly, in 1980 while Archbishop of Munich and Freising (in whose diocese Oberammergau sits) from 1977 to 1982, and again in 2000, Cardinal Joseph Alois Ratzinger, soon after to be named Pope Benedict XVI in 2005, attended the play.

So much is the play affiliated with Roman Catholicism that Helena Waddy titles the first chapter of her book *Oberammergau in the Nazi Era* "Catholics."[7] For much of its history, only Roman Catholics in good standing with the Church could participate in the Passion Play. Even more so than the famed residency requirement was the prerequisite for participation that the cast and crew be good Catholics, only revoked in 2000, allowing non–Catholics and non-practicing Catholics to be involved in the play for the first time.

Despite non-Catholics not being allowed to perform in the play, in the early twentieth century the play began to be presented as both Catholic and more general non-denominational Christian:

> By 1930 both Protestants and Catholics embraced Oberammergau as an embodiment of Christian ecumenism: a place that replicated the best of the Middle Ages; a place where the sacred penetrated ordinary life; a place that transcended the modern fragmentation of Christianity; and a place mystically suffused with the peace of Christ. Of all religious liberals, only Jews dissented publicly from this celebration of Oberammergau. For them, Oberammergau represented the worst Christian "medievalism": violence, hatred, and superstition.[8]

The play was perceived as being for all Christians, despite remaining very firmly rooted in medieval Catholicism. "This celebration of the 'catholicity' of the Passion Play obscured the extent to which the production was actually Catholic with a capital 'C.'"[9] As Helen Waddy discerns, it is a Catholic play that is safe for Protestants: Peter is not central, nor appointed to be "the rock upon which I build my church," and Mary is simply the mother of Jesus, not the Queen of Heaven.[10] Theological differences between Roman Catholics and Protestants are downplayed, and have been since the beginning of the twentieth century when more and more Protestants began to attend the play.

By focusing solely on a generic Christian representation, while Protestants felt welcome, all other faiths had been excluded. Page Laws, reviewing the 2000 production for *American Theatre* magazine, observed, "The Oberammergau passion play tacitly assumes its audience to be co-participants—Christian co-participants—in the greatest story ever ritually retold. As a work of art that is both its sin and its salvation."[11] The devotion to the telling of the Passion story makes for a wonderful play, but also makes for an exclusionary experience if one is not of the faith tradition.

As the quotation above notes, the problem for Oberammergau was not doctrinal differences between different denominations of Christianity. Oberammergau had also inherited the Church's historic anti-Semitism, especially in depictions of the Passion. In the years before the Second World War, Jews protested the anti-Jewish nature of the play which, as Spear argues, above, represents the worst of Christianity's attitudes toward the Jews, all of which was occurring as Germany embraced Hitler and the Nazis, with Bavaria forming the heart of the Nazi movement.[12]

Catholics, How They View the Jews and How the Jews View Them

It is important to remember, as Gordon R. Mork notes, that "the word 'anti-Semitism' itself was unknown before Wilhelm Marr coined it in 1879," and thus that the Oberammergau villagers "had no intention of presenting an especially anti–Semitic play."[13] The villagers presented history as they had been taught it by the Church. This is neither to excuse nor justify the anti–Semitic elements of the play or medieval Catholic culture, merely to state that the Passion Play was the product of its time. Marvin Perry and Frederick M. Schweitzer see Oberammergau as "typical of this uninterrupted flow of contempt and vilification of Jews that links historic Christian anti–Judaism with twentieth-century racial-nationalist anti–Semitism."[14] It is only in the twentieth century and especially in the wake of the Holocaust that the larger world expected changes to the play.

A long history of anti–Jewish stereotypes plagues medieval Catholic theatre. A. James Rudin reports, "Passion Plays and their almost universally negative portrayal of Jews and Judaism have been flashpoints in Christian-Jewish relations for centuries," both in terms of Jewish critiques of Christian representations and, much more ominously, in terms of motivating Christian violence toward the Jews in their community.[15] Rabbi Krauskopf argues that on Easter in Europe atrocities are committed in Jewish quarters "perpetuated by hands scarcely dry from the holy water with which they crossed themselves in church."[16] The concern being that Oberammergau, by perpetuating stereotypes, was, in fact, giving tacit approval toward anti–Jewish violence, a historic reality for much of European theatre history.

This anti–Semitism is rooted in a long history of Christians separating themselves from other monotheistic religions, starting with the letters of Paul in the Bible. Further problematizing the issue is the need in drama for protagonists and antagonists. When the protagonist is the incarnation of God, the antagonists must truly be evil. Dramatized accounts of the death of Christ have historically always contained anti–Jewish elements. Kevin Madigan summarizes thus: "Jews are meant to embody the forces of Satan, as well as to illustrate their wanton tendencies to blindness and refusal to believe. In addition, they were portrayed as Christ killers and meant, thus, to bear all the guilt for the suffering and death of Jesus."[17] As Kevin Madigan observes, acting instructions for Passion Plays from the medieval period encourage performers to play Jewish characters as different physically from Christian characters, "to pose awkwardly and menacingly, to gesture monstrously, to make fiendish noises."[18] Jews were literally to be represented differently on stage through the actors' performances. Such physical differences continued into the twentieth century, with Jewish high priest costumes having horns, and the performances of those playing such characters focusing on the malevolence of the characters as embodied in the physical and vocal performances. This was the legacy the defenders of the traditional text in Oberammergau were protecting, arguing the village simply was performing the play as it always has—it was the critics who had the problem.

Shapiro argues that the villagers who decry critiques of the play as criticisms of Christianity and the gospels themselves, and argue the play concerns a "portrayal of who killed Jesus, prefer ... to see this as a Jewish problem, rather than what it was, a Christian problem with profound implications for interfaith relations in a post-holocaust world."[19] The primary argument against Oberammergau being that since they were the ones continuing to present dangerous and offensive stereotypes and propaganda in the play, they were the ones who had to change. Instead of finding refuge in the Church, defenders of tradition found even the Vatican was changing how it perceived Judaism.

The Second Vatican Council radically changed the relationship between the Catholic Church and Judaism. *Nostra Aetate* (In our times), also known as *The Declaration on the Relationship of the Church to Non-Christian Religions*, offered the definitive statement of the Church toward the Jews:

> True, authorities of the Jews and those who followed their lead pressed for the death of Christ (cf. Jn. 19:6); still what happened in His passion cannot be blamed upon all the Jews then living, without distinction, nor upon the Jews of today. Although the Church is the new people of God, the Jews should not be presented as repudiated or cursed by God, as if such views followed from the holy Scriptures...
>
> The Church ... deplores the hatred, persecutions and displays of anti–Semitism directed against the Jews at any time and from any source.[20]

John XXIII had specifically instructed the Secretariat for Christian Unity "to deal with relations with the Jews."[21] He sought to change the relationship between the Church and Judaism and also saw that "too often Catholic preachers had accused the Jews of deicide and presented them as accursed and rejected by God."[22]

Tangentially, another German play gave the Vatican pause in the sixties. John W. O'Malley argues Hochhuth's 1963 play *Der Stellvertreter* (*The Deputy*) "deeply disturbed the Vatican and troubled perhaps nobody more deeply than Paul VI, who ... worried that the council's declaration [condemning anti–Semitism] might be taken as a validation of Hochhuth's position."[23] The Church's historic anti–Semitism was untenable by the mid-twentieth century, and the Second Vatican Council disavowed it in all forms.

Thus the Catholic Church had condemned the Blood Libel (the idea that all Jews historically bore responsibility for the death of Christ) and anti–Semitism in all forms by the mid-sixties. Oberammergau, however, continued to maintain the lines which invoked the blood libel and continued to present stereotypes of Jews on stage, even in the wake of the Church's renunciation.

In 1960 concerns about the representation of Jews were brought to the village from various American and other Jewish advocacy groups, most notably the Anti-Defamation League (ADL). These groups demanded significant changes to the Oberammergau Passion Play as related to the depiction of the Jews. By 1970, the failed attempts at reform resulted in the ADL demanding a boycott of the show.

Multiple criticisms of Oberammergau in 1970, 1980, 1990 and even 2000 is that the Judaism of Jesus was erased and that first-century Palestinian Jews are presented as a monolithic bloc, savage in their collective hatred of and opposition to Jesus, whose historical name we should recall, is Yeshua, a Hebrew name. The Jesus of pre–2010 Oberammergau was an outsider to Judaism, seeing the rabbis and people of Jerusalem as a "them," countered by the "us" of himself, his disciples, and the audience.[24]

Gordon R. Mork argues that the construction of religious identity in the play is that the Jews are "Wicked Jews" but the Christians (by which he means the Jewish characters who are supporters of Christ: Mary Magdalene, the Virgin Mary, the apostles and disciples) are "Suffering Christians."[25] The Jews are seen to delight in the suffering of Christ whilst the same spectacle causes Christians to suffer. A distinction is made between "Jews" who are the enemies of Jesus, and his supporters, who despite actually being Jewish as well are never acknowledged as such in the Passion Play.

Writing of the previous productions of Oberammergau in comparison with Mel Gibson's *The Passion of the Christ*, Gordon R. Mork set as one of the criteria for critically understanding a passion play is "do the presenters make clear the Jewishness of Jesus and his followers."[26] In the case of Oberammergau he concludes:

> The traditional play also made a clear and visual distinction between "Christians" and "Jews" on stage. Jesus, his apostles, Mary, and the other women followers were dressed in modest earthtones, humble but honorable. Jesus' opponents, whether priests, members of the high council, temple traders, or the crowd before Pilate were dressed in "oriental" styles, with garish colors and elaborate headgear (some of which suggested the horns of the devil himself). Jewish symbols, like the menorah, were associated with the high council which condemned Jesus. A particularly nasty opponent of Jesus was named "Rabbi." There was little to suggest the Last Supper was a meal to commemorate the Passover.[27]

Mork, writing in 2005, was obviously referencing an older performance tradition, as some of the design elements he observes had been removed by the 2000 performance.

The same call for change was made previously by Saul Friedman in his volume tellingly entitled *The Oberammergau Passion Play: A Lance Against Civilization*. Friedman advocates that Oberammergau "introduce properly pronounced Hebrew words or greetings" and "place Jesus within a Jewish religious and historical milieu, including identification of the Last Supper as a Seder of freedom, replete with matzos, *tallisim* and *barochot*."[28] Interestingly, Friedman also suggested that the production "incorporate a Kaddish somewhere in the Crucifixion scene."²⁹ In other words, Jesus' followers should say the Hebrew prayer for mourners after the death of someone.³⁰

One should note that the 2010 production actually reversed many of Mork's concerns and employed many of Friedman's suggestions, as will be elaborated upon below: the menorah is associated with Jesus (as are other elements of Jewish material culture, including the Torah scroll), Jesus is the one called "Rabbi," and the Last Supper is obviously a Passover Seder. Mork's charge is that these elements in earlier productions demonstrate that Oberammergau has ignored the Jewishness of Jesus. Twenty-ten instead reversed many of the same elements and focused on the Jewishness of Jesus.

Interestingly, while the call to emphasize the Jewishness of Jesus came from Jewish advocacy groups, the Catholic Church took a different approach, advocating that Jesus's opponents be made less Jewish. Saul L. Friedman reports that the Secretariat for Catholic-Jewish Relations of the National Conference of Catholic Bishops in America prepared a series of position papers criticizing Oberammergau and offering guidelines for the change of the play as early as 1968.³¹ Among the suggestions were to decrease the focus on the "Jewishness" of Jesus' enemies by not giving them "exclusively ... recognizably Hebrew Bible names," "not give the impression that most of Jesus' opponents were Pharisees, nor should there be any 'rabbis' among his opponents," and "avoid creating the impression that most Jews of Jesus' day willed his death."³² Instead, they argued, Oberammergau should "not conceal the fact that Jesus is a Jew (that is, Jesus and his followers should look and act like the Jews they were)."³³ This last line is crucial to the requested change. Jesus and the apostles are not simply changed through new and improved costume designs. They need to "act like the Jews they were"—Jesus, his apostles, and his supporters in the crowd needed to "act Jewish." In order to do so, Jewish ritual culture and Jewish material culture needed to be injected into the play.

Strikingly, one of the suggestions by the Secretariat for Catholic-Jewish Relations of the National Conference of Catholic Bishops in America, as reported by Saul Friedman, was that the conflict between Jesus and religious authorities *not* be presented as a struggle within Judaism: "In summary, Passion plays should not portray the events leading to the death of Jesus as a struggle among Jews. It should make Gentile Christians grateful that they have been led to the one true God and to God's teaching through the Jew, Jesus."³⁴ The Bishops did not want the origins of Catholicism to be posited as a sectarian struggle among Jews, which in and of itself leads to a slippery slope of supersessionism.

Several Jewish scholars have attended the Oberammergau Passion throughout its performance life. Rabbi Joseph Krauskopf, an American reform rabbi who attended the 1900 performance and returned to Congregation Keneseth Israel in Philadelphia gave a series of lectures on what he saw. In his book *A Rabbi's Impression of the Oberammergau Passion Play*, he argues that not only is the play historically false, theologically false, and the actor playing Jesus is "a little too Teutonic and not enough Jewish,"[35] but he also argues that the Oberammergau Passion Play offers proof that Christianity fundamentally misunderstands Judaism and is theologically problematic, especially the "blood libel" in Matthew.[36] To put it somewhat flippantly, his understanding of Christian understandings of the Torah and the prophets is "Boy, did you guys get it wrong." He states he wrote the book because "if the Jew does not defend himself or cannot, how should the Christian know that he is wronging him?"[37] Much of the postwar dialogue about Oberammergau has been precisely that: Jewish authorities informing the Christians of Oberammergau that the play wrongs them.

We should note tangentially the fascinating suggestion by Saul Friedman, among many, many others, who argues that the blood libel lines should be removed. He then advocates for the inclusion in the Oberammergau Passion Play of "Christ's lines of forgiveness offered from the cross, lines which have been notably absent from the traditional Oberammergau Passion."[38] He is, of course, referring to Luke 23:34, "Jesus said, 'Father, forgive them; for they do not know what they are doing.'" As opposed to the blood libel of Matthew, which places the blame for the death of Jesus on all Jews, and remains a presence in virtually all Passion Plays from the Middle Ages to the present, Luke's gospel offers forgiveness for all involved and no blood libel. Interestingly, the 2010 Oberammergau Passion Play does, in fact, include words of Luke spoken from the cross but does not include the blood libel.[39]

In 1930, another American Rabbi, Philip Bernstein saw the play and published an essay about it in Harper's magazine. He states the play is "so beautiful, so reverent, so moving ... it gave me an appreciation for the soul of the devout Christian." But he is saddened because he believes (correctly so) that Christians come away from the play without a love or appreciation of Jews in their hearts. For almost all of its history, the Oberammergau Play has been charged with being anti–Semitic, a charge true for its entire history and exacerbated by the rise of the Nazis.

Many in the village itself resisted much of Nazism and there were huge conflicts within Oberammergau between those who embraced Hitler and those who saw his policies as being problematic for Catholics as outlined in Helena Waddy's fascinating *Oberammergau in the Nazi Era* (when Hitler came to the village, for example, the village priest refused to meet with him). Oberammergau was first and foremost a Catholic village, then a German one. Yet Hitler embraced the play, even as many in the village admittedly embraced Nazi anti–Semitism. In 1934, the script did not have to be changed. It was already anti–Semitic. Hitler met the cast onstage after seeing the play, and said, "You must preserve this passion play unchanged in spirit and production," indicating that the play demonstrated the dangerousness of the Jewish race: "To save future generations it is vital that the Passion Play be continued at Oberammergau for never has the menace of Jewry been so convincingly portrayed as in the presentation of what happened in the time of the Romans."[40] Even Mayor Raymond Lang announced in 1936, "The Passion Play is also no Jewish play but rather as many leading men have already declared the absolute opposite. It is the most anti–Semitic play we have."[41] Goebbels insisted the play be "Nazified" for the 1940 production, although the war prevented production of the play that year.[42] In other words, the Nazis thought the play was wonderfully anti–Semitic, they now wanted it to be more reflective of Nazi values in other ways.

Even as late as 1990, the text remained thoroughly anti–Semitic. The tableau featuring Cain and Abel contained the line "Abel the upright was hated by his brother Cain, even as Christ was despised by his brothers, the Jews."[43] Tangentially, in 1980, Cardinal Josef Ratzinger, now Benedict XVI, declared, "There is nothing anti–Jewish in the play anymore."[44] In texts based on Daisenberger's script, Cain, Judas and Caiaphas were Jews, Jesus and his followers were, for all practical purposes, Catholic.

The history of concerns of anti–Semitism is detailed quite thoroughly in James Shapiro's *Oberammergau: The Troubling Story of the World's Most Famous Passion Play*, which catalogues the ongoing concerns of the ADL and other Jewish organizations before and after the 2000 production. The ADL and other organizations implore Oberammergau every year to change the play, to eliminate offensive lines, to emphasize the Judaism of Jesus, to at least make the last supper less of a Da Vinci painting and more of a Passover Seder. In his book *Christ Killers*, Jeremy Cohen demonstrates that the revisions to the play to make it less anti–Semitic consisted primarily of reduction and removal: lines that condemned the Jews were removed.[45] But the anti–Semitism remained as, if you will pardon the phrase, as a sin of omission rather than commission. The Jewishness of Jesus was always overshadowed by the Catholicity of the play.

Adding to the challenge, in the wake of Vatican II, *Nostra Aetate*, and historical Catholic theology exploring the Judaism of Jesus, the village was in a bind. It had been insisting in the historical accuracy of its representation of the last days of Jesus Christ. To change the play would mean to transform not only tradition but Bavarian Catholic theology. Twenty-ten represented a perfect storm of factors that radically changed the play. A decision was made for the 2010 play to approach the representation of Jesus differently than had been the tradition. Adaptor and Deputy Director Otto Huber announced, "In 2010, on the other hand, we are attempting to place greater emphasis on his call for a radical change of ideas, his commandment to love God and man."[46]

Oberammergau 2010: A Jewish Jesus in a Catholic Play

Beginning with the 2000 production, genuine and sincere attempts were made to remove the anti–Semitic elements from the play, which proved difficult. One of the key realizations for the playmakers, however, was the need not just to remove the perceived offensive elements but also to recognize the culpability of Christians in general of perpetuating anti–Semitic violence and culture. Christian Stückl stated:

> Oberammergau is the story of the man whose message set worlds in motion for two thousand years.... But this is also the story of a man whose followers, the Christians, brought unbelievable suffering into the world. Their religious zeal recoiled from no act of violence and left a bloody trail through the centuries. Millions of Jews—the people who shared the faith of Jesus—died in the twentieth century. They had to die because the Church and yes the Passion Play for centuries sowed the seeds of anti-Semitism, of Jew-hating. The Nazis harvested a well-fertilized field.[47]

Acknowledging Oberammergau's role in spreading anti–Semitism and invoking the Nazis made for both a startling confession and a need to address and redress the past problems with the representation of Jews and Jesus.

The village as a collective whole agreed with Stückl and sought remedies to the problems with the text that had continued through 2000. Fifty villagers travelled to Israel in September 2009 accompanied by a Vatican theologian to carry out research for the production as well as to better understand contemporary and historic Judaism in situ. Before the play was even made public, the public faces of Oberammergau began to focus on the Judaism of Jesus. Frederick Mayet, one of the two men playing Jesus and one of the public relations representatives of the Passion Play, "described the Passion Play first and foremost as 'an inner Jewish story' that dramatizes religious conflicts within Jerusalem during the Roman occupation."[48] The script would reflect this shift.

Unlike previous versions of the script, in which the Jewish elements were removed for being anti–Semitic, Stückl Huber radically altered the text in order to emphasize the Jewishness of Jesus. Indeed, the Council of Centers on Jewish-Christian Relations (CCJR) in their *Ad Hoc Committee Report on the 2010 Oberammergau Passion Play Script* singled out three aspects for praise, despite concern for the presence of ongoing anti–Jewish elements in the script. In addition to presenting "the diversity of late Second Temple Judaism" and a "highly nuanced" and "quite realistic" relationship between Pilate and Caiaphas that rendered the latter less cartoon villain and more "sophisticated politician" in a challenging political situation, the script for 2010 is singled out for "the Jewishness of Jesus"[49]:

> In comparison to previous scripts, Jesus himself is placed much more convincingly in his Jewish milieu, as a Jew among Jews in a Jewish society. Although he is shown to

be in conflict with a variety of Jewish groups, from Zealots to the Temple priesthood, the script never loses sight of Jesus' essential character as a worshipful Jew. Although perhaps a bit anachronistic, he is called "rabbi" more than 45 times during the play. He is also credited with preaching the commandments. He prays in Hebrew, providing the correct b'rachot for the onset of Passover and for the bread and wine of the meal; his Last Supper is lit by a menorah. Although the crowd's praying the sh'ma in the "Expulsion of the Temple Merchants" scene problematically lacks context, its inclusion is notable. Handled properly in staging and emphasis, these decisions tend to make the conflict around Jesus more a matter of internal turmoil within the Jewish community and less a confrontation of a "Christian" Jesus with "Judaism."

Oberammergau 2010 transformed the Catholic Jesus of previous performances into a devoted, practicing Jew. He is referred to or addressed as "Rabbi" by both his followers and the people of Jerusalem. He emphases his own knowledge of Torah and Jewish ritual. He speaks Hebrew.

The published script, given to everyone who attends the play, contains a preface by Professor Doctor Ludwig Mödl, the theological advisor of the 2010 Oberammergau Passion Play, in which he writes: "The staging of 2010 has newly revised Joseph Daisenberger's Passion text in order to show more clearly: Jesus, the Jew, sought to renew the religion of the fathers, a religion built on the foundation of the law and the prophets, by showing that the personal relationship to the Eternal Father-God represents the core of all religious activity."[50] Everyone involved in Oberammergau 2010 seemed to be working toward creating this image of "Jesus, the Jew." The CCJR report was based upon the published script in English. In performance these elements stood out far more, and in fact emphasized the Jewishness of Jesus.

The play begins with the cleansing of the temple, which in previous productions had been a Catholic Jesus challenging Jewish moneylenders. Instead, for the 2010 production, the action is rooted in Judaism itself:

> JESUS: Away with you! I want this desecrated place to be restored to the worship of my father!
> PETER: *[entering with Torah, which he hands to Jesus]* Sh'ma Israel!
> JESUS: Sh'ma Israel Adonai elohenu Adonai echad. Baruch schem kavod, malchuto le O lam va Ed. V'havta et Eloheicha, bechal leva vecha ufchal nafsche cha ufschal Meodecha. Sh'ma Israel.
> ["Hear, O Israel—the Lord, our G_d, the Lord is one. Blessed is the Name of the Glory of His Kingship, forever!"][51]

The Sh'ma is from Torah, specifically Deuteronomy, and it is a Mitzvah to say it twice a day, as well as just before one dies. It states the centrality of monotheism in Judaism, as well as the special relationship between Israel and God. Twenty-ten Jesus drives not moneylenders (perhaps another insidious stereotype) but those who are not observant Jews from the Temple. (As a side note, Jesus in Mark 12:29 cites the Sh'ma as one of two great commandments, the other being "Love your neighbor as yourself," so in theory the Sh'ma is a central tenet of Christianity as well.) These lines alone represent a radical transformation of Jesus' identity in the play, the fact that some of his first lines are in Hebrew only accentuates that identity.

We might also note the presence of the material culture of Judaism in this moment. Peter carries the Torah scrolls, hands them to Jesus, who holds them up while proclaiming the Sh'ma. Visually, Jesus is identified with the Torah, aurally he is identified with Hebrew. This Jesus is not the Jesus of the Gospel of John, the eternal word who is one with the Father, this is a Jesus devoted to the special relationship between Israel and God.

Another scene new to the 2010 Passion shifts the focus and the blame within the Passion Play. Pilate enters much earlier than he had in previous productions, entering during Act III, immediately following the cleansing of the temple. After Jesus and his disciples exit, the merchants and the High Council demand Caiaphas do something about Jesus. Caiaphas resists action, telling them, "This man has too many followers," and "This could lead to a dangerous battle and provide the bloodthirsty Romans with an excuse to put an end to the uprising with their swords."[52]

Pilate then enters the temple forecourt in a scene not from scripture. Pilate demands to speak with Caiaphas alone and then questions him about Jesus and Caiaphas's inaction. Caiaphas calls Jesus "an insignificant itinerant preacher," and assures Pilate that no one is planning to rebel, riot, or revolt against Rome. Pilate responds:

> No one? No one? I know you. What was your people before I took over? An unruly mob—without obedience, without leadership. And there was no peace in this goddamned land until I crucified all those rebels and had all their collaborators executed as well...
> I let you remain in the position of High Priest; I put you in charge of watching over peace and order in this city; I gave you everything you asked for...
> If order is not restored in the city I will take everything from you I have given to you.[53]

This exchange transforms the relationship between Jesus and Caiaphas, allowing for much greater nuance and removing the oversimplified adversarial context, not to mention previous productions' absolving of Pilate for his role in the events. It is clear that it is no longer "the Jews" after Jesus—Caiaphas sees Jesus as "insignificant." Pilate puts Caiaphas in charge of maintaining order and any breaches of the peace are his responsibility. Thus the Romans placed the Jewish religious authorities in a position in which any public disturbance was their fault. It is also clear that Pilate himself is anti–Semitic, despising "an unruly mob." Lastly, Pilate is the one who is the devotee of crucifixion: the idea is planted in the mind of the audience that Pilate is the one who crucifies, not the Jews. Even later, when some in the crowd cry out, "Crucify him," they are simply encouraging Pilate to do what he wants to, what he does best, what is his solution to any political problem with the Jews. It also oddly emphasizes the fact that Jesus was not the first one crucified by Pilate, nor the last, just another "rebel" as far as the Romans were concerned.

Jesus' Jewish identity is further established at the Last Supper. The disciples gather, lay out unleavened bread, light the candles and clearly prepare not for a da Vinci painting, but a Seder. The original script reads:

Scene IV The Last Supper
JOHN: Blessed be the light that always burns in the innermost recesses of the heart.
THOMAS: Blessed be the heart that maintains its dignity. Blessed be the match that consumes itself as it ignites the light.
JOHN: Baruch atta adonai elohenu, melech haolam, ascher kiddeschanu bemizvotav vetzivanu lehadlik ner schel yom tov.[54]

John's last line is Hebrew. It is the prayer for lighting the candles at the beginning of the Pesach Seder: "Blessed are you, o Lord our G_d, King of the Universe, who has sanctified us with his commandments, and commanded us to kindle the light of yom tov. ["Good day" = can be replaced with holiday name]." After John lights the Passover candles, the Last Supper does not follow any of the gospel accounts. Instead, there is a conversation which focuses on the Jewish celebration of Passover, which is still unfamiliar to most Germans (and, I suspect, to many of the North American tourists as well):

JESUS: Most fervently I have longed to celebrate this Passover meal with you.
PETER: Praised be you, our G_d, who blessed your People Israel.
JOHN: Why is this night different from all other nights?
PETER: This is the night when the Lord led Israel out of Egypt with a mighty hand and an outstretched arm.
ANDREW: He separated the sea of reeds into two parts and led Israel safely between the waters.
JUDAS: He guided his people though the desert and gave the land as inheritance to Israel, his servant.
JOHN: This is the day the Lord has made.
JESUS: Our Father in the heavens, your name be holy, your kingdom come.
PHILIP: On Earth your will be done, as it is in heaven.
THADDEUS: Give us each day the bread we need!
JUDAS: Forgive us our sin, as we forgive those who have sinned against us.
PETER: Lead us not into temptation but deliver us from evil...[55]

Three key things should be taken away from this exchange: First, after Jesus firmly establishes that this is not a traditional Christian vision of the Last Supper, but a "Passover meal," John asks the Ma Nishtana, the question traditionally asked by the youngest child present that leads to the four questions that are asked and answered during the Seder: "Why is this night different from all other nights?" The purpose of the Ma Nishtana is to fulfill the commandment of Exodus 13:8, "You shall tell your son on that day, saying,

'It is because of what the LORD did for me when I came out of Egypt.'" John, Peter, Andrew, Jesus and Judas begin to tell the story of the Exodus, as is required at a Seder.

Second, we must note the repeated use of the term "Israel" to describe God's chosen people, four times in five lines. Not only are these lines from the *haggadah*, the text that sets the order of the Seder, they serve to identify for the audience, perhaps less familiar with Seders and *haggadahs* that they are watching a Jewish ritual performed by Jews.

Third, the Lord's Prayer is transposed from the Sermon on the Mount, much earlier in the Gospel accounts, to this Passover Seder, linking the most important prayer in Christianity to this moment when the Judaism of Jesus and the apostles is foregrounded. It links the Lord's Prayer to the Passover Seder and God protecting his chosen people. The implication is that the prayer most identified with Jesus is in fact an outgrowth of the Passover Seder, and not part of the separate teachings of Jesus.

Remarkably, after the Lord's Prayer, the first suggestion of a Catholic Last Supper, as represented by the traditional Eucharistic prayers, is presented, but it is wrapped in the celebration of Passover. The Last Supper becomes a literal Last Seder:

> JESUS: Baruch atta adonai elohenu melech haolam, hamozi lechem min haarez. *[He breaks the bread and gives it to them.]* Take! Eat! My body! This bread is my body that I shall give for the life of the world.
> Baruch atta adonai elohenu melech haolam, boray pri hagafen. *[He lifts the cup]* Praised be to you, Eternal One, our G_d, King of the World, who creates the fruit of the vine.... Drink! My blood!...
> JOHN: Rabbi, so this is your last Passover feast?[56]

Stückl told the actors to act confused by the "eat my body, drink my blood" stuff, so as to suggest that as observant Jews, they recognize the lines of the Seder prayers, but not the Catholic understanding of mass. The audience, presumably predominantly Christian, becomes the Other to the onstage Self.

Lastly, as Raymond Goodburn asserts, "at the Last Supper, a Menorah was prominently displayed."[57] The Menorah used is not the modern, eight-branched menorah of Hanukkah but the seven lamp version used by the Temple in Jerusalem and described in Exodus 25:31–40. In other words, the drive to emphasize the Judaism of Jesus manifested in every aspect of the scene, down to the level of the stage properties.

The end result of these textual, performative and material changes is that the emphasis shifts from Jesus bringing a religion that supersedes Judaism to Jesus as Jewish reformer. It is not an unproblematized structure. One can still see the play as offering a form of replacement theology, but the overall effect is to displace the Catholic identity which has dominated the play until now. Furthermore, in making Jesus a reformer of Judaism from within, Oberammergau 2010 also makes the play more Protestant, or at least indicative of Martin Luther. It is a play that celebrates those who seek to purify an organized religion grown stale and corrupt, honoring the letter of God's law but not its spirit.

It should be noted that Otto Huber, the adaptor and assistant director, argues that the counterpoint of the Living Tableau from the Hebrew Bible, separating out the scenes from the gospels are not intended to be read as supersessionism: "These comparative flashbacks to the faith experiences of the Israelites also help to bring His [Jesus's] faith closer in an emotional way."[58] In other words, the Living Tableau are designed to reinforce the Judaism of Jesus by linking his faith tradition to that of the ancient Israelites. In previous performances, the tableaux have highlighted supersessionism, most notably showing scenes such as Esther 1–2, in which Ahasuerus exalts Esther and casts Vashti from him, a tableaux cut after 1980.[59] In the 1984 text, the chorus sang, "Abel the upright was hated by his brother Cain, even as Christ was despised by his brothers, the Jews."[60]

So what's going on here?

Several factors came into play in the transformation both of Jesus' identity in the play and the play's identity in the village, most of which are rooted in the village's identity in the world. Usually the forces of tradition win out over progressive elements in Oberammergau that want to update the play, but for 2010 there was a vote in village not only to change the historic script but also to change the entire way in which the play was presented. Second, Huber and company met with Ludwig Mödl, theological advisor to the Archbishop of Munich, who offered a contemporary theological understanding of the historic Jesus: "Jesus, the Jew, sought to renew the religion of his fathers," and the trial and execution of Jesus was "an inner-Jewish conflict during the Roman occupation that the Romans stepped in to resolve." If Jesus became more Jewish, so to speak, Pilate became the bad guy: Huber introduces him much earlier in the narrative than in the Gospels and Pilate becomes the first person to demand that Jesus be silenced. He threatens Caiphas with terrible retribution against Jerusalem if they cannot control Jesus.

Finally, the multicultural audience of 2010, from both within and without Germany, required a more sophisticated approach to the identity of Jesus. Most of the people I met were American evangelicals and German students. Jeremy Cohen reports that the majority of Oberammergau attendees in 2000 were from North America.[61] Twenty-ten repeated this demographic. In short, the audience expected a less Catholic Jesus, and in response to decades of criticism before 2010, Stückl and Huber gave them a Jewish one.

While initial responses from Jewish advocacy groups were not positive, the critics who saw the production had a much different response. In February of 2010, the ADL and the American Jewish Committee objected to implications on the Oberammergau website that the two organizations had approved of the new script and 2010 production:

> The American Jewish Committee and the Anti-Defamation League have not approved the 2010 Oberammergau Passion Play. After our rabbinic team met in Oberammergau with the directors and church (Catholic and Lutheran) theological advisor in October 2009, we made clear a number of issues of great concern regarding the play's text, visual images and significant plot changes that we believe can transmit toxic anti–Jewish images and perceptions. We notified them about our concerns in a Nov. 4, 2009 letter, and have never received a response.
>
> Although we engaged in significant discussions regarding a host of issues, it would not be possible to render our final evaluation regarding the 2010 Passion Play until a team of Christian and Jewish scholars can study a completed text and translation and receive a clearer picture of the set designs, costuming and plot changes. Until then we cannot offer a final evaluation of the 2010 Passion Play.[62]

Two and a half months later, at a preview performance, the ADL and AJC found the 2010 production to be still highly problematic, as reported in the press: "The Oberammergau Passion Play, the world's oldest and most famous, "continues to transmit hostile stereotypes of Jews and Judaism," according to the Anti-Defamation League (ADL) experts who attended a preview of the six-hour production in Oberammergau, Germany on May 8."[63] While representatives from the ADL found a few things to praise, they felt the depiction of the Jewish characters were still too stereotypical and unfair:

> "There have been welcome changes that emphasize that Jesus of Nazareth and his disciples were practicing Jews within a vibrant Jewish context under cruel Roman occupation," said Professor Levine. "Sadly, the play continues to depict damaging stereotypes of Judaism and presents Jewish leadership as deceitful, legalistic, vindictive and xenophobic."
>
> Rabbi Greenberg added, "Most disturbing is the portrayal of the Jewish High Priest Caiaphas as a lying, manipulative, mean-spirited politician and his father-in law, the former High Priest Annas, as an equally vindictive character. They are supported by equally malicious extra-biblical priestly figures."[64]

Despite the denunciations by the ADL and the AJC, reviewers picked up on the shift of the Jewishness of Jesus and found 2010 to be a radically different Oberammergau Passion Play and disagreed with the Anti-Defamation League's assessment. A.J. Goldmann, noting the ADL's statement, called the 2010 production "an intelligent, beautiful and moving work of art that didn't smack of the racist accusations historically leveled against it."[65] Elizabeth Johann Montgomery saw the crowd scenes that open the play indicative of a shift in identity within the play. By having Jesus enter triumphantly in the beginning, and demonstrate the (Jewish) crowd's support for him, it "subtly undercut later crowd scenes, where the masses called for their former hero's crucifixion."[66] Montgomery further picked up on the costume design as a source of combating anti–Semitism, arguing that the crowds were dressed in simple blue robes, which set them apart from the elaborate costuming of the priests and the military costumes of the Romans.

Lewis Segal, writing for the *Los Angeles Times*, observes: "By making Jesus and his disciples unmistakably and devoutly Jewish, 2010's director, Christian Stückl, and his collaborators completely undercut the accusations of anti-Semitism that, for good reason, tainted the Passion play throughout much of its history. In this very German retelling, Jesus—like Martin Luther—tries to reform a corrupt, inflexible religious establishment from within."[67] In other words, the characters were more Jewish, the experience more Protestant, and the overall effect was to allow audiences to experience the story in a new manner.

Catholic—But for How Much Longer?

Yet, the village's Catholic identity was also undergoing a complex shift, and not merely due to the multiculturalization of the area. As the *New York Times* pointed out, as the play was in rehearsal for 2010, a scandal broke in which it was revealed that fifteen monks at the Ettal Benedictine Monastery nearby had physically and sexually abused over a hundred students.[68] Nicholas Kulish reported, "Many [villagers], too, are feeling alienated and angry at the church not only for what some see as an inadequate response to the most recent sexual abuse crisis, but also for a broader failure to connect with Catholics living in modern Europe."[69]

Kulish reports that Frederick Mayet, who was one of the two actors playing Christ, sought to leave the Church officially in 2009, after Benedict XVI reinstated four German bishops who had been excommunicated, including Bishop Richard Williamson, a Holocaust denier. "I didn't want to be a member of a church that welcomed Holocaust deniers with open arms," Mayet told Kulish.[70] Instead, Mayet and Stückl chose to remain within the church as inactive members, due to their lifetime connection to the faith. "I can't just change my faith like I'm changing a pair of underwear," Stückl irreverently quipped.[71] There is a hope in the village that the scandal will lead to greater reform within the Church.

Likewise, Andreas Richter, who also plays Christ, reports the performance experience has less to do with religion and more about his identity as an Oberammergauer, Oana Lungscu reporting that "this is about tradition, rather than faith."[72] Andreas told her, "It's a big pride to play this part, the community chose me to play this role.... Every ten years, fathers and grandfathers and children come together and go out on stage and play this important story. It's part of our life. It fixes the community."[73]

The village's identity is shifting away from Catholicism. Stückl reports going "to the skateboarding half-pipe and say, 'You're an angel. You're an apostle.'" to the young people there, who then join the cast. "There's an entire generation that has very little connection to the Church," he observes, but the play is a means to connect them to another aspect of village identity.[74] The millennials performing in the play do not perform as an act of (Catholic) faith—they perform as a part of community identity. This play is what one does if one is from Oberammergau, regardless of religious faith or lack thereof.

Many of the reviews for 2010 focused on the changing, increasingly multicultural, multiethnic nature of the village. Since the requirement was changed from having to be born in the village to simply having lived there twenty years, as well as the presence of the local international school, the cast has grown more varied in terms of ethnicity. Oana Lungescu, reporting for the BBC, interviewed several cast members she described as "not your typical Bavarian."[75] She spoke with Anton Lel, who was born is Kazakhstan, who took time off from university to play one of the temple guards. He "describes Oberammergau as "the greatest village ever," noted "it feels pretty good" to be in the play, and that "it's a lot more fun to play a bad guy!"[76]

It is this last statement that is particularly interesting. He acknowledges that in playing one of the Jewish temple guards who capture Jesus in Gethsemane and hand him over to the Romans that he is playing "a bad guy," but he does not give any indication of the Jewishness of the character being the reason for being "a bad guy." Instead, a shift might be perceived in the presentation of "the bad guys" that religious or ethnic identity does not enter into. Lel's own religious identity is never stated, but the implication is that he is Muslim. His performance has nothing to do with presenting Catholic anti-Semitism and everything to do with playing one of the "bad guys" in a really interesting story. There is no sense of exclusion in the village—he is part of a community telling a story, not part of a group of Catholics fulfilling a religious vow. The village identity of Oberammergau has shifted considerable in the last century.

If, as Elizabeth Johann Montgomery posits, "the Oberammergau Passion Play 2010 was inextricably and uniquely linked to a collective performance of the town's identity," then the town's identity as Bavarian Catholic has transformed even within the past ten years.[77] As Protestants, married women, and those not born in the village (but who have maintained residency for two decades) have been allowed to join the production, a changing, multicultural Germany is reflected in the production and the village identity it now posits. While there is not a substantial Jewish population, "gastarbeiters" and their children who have stayed permanently have already begun to shift Oberammergau's cultural and religious identity.[78] Montgomery observes "while the reframing of Jesus helped offset anti-Semitic undertones, it also reflected a growing acceptance of other cultures that has become part of the fabric of an increasingly multicultural Germany struggling to integrate."[79] That, combined with a continually shrinking globe (and a village whose younger generation have embraced a larger world), will continue to transform the identity of Oberammergau.

NOTES

1. Helena Waddy, *Oberammergau in the Nazi Era: The Fate of a Catholic Village in Hitler's Germany* (Oxford: Oxford University Press, 2010) 12.
2. Waddy 31.
3. Gordon R. Mork, "Christ's Passion on Stage—The Traditional Melodrama of Deicide." *Journal of Religion and Film* 8.1 (2004): http://www.unomaha.edu/jrf/2004Symposium/Mork.htm.
4. James Shapiro, *Oberammergau: The Troubling Story of the World's Most Famous Passion Play* (New York: Vintage, 2000) 61.
5. Shapiro 61.
6. Waddy 23.
7. Waddy 3.
8. Sonja E. Spear, "Claiming the Passion: American Fantasies of the Oberammergau Passion Play, 1923–1947." *Church History* 80.4 (December 2011): 844.
9. Spear 839.
10. Helena Waddy, *Oberammergau in the Nazi Era: The Fate of a Catholic Village in Hitler's Germany* (Oxford: Oxford University Press, 2010) 20.
11. Page R. Laws, "The Power and the Glory." *American Theatre* 17 (November 2000): 34.
12. When considering Oberammergau and anti-Semitism, it pays to remember that the Nazis began in Bavaria, and the Beer Hall Putsch took place in Munich, just an hour from Oberammergau.
13. Mork, "Christ's Passion on Stage."
14. Marvin Perry and Frederick M. Schweitzer, "The Medieval Passion Play Revisited" in *Re-Viewing the Passion: Mel Gibson's Film and Its Critics*. Ed. S. Brent Plate (New York: Palgrave, 2004) 6.
15. James Rudin, "Oberammergau: A Case Study of Passion Plays" in *Pondering the Passion: What's at Stake for Christians and Jews?* Ed. Philip A. Cuningham (Lanham, MD: Rowman & Littlefield, 2004) 97.
16. Krauskopf 95.
17. Kevin Madigan, *Medieval Christianity: A New History* (New Haven: Yale University Press, 2015) 356.
18. Madigan 356.
19. Shapiro 79.
20. Walter M. Abbott, S.J., ed., *The Documents of Vatican II* (New York: Guild Press, 1966) 666–7.
21. John W. O'Malley, *What Happened at Vatican II* (Cambridge: Belknap Press, 2008) 195.
22. O'Malley 220.
23. O'Malley 221.
24. See Jeremy Cohen, *Christ Killers: The Jews and the Passion from the Bible to the Big Screen* (Oxford: Oxford University Press, 2007) 226.
25. Gordon R. Mork, "'Wicked Jews' and 'Suffering Christians' in the Oberammergau Passion Play" in *Representations of Jews through the Ages*. Eds. Leonard Jay

Greenspoon and Bryan F. LeBeau (Omaha: Creighton University Press, 1996) 153–170.

26. Gordon R. Mork, "Dramatizing the Passion from Oberammergau to Gibson." *Shofar* 23.3 (2005): 86.
27. Mork, "Dramatizing the Passion: 87–8.
28. Friedman 185.
29. Friedman 186.
30. His point is well taken, but technically would not have happened, as a *minyan* is required for Kaddish, since it is a public sanctification. The only group with ten men present at the crucifixion with ten men would be those who were the opponents of Jesus and less likely to publicly say Kaddish for him. Still, the idea is intriguing.
31. Saul Friedman, *The Oberammergau Passion Play: A Lance Against Civilization* (Carbondale: Southern Illinois University Press, 1984) 47.
32. Friedman 47–8.
33. Friedman 48.
34. Friedman 48.
35. Joseph Krauskopf, *A Rabbi's Impression of the Oberammergau Passion Play* (Philadelphia: Edwards Stern & Co, 1901, Forgotten Books, 2008) 27.
36. The "Blood Libel" refers to Matthew 27:25, "Then the people as a whole answered, 'His blood be upon us and on our children,'" which has been used to justify anti-Semitism and accuse all Jews of being "Christ killers." John Dominic Crossan argues the Blood Libel is "neither prophesy nor history but Christian propaganda, a daring act of public relations faith in the destiny of Christianity not within Judaism but within the Roman Empire" (*Who Killed Jesus? Exploring the Roots of Anti-Semitism in the Gospel Story of the Birth of Jesus* [San Francisco: Harper, 1995] 159). It helps to remember that all of the gospels, including Matthew, were written after the fall of Jerusalem, in the context of a strong Rome and a dispersed Jewish nation. See also Cohen.
37. Krauskopf 16.
38. Friedman 186.
39. *Passionsspiele 2010 Oberammergau Textbook*, trans. Ingrid Shafer (Oberammergau: Gemeinde Oberammergau, 2010) 113.
40. Quoted in Perry and Schweitzer 7.
41. Qtd. in Waddy 184.
42. Perry and Schweitzer 7.
43. Qtd. in Cohen 219
44. Qtd. in Friedman 179
45. See Cohen, *Christ Killers*.
46. Otto Huber, "Welcome to Oberammergau" in *Oberammergau 2010: The Village and Its Passion Play* by Raymond Goodburn (Woodbridge, Suffolk: Pilgrim Book Services, 2010), 5.
47. Quoted in Perry and Schweitzer 8–9.
48. A.J. Goldmann, "New Kind of Passion in an 'Alpine Jerusalem.'" Forward.com May 26, 2010. http://www.forward.com/articles/128345. Accessed December 12, 2010.
49. Council of Centers on Jewish-Christian Relations. *Ad Hoc Committee Report on the 2010 Oberammergau Passion Play Script*. May 14, 2010. http://www.ccjr.us/images/stories/CCJR_Oberammergau_Report_2010May14.pdf. Accessed March 23, 2014. 6–7.
50. *Passionsspiele 2010 Oberammergau Textbook* 7.
51. *Passionsspiele 2010 Oberammergau Textbook* 33.

52. *Passionsspiele 2010 Oberammergau Textbook* 34.
53. *Passionsspiele 2010 Oberammergau Textbook* 35.
54. *Passionsspiele 2010 Oberammergau Textbook* 47.
55. *Passionsspiele 2010 Oberammergau Textbook* 49.
56. *Passionsspiele 2010 Oberammergau Textbook* 49–50.
57. *Oberammergau 2010: The Village and Its Passion Play* (Woodbridge, Suffolk: Pilgrim Book Services, 2010), 21.
58. Huber 5.
59. Cohen 218–9.
60. Cohen 219.
61. Cohen 217.
62. Anti-Defamation League. "American Jewish Groups: We Have Not Approved 2010 Production Of Oberammergau Passion Play." February 18, 2010. http://www.adl.org/press-center/press-releases/interfaith/american-jewish-groups-we.html#.Vl1g9HarSM8. Accessed June 13, 2013.
63. Anti-Defamation League, "Despite Changes."
64. Anti-Defamation League, "Despite Changes."
65. Goldmann, "New Kind of Passion in an 'Alpine Jerusalem.'"
66. Elizabeth Johann Montgomery, "Oberammergau Passion Play 2010." *Theatre Journal* 63.2 (May 2011): 261.
67. Lewis Segal, "A Village's Long Passion Matures." *Los Angeles Times* (August 15, 2010): E7.
68. Nicholas Kulish, "Church Crisis Shakes German Town Long Faithful to Tradition." *New York Times* (May 15, 2010): A4.
69. Kulish A4.
70. Kulish A7.
71. Kulish A4.
72. Oana Lungescu, "Bavarian Passion plays to global crowds." BBC News Europe. 31 May 2010. www.bbc.co.uk/news/10198502. Accessed April 25, 2012.
73. Lungescu, "Bavarian Passion."
74. Kulish A7.
75. Lungescu, "Bavarian Passion."
76. Lungescu, "Bavarian Passion."
77. Montgomery 260.
78. Montgomery 261.
79. Montgomery 261.

Dialectical Aesthetics of Change and Continuity in the 2010 Oberammergau Passion Play

S̲H̲A̲R̲O̲N̲ A̲R̲O̲N̲S̲O̲N̲-L̲E̲H̲A̲V̲I̲

In the final moments of the documentary *Die Große Passion* by Jörg Adolph (2012), which follows the preparations, rehearsals, and complex dynamics of the 2010 Oberammergau Passion Play, the camera catches an intimate post-production dialogue between Christian Stückl, the charismatic director of the production over the past three decades, and his close collaborator, dramaturge and deputy director, Otto Huber. As the two men speak, the camera moves from capturing their postures to showing the great shadow of the Oberammergau Kofel Mountain, which becomes background to their voices (Figure 2).

In their understated dialogue, Stückl brings up the hypothetical option that Jesus would return once again nowadays:

> STÜCKL: What if the situation was reversed and after 2000 years he were to say, "I have to stop in one more time before I return once and for all." If God were to say, "I have to make another stopover..." Do you think he'd be happy with what has become of us? Do you think he'd be happy?
> HUBER: You could've carved figurines instead...
> STÜCKL: No...
> HUBER: No, I think he'd be satisfied with you, don't you?
> STÜCKL: I don't mean personally, but ... nice of you, but I don't think he'd be happy with me either. But it's nice of you that you're trying to convince me with the opposite. Well, I think ... and that's the crazy thing about it for me, that after 2000 years of Christianity ... after 2000 years of Christianity mankind overall, with that I mean Christians as a whole, haven't really changed much.

Figure 2. Video still of the final moments of Jörg Adolph's 2012 documentary *Die große Passion* (Doc Collection; image is background to Christian Stückl's voiceover).

HUBER: I wouldn't say that.
STÜCKL: I really don't think so Otto.
HUBER: I think there are a lot of good people.
STÜCKL: But I think there were just as many back in the days of Jesus. I think Jesus would laugh his head off if he were here today. He didn't want a Catholic Church.
HUBER: Well, let's say...
STÜCKL: He told us to regard other people, to regard each individual! And if he taught us anything he taught us to care about others. When that happens, his kingdom will have come. But it won't be a Catholic Kingdom!
HUBER: Christian, Christian.... I think if this fellow from Nazareth really existed... [End of Film][1]

In this minute and understated conversation, Stückl repeats his thoughts about what he believes to be the essence of Jesus' ideas and ideals—"regarding other people" and "caring about others." Through these concepts Stückl expresses the underlying principles that guide his theatrical vision during the process of creating the Passion Play. This process is based on his deep commitment not only to staging the play, an enormous task in itself, but also to turning this artistic endeavor into one that aspires to promote an engaged community, a community that focuses on the ethical and artistic significance of the performance in addition to or even rather than its financial aspects. In this sense, the image that the film director conveys makes a clear association between Stückl, the artistic director of the production, and the idea of a (new) "Sermon on the Mount," a biblical text Stückl himself constantly refers to when he addresses the Oberammergau community during the preparations of the performance.[2] On a larger scale, however, this image also suggests the role of artists in society as influential cultural agents, even leaders, who see art and aesthetics in general and theatre specifically, as social spaces for grappling with questions of identity. This appears to be the case even within a conservative religious context such as the Oberammergau Passion Play, especially under the directorship of Stückl. Notably, in his 1918/1921 *Mystery Bouffe*, a play that relies on the biblical story of the flood as a metaphor of the revolution in Russia, Vladimir Mayakovsky performed himself in the role of "the Man of the Future," similarly paraphrasing the Sermon on the Mount. The rebellious unclean workers notice a man walking on water (Mayakovsky), approaching and addressing them:

> Who am I?/I'm of no class,/no tribe,/no clan.
> I've seen the thirtieth century/and the fortieth.
> I'm simply the man of the future.
> I came to fan/the flames in the forges of souls.
> For I know/how hard it is/to try to live.
> Listen!/A new Sermon on the Mount...[3]

Seeing in art and performance cultural sites that are related to ideological change is a significant modern phenomenon. This potentiality becomes particularly intriguing when performance engages with "closed" narratives such as religious and biblical ones, which are not only inscribed in cultural consciousness, but also continue to be relevant narratives and icons for believing spectators.[4] Through this perspective two interrelated factors can be seen as substantial to the Oberammergau Passion Play under the directorship of Stückl and his collaborative team, particularly Otto Huber and stage and costume designer Stefan Hageneier[5]: (1) the emphasis on the potentiality of art (color, design, and aesthetic effect overall) to create a sophisticated and thought-provoking mise-en-scène that touches upon questions of identity that are embedded in the history of the Oberammergau Passion Play; and (2) the commitment to dramaturgical adaptation and change as an artistic means to address cultural, political, and religious questions that are at stake.

In other words, despite the impression of a straightforward and even conservative theatricality the Passion Play might convey, it is actually based on a complex set of anachronisms, metaphors, and iconography that dialectically call spectators' attention to deeper questions that underlie the play in the twenty-first century. One of the scenes in Jörg Adolph's documentary follows a discussion between the artists and other city officials about ways to market the performance; in addition to suggestions to emphasize the play's long run and religious significance, Huber adds that "it's about change. Both change and continuity."⁶ As in religious theatre in general, here too, a profoundly anachronistic design of dramatic time enables the artists to create timeless images, that simultaneously refer to an imagined past of the sacred history as well as to a more concrete present. Significantly, such a dialectical concept of theatre is also related to German theatrical experimentalism in the second half of the twentieth century,⁷ to which Stückl is connected no less than to his roots in Oberammergau, including his experience as manager of the Munich Volkstheater and as director of numerous classical and contemporary plays.⁸

In order to examine the ways artistic choices and aesthetics become a means to address contemporary social, religious, and ethical questions, I will first focus on the theatricality that was designed to emphasize Jewish elements in the "character" of Jesus. My argument is that Stückl and Huber use this element of the scriptural narrative, Jesus being Jewish, in order to create an interreligious stage persona of Jesus from a contemporary point of view. This is done as an attempt to transmit a universal message of tolerance as well as a positive image of Judaism without giving up the retelling of the story of the Passion. In order to examine the various references this stage persona potentially evokes, I will look comparatively at a few examples of Jewish art and theatre that depict the Passion, mixing Jewish and Christian iconography, and will discuss the similarities and differences between these works and the dramaturgical and theatrical choices at Oberammergau. Although the Jewish artists do not create within a conservative and religious framework such as that of Oberammergau, they set significant examples for the complex meanings that underlie religious representations nowadays. Artists such as Marc Chagall, Barnett Newman, Hanoch Levin, and Adi Nes depict Christian iconography from a Jewish perspective, referring in their works to the Holocaust, anti–Semitism, and the meaning of suffering and sacrifice, expressing through the interreligious iconography a radically human perspective and quest for a moral and just society. Notably, Stückl is interviewed time and again emphasizing the fact that Jesus was Jewish, and in Adolph's documentary he is shown talking to a group of spectators before the performance, explaining to them that

> Jesus was a Jew from the day he was born to the day he died. On the eighth day his mother and fa ... or rather Joseph, had him circumcised. He didn't receive First Communion or Confirmation. He celebrated his Bar Mitzvah at age 12 [sic] like every devout Jewish boy. And he died on the cross as a devout Jew uttering the words of Psalms 22 "My God why hast thou forsaken me?" It was crucial to make it very clear, down to the costumes, that this isn't about Jews against Christians. It's an entirely Jewish story...⁹

The lively way Stückl talks about Judaism is connected to the present no less than to a scriptural past. In addition, the image of Judaism he conveys differs significantly from the one that used to be projected through the Oberammergau performance in earlier decades and times.[10] However, this perspective and dramaturgical choice also evoke questions about the meanings and potential implications of emphasizing Jesus' Jewishness from a contemporary Christian perspective. I would like to suggest that the performance does not aim to offer a theological reformulation of Jewish/Christian thought,[11] but rather an artistic exploration and representation of the "Other" in order to promote a deeper understanding and positive relationship between the two religions. Based on this assumption, I will also examine the performativity and aesthetics of the tableaus in the Oberammergau 2010 Passion Play, arguing that their striking colors and haunting imagery evoke an effect that exceeds doctrinal pre-figuration and calls attention to the artistic mechanism itself and its attempt to face the complexities of performing religious theatre in the twenty-first century.

A Jewish Jesus

As mentioned, one of the dramaturgical emphases in the 2010 production, particularly during the first part of the performance, is Jewish performativity that is attributed to Jesus. Although this characterization conforms to the "historical" narrative (i.e., that Jesus was Jewish), the stage iconography and performative gestures that are used to depict this identity are a matter of choice, proportion, interpretation, and design. The most explicit signifiers on stage include the actor in the role of Jesus holding wide-open a biblical scroll (Old Testament), a *menorah* with lit candles on the table of the last supper (Figure 3), and the fact that the blessings on the wine and bread that the actor in the role of Jesus performs during the last supper are performed in *Hebrew*.[12] In Adolph's documentary Huber and other Oberammergau officials are shown visiting the Vatican with a gift for the Pope, a picture from the performance. The scene that is chosen is the one with the menorah on the table of the last supper. This is also the image that appears on the back cover the 2010 picture album of the performance.[13] These icons and gestures refer simultaneously to an image of the past *and* to contemporary signifiers of the Jewish religion. Although the idea is to convey an image of Judaism by using icons that can be recognized by contemporary audiences "as Jewish," thus creating stage anachronisms that are typical of religious theatre, still, these are quite bold signifiers that lead to deictic moments in the performance that point at their own theatricality and call attention to the complex theological, historical, and cultural relations between the two religions in general and to the history of the Oberammergau Passion Play particularly. In addition, reciting the ritualistic blessings in Hebrew stands out in strike

Figure 3. A *menorah* at the center of the table, "The Lord's Supper" (http://www.passionplay-oberammergau.com/uploads/media/Last_supper_02.jpg, accessed June 10, 2014).

contrast to the fact that the rest of the dialogue is in German. These theatrical gestures (perhaps even *gestus* to use the Brechtian term) turn the character of Jesus in the performance into a complex, interreligious, and multi-layered sign, which does not easily conform to conventional depictions of either Jewish or Christian iconography. During the second part of the performance, as the play moves into the scenes of the Passion, Crucifixion, and Resurrection, the iconographic emphases of Jesus' Jewishness lessen and the representation coheres more straightforwardly with conventional Christian iconography. This leaves the questions about "Jesus' Jewishness" and their implications somewhat open and unsettled. In this sense, the performance should be seen as a work of art that problematizes issues at stake, in an attempt to transmit a message of religious tolerance while keeping the Christian narrative intact.

It is interesting to compare this interreligious depiction of Jesus at Oberammergau with works of art created by Jewish artists who blend Jewish and Christian iconography in their art. At Oberammergau this theatrical gesture is principally intended to offer a corrective depiction of anti–Semitic representations of the Jews, a plea for a respectful dialogue between the two religions, and an attempt to take into consideration the deeper connections between ideas that appear in both Judaism and Christianity. Similarly, Jewish artists who depict Jesus as simultaneously Jewish and Christian do so in order to express ethical and philosophical questions by problematizing and alienating deeply embedded cultural, religious, and mythological icons.[14]

Perhaps most famous are the paintings of Marc Chagall (1887–1985). In his *White Crucifixion* (1938) the central image is the Crucifixion, around which are scattered images of the "burning Jewish town," including men and women in traditional Jewish attire, running away and crying for help clinging to Torah scrolls, a lit Shabbat candelabra, and more. Most significantly, the figure of Christ has a Jewish prayer shawl (*tallit*) instead of the conventional loincloth; the cross itself, typical of Chagall's surrealism, seems to be floating in the air, and a ladder leaning on it, refers simultaneously to the act of carrying out of the Crucifixion as well as to Jacob's ladder. On the right top corner is a burning synagogue, most likely referring to the events of *Kristallnacht* (Night of the Broken Glass) that took place in Germany during that year.

In his *Yellow Crucifixion* (1943) the Crucified Jesus has phylacteries on his head and left arm, a drip of blood on his right chest, a blue loincloth, and he holds wide open a Torah scroll; In front of the Torah there is a flying angel holding a lit candle in its left hand and in its right hand holding and blowing a shofar (ram's horn). At the lower part of the painting, a family is fleeing; the mother's face is blue (probably referring to Mary) and she holds a child and a baby in her arms. The background yet again depicts scenes of the "burning *Shtetl*." Chagall's irony, despair, and critique are evident, and yet, because of the way he creates the Jewish/Christian hybrids, the message that comes through is a complex one, raising deep ethical questions about suffering, sacrifice, and actions that are taking place without any signs of redemption.[15]

Unlike Chagall's surrealistic paintings of the war and anti–Semitism in Europe, the works of the American and Jewish artist Barnett Newman (1905–1970) are characterized by minimalist abstract qualities. In his 1958–1966 series titled *Stations of the Cross: Eli Eli Lema Sabachthani* he takes a radically human perspective to examine Jesus's turning to God on the cross, questioning why he has been forsaken.[16] In Newman's statement accompanying the Guggenheim exhibition of the installation in 1966 he writes:

> Lema Sabachthani—why? Why did you forsake me? Why forsake me? To what purpose? Why? This is the Passion. This outcry of Jesus. Not the terrible walk up the Via Dolorosa, but the question that has no answer. This overwhelming question that does not complain, makes today's talk of alienation, as if alienation were a modern invention, an embarrassment. This question that has no answer has been with us so long—since Jesus—since Abraham—since Adam—the original question. Lema? To what purpose—is the unanswerable question of human suffering.[17]

Although in Newman's *Stations of the Cross* conventional religious iconography (Jewish or Christian) is nullified and replaced by abstract-expressive variations on a similar and repetitive theme—black or white stripes on raw canvases, his works have been contextualized by Thomas Hess in relation to

Jewish thought, including Jewish mysticism and the Kabbalah. Hess interprets the *Stations* and their relation to Newman's Jewish cultural heritage:

> *Be* is the imperative of God of the Jews. Man should *be*; he should work in the Lord's ways in order to be able to stand before Him—as a man, in a place (*Makom*), just as the orange stripe—the color which for Newman represented man since *Onement I*, 1948—stands across the white field from its sever counterpart in black.... Christ for Newman in the Stations is not the Messiah, nor is the Passion a ritual of fourteen steps on the road to Resurrection. Rather, Christ is man; prototypical man born to suffering. He has lived from the beginning of the world until now. He suffers the torments of the artist, for "the first man was an artist." And the goal for all men is to be artists. He forgives enemies, but after life's humiliations and pains have become unbearable, he asks God the unanswerable question—Lema Sabachthani? And God replies: *Be!*[18]

However, Newman's conscious reappropriation of a Christian narrative as specifically mentioned in the title of the installation is most likely done in an attempt to express a human, universal, and existentialist message, turning this icon into a complex sign, overflowed with potential meanings and references that go beyond an either Jewish or Christian context. This installation turns the artistic viewing experience into one of contemplation, yet one that resists and even undermines religious practice.

Another variation of this phenomenon is a radical play by Israeli playwright Hanoch Levin (1943-1998), *The Torments of Job* (1981), which retells in a troubling and grotesque way the biblical story of Job, trying to touch upon the essence of humiliation and suffering. In contrast to the Biblical version, Levin's Job cannot bear his torments and denies the existence of God. His friends try to comfort him and convince him to reassert his belief, which he does, imagining that God is caressing him as if God were his own father. Unwilling to give up this revelation, he is then confronted with soldiers who threat, at the order of the Emperor, to skewer any Jew who will not deny the Jewish God. Although Job's life can be saved by denying God as he did just a short while ago, he refuses to do so and is skewered in an extremely humiliating ritual, which turns into a grotesque version of the Crucifixion.

Eventually, unlike the biblical story of Job once again, he is left to die and is not redeemed. However, in Levin's play the sacrificial figure that is created is more complex than a mixture of Job and Jesus (a Christian conventional prefigurative paradigm), but also the play contains modern references through this character to a Holocaust victim. For example, "Job's" tormentors pull out his "golden teeth"[19] or humiliate him by shoving a boot into his face. By adding the reference to modern Jewish history, Levin further complicates the timeless and interreligious sacrificial figure.

Whereas these three examples differ in artistic means of expression but share an ethical and philosophical encounter with existentialist questions about the nature of human suffering, sacrifice, and victimhood by reinterpreting and even profaning religious concepts and specifically by depicting interreligious Jewish/Christian figures, my final example straightforwardly addresses identity politics. Israeli Photographer Adi Nes (1966–) is famous for his staged photographs and tableaus, in which he conflates contemporary political and social issues with iconic referential systems and often with religious iconography. His series *Biblical Stories* (2003–2006) is composed of "restagings" of figures and stories mostly from the Old Testament, and yet many of his works rely on Christian art and iconography.[20] One of his worldly renowned works from a previous series titled *Soldiers* is *Untitled (Last Supper)* (1999) in which the religious figures of the Last Supper are replaced by Israeli soldiers, signifying the coming death of the soldier in the middle who gazes contemplatively in the air. Perhaps most relevant to the discussion here, however, is Nes's *Untitled (Christ)* (2009),[21] which is a portrait of a bearded and long-haired man looking down with a serious and contemplative expression. He also has a notably long nose. Despite the lack of signifiers other than the beard and the long hair, even without the subtitle of the "untitled" photograph, it is hard to miss the reference. However, because of the long nose of the man in the portrait, this work, much like many others by Nes's, calls attention to cultural signs and the ways they construct and take part in constructing social relations and stereotypical prejudice. The fact that the man in the photograph has a long nose most likely refers to anti–Semitic images of Jewishness, turning this photo into an interreligious, ironic, and deconstructive expression about the ways identities are imagined, fixated, and performed.[22] The medium of photography, like theatre, refers simultaneously to the real human being who is the performer and to the culturally inscribed image of the "character." This is what makes the image unsettling and one that cannot be simply experienced as a typical iconographic reiteration, but rather one that relies on cultural knowledge and stereotypes in order to problematize questions regarding identity politics and Otherness.

The works examined so far have all been created not as "religious art" for ritualistic purposes but rather within secular, avant-garde, and experimental *artistic* contexts. The Oberammergau Passion Play is, however, obviously much more related to conventional and conservative paradigms of religious art and performance. And yet, it seems that the concept of art and performance brought forth by the directorial team at Oberammergau similarly embraces the potentiality of art as a social and performative site rather than a merely representational one. This concept enables interpretation and adaptation of "closed" narratives and images in ways that are comparable with more radical examples of a similar phenomenon. Moreover, as in the other works examined here, the emphasis on Jewish elements in the performativity of Jesus in the 2010 production, demonstrates the complexities and potentialities that are embedded in this theatrical choice.

The Tableaus

The scenes in the 2010 Oberammergau play that retell the narrative of the passion from Jesus' entrance to Jerusalem to the Resurrection are designed by employing a serene and deep color palette. There is a great emphasis on a deep blue that serves as the dominant background of the performance, as well as a sophisticated and subtle color-degradé of blue, black, white, and golden-orange for the costumes. In contrast, the tableaus that represent events from the Old Testament are designed in strikingly bright colors and expressive aesthetics. Each one of the tableaus has a different bright background color, including yellow, green, red, orange, and more. In addition, the design of the tableaus themselves, beyond the colors, is expressive, suggestive, and at times almost surrealistic. For example, the tableau of the Passover meal before fleeing Egypt is designed with a striking red background, a bleeding sheep in the center, and a big skull in the front.[23]

The aesthetic dissonance between the tableaus and the narrative parts of the play clearly distinguishes between pre-figurative events of the Old Testament and those of the New Testament, just as the stillness of the tableaus differs from the more "realistic" acting in the narrative scenes. And yet the striking colors and overall design of the tableaus in this production, which are innovative in comparison to earlier productions of the Passion Play, emphasize the artistry of the event and point at the dialectical and unsettling issues the performance raises. It is yet another expression of the centrality of art in this production as a means to question religious representations in the twenty-first century.

Moreover, it was under the directorship of Stückl that the events of the 2000 Passion Play included Robert Wilson's avant-garde installation *14 Stations*,[24] similarly positioning a modernist aesthetics alongside a conventional and conservative one.

Following its presentation at Oberammergau, it was positioned at Mass MOCA (Massachusetts Museum of Contemporary Art), about which James D. Herbert writes: "Wilson's *14 Stations*, installed here [at Mass MOCA], represents religion—both repeating and reversing it—held before the scrutiny of contemporary art."[25] About its inclusion in the 2000 Oberammergau event Herbert adds that "the commissioning of *14 Stations* thus allowed the community to make a gesture of atonement, not in spite of but because of the work's jarring incongruity. The Passion play may have stood steady on its timeless foundations, but the full experience of the packaged tour promised the dialogue between tradition and modernity so problematically reduced to a whisper within the drama itself. Oberammergau needed Wilson less as a reiteration of the Passion (though it was that) than as an artistic counterweight to it."[26] It seems that whereas in the 2000 performance, for obvious reasons, Stückl and Huber were somewhat reluctant to introduce major artistic innovations into the performance itself, in the 2010 production, based on the trust they built with the community, more artistic freedom was allowed. Interestingly, rather than designing scenes from the Old Testament as "old," the bright colors and visual images are expressed by a "new" and even futuristic artistic style.

In conclusion, through the lens of art, theatricality, and aesthetics religious representations in the twenty-first century can become a site that enables simultaneous—if dialectical—"change and continuity." Art cannot change history, but it can call attention to its own mechanisms and accordingly to ethical questions that are being negotiated. In the case of religious performance such as the Oberammergau Passion Play, which is struggling to find its meaning nowadays, it seems that art and aesthetics as have been discussed in this chapter are embraced because of their potentiality to problematize cultural, historical, and religious issues.

Notes

1. The conversation is in German and the quotes are from the film's English subtitles. Jörg Adolph, *Die Große Passion: Hinter den Kulissen von Oberammergau* DVD 2012; 144 min.
2. There are two DVDs that were created in relation to the 2010 production. In 2010 part of the merchandise at Oberammergau included a DVD with two 45 min. films; the first film is about the preparations of the performance and the history of the Passion-Play and the second one documents the trip to Israel (the Holy Land) that Stückl and a group of thirty leading actors make in preparation of the performance. This film documents not only visits to religious holy sites (Christian and Jewish), but also a visit to the Yad Va Shem Holocaust Memorial Museum in Jerusalem. See *Die Oberammergauer Leidenschaft* (Passionate Oberammergau); directed by Jörg Adolph and Ralph Bücheler, 2010. The second and fuller documentary, from which I quote in this essay, is Jörg Adolph's 2012 two-and-a-half-hour film, *Die große Passion: Hinter den Kulissen von Oberammergau*.
3. Vladimir Mayakovsky, *Mystery Bouffe* in *The Complete Plays of Vladimir Mayakovsky*, trans. Guy Daniels (New York: Simon & Schuster, 1971), 86–87.
4. See more on this issue in my essay "Religious Theatre and the Potentiality of Live Art," in *Inter-Art Journey*, ed. Nurit Yaari (Brighton: Sussex Academic, 2015) 163–79.
5. For details about the artists see the 2010 Oberammergau Passion Play Press Kit, especially pages 13–14. http://www.passionplayoberammergau.com/uploads/media/english_Press_kit_28_November_01.pdf (accessed June 10, 2014).
6. Jörg Adolph, *Die Große Passion* min. 50.
7. Clearly the theories and practices of Bertolt Brecht have had immense impact on German experimental theatre in the second half of the twentieth century; see also Marvin Carlson's *Theatre Is More Beautiful Than War: German Stage Directing in the Late Twentieth Century* (Iowa City: University of Iowa Press, 2009).
8. Http://www.goethe.de/kue/the/reg/reg/sz/stu/enindex.htm (accessed June 10, 2014); https://www.muenchner-volkstheater.de/ensemble/regisseure/christian-st%C3%BCckl (accessed June 10, 2014).

9. Jörg Adolph, *Die große Passion* min. 2:02:50.

10. See, for example, James Shapiro's *Oberammergau: The Troubling Story of the World's Most Famous Passion Play* (New York: Vintage, 2001).

11. These issues are seriously studied and being discussed in contemporary Christian discourses, particularly under the papacy of Pope Francis. See, for example, http://www.religionnews.com/2014/06/13/pope-francis-inside-every-christian-jew/ (accessed June 20, 2014).

12. See the 2010 *Passionsspiele Oberammergau Textbook* (Oberammergau: Gemeinde Oberammergau, 2010), 47–51 ("The Lord's Supper"). See also Kevin Wetmore's essay in this volume.

13. *Passionspiele 2010 Oberammergau* (Munich: Prestel, 2010).

14. See, for example, Zev Garber, ed., *The Jewish Jesus: Revelation, Reflection, Reclamation* (Indianapolis: Purdue Press, 2011); Neta Stahl, ed., *Jesus Among the Jews: Representation and Thought* (New York: Routledge, 2012); especially Amitai Mendelsohn's "Jesus of the Sabra Thorns: The Figure of Jesus in Israeli Art," 203–215; Marina Hayman, "Christ in the Works of Two Jewish Artists: When Art in Interreligious Dialogue," *Studies in Jewish Christians Relations* 4 (2009): 1–14.

15. For a recent discussion of these and other related works by Chagall see Susan Tumarkin Goodman's *Chagall: Love, War, and Exile* (New York: The Jewish Museum, 2013).

16. *The Stations of the Cross: Lema Sabachthani* was first presented in 1966 at the Guggenheim Museum in New York City.

17. Quoted in Thomas B. Hess, *Barnett Newman* (New York: The Museum of Modern Art, 1971), 98.

18. *Ibid.*, 103–104. See also Mathew Baigell, "Barnett Newman's Stripe Paintings and Kabbalah: A Jewish Take," *American Art* 8:2 (1994): 32–43.

19. Hanoch Levin, *The Torments of Job*, trans. Barbara Harshav, in *The Labor of Life: Selected Plays of Hanoch Levin* (Palo Alto: Stanford University Press, 2003), 62–63. See also Sharon Aronson-Lehavi, "Transformations of Religious Performativity: Sacrificial Figures in Modern Experimental Theatre," *Performance and Spirituality* 3:1 (2012): 57–70.

20. See Dorit LeVitte Harten, "'Less the Horror than the Grace,'" in *Adi Nes: Biblical Stories, The Tel Aviv Museum of Art*, Curator: Mordechai Omer, 2007; 146–128; and Susan Chevlow, "Adi Nes's Biblical Stories," in *Adi Nes: Biblical Stories* 126–116.

21. Http://www.jackshainman.com/artist-image279.html (accessed June 10, 2014).

22. In this context see also Douglas Rosenberg, "Self Portraits (As a Jew)," *TDR* 55:3 (2011): 68–71.

23. *Passionspiele 2010 Oberammergau* (Munich: Prestel, 2010), 36–37.

24. Robert Wilson, *14 Stations* (Munich: Prestel Publications, 2000).

25. James D. Herbert, *Our Distance from God: Studies in the Divine and Mundane in Western Art and Music* (Berkeley: University of California Press, 2008), 134.

26. *Ibid.*, 135.

PART 2

Comparative Oberammergaus

Spiritual Voyeurism and Cultural Nostalgia
Anglophone Visitors to the Oberammergau Passion Play, 1870–1925 and 2010

Joshua Edelman

When I visited the Oberammergau Passion Play in the summer of 2010, I was struck by the hybridity of the experience. I was attending an international meeting of theatre scholars in Munich, and two busloads of us made the two-hour trip for the day's experience. What we saw was like no other event we had witnessed before. It was, in parts, a religious pilgrimage, a local cultural festival, a historical tribute, a crafts fair, a tourist trap, and the largest and most elaborate piece of amateur dramatics any of us had ever seen. These impulses behind these different aspects—religious devotion, cultural pride, artistic grandeur, and economic development—sat in a tension that fascinated us as observers of theatre as an artistic and social practice.

But there was one other aspect of the day that we could not ignore. The mechanics of welcoming and caring for thousands of audience members from across the world—a group larger than the village's population—were handled remarkably smoothly. Transport, refreshments, souvenirs, programs, tickets, and seating all went off without a hitch. While the performance was only in German, every other need a visitor might have could be catered for in half a dozen languages. During the dinner break, the restaurants were plentiful and quick, and everyone had time to finish their ice cream and browse the shops before the bells rang for the second half. I have never been to a theatrical event in New York or London that was this well-organized. But then, this was clearly no ordinary piece of theatre.

These two traits—hybridity and organizational smoothness—appeared as two sides of the same coin. As visitors, our impression was not that of a hybrid performance which was built on its own and had only later opened up to an audience of tourists and pilgrims. Rather, the two seemed to have grown in tandem: the need to cater for such a diverse and international audience had led to the hybridity of the event. As theatre scholars, we were also aware that this is how performance traditions develop: audiences, performers, organizers, and communities develop their practices in dialogue with one another, especially for performance traditions that have develop through many years and many iterations as has the Oberammergau Passion.[1]

So the twin questions of how this act of religious devotion became such a fascinating hybrid of culture, heritage, commerce and faith, and how the performance grew to become so central a tourist institution as to completely dominate the life of the village are, in fact, one and the same. If we could trace out the ways in which the audience for the Passion developed, we would be tracing out the development of the play itself. This is known as 'reception history' in theatre studies, and this chapter hopes to make a contribution to it.

Many histories and critical appraisals of the Passion exist in the literature. The most modern and helpful for the contemporary reader is James Shapiro's *Oberammergau: The Troubling Story of the World's Most Famous Passion Play* (2000). While Shapiro's book has a broad scope, its focus is on the twentieth century, and in particular, on Oberammergau's role in the rise of Nazism and in the controversies around Catholic anti–Semitism in the decades following World War II and the Second Vatican Council. These are, clearly, the areas in which the Passion has generated the most controversy, and Shapiro's narrative teases them out well. But in order to understand the development of Oberammergau as an international cultural and tourist destination, I would like to go back a bit farther, to the late nineteenth century, when technological and economic developments led to the globalization of the Passion for the first time in its history.

In particular, this essay will look at the responses that American and especially British audiences had to these productions. From 1870 to about 1925, a considerable corpus of popular and semi-scholarly literature emerged from those who had made the journey to the Oberammergau Passion, and were eager to report back on their experiences to others. In some ways, they resemble the narratives of the Hajj, the Muslim pilgrimage to Mecca that had long existed in the Islamic world but began circulating around Europe in the late Victorian and Edwardian eras. In other ways, they resemble the exoticized orientalist travel narratives that also found great popularity in Europe at this time. They could also serve as commercial advertisements and guides for future visitors. But occasionally, they also take the form of the letters of a pilgrim, seeking to capture a profound religious experience for their own continued devotion and to share it with their friends and fellow believers. We can trace these tensions out in this literature, and through it, a sense of what the Oberammergau Passion meant for its new audiences.

* * *

Passion Plays, of course, were common in Bavaria, as in much of Catholic Europe, from the Middle Ages well into the eighteenth century. But there were three developments that helped to position the Oberammergau Passion as a particularly attractive one around which to build an international market.

First, there was a reduction in competition. In the late eighteenth century, the Catholic Church began banning passion plays as potential sources of heresy and as inappropriate for the laity. The 1770 Oberammergau Passion was not performed as a result. The Oberammergauers, however, were able to negotiate a dispensation from the Catholic authorities by pruning all "objectionable and unseemly mater" from the performance,[2] and by 1800, Oberammergau was effectively the only Passion left in Bavaria.

Next, the Passion developed a remarkable following within and around Bavaria. The excitement was so great that in 1870, King Ludwig II of Bavaria commissioned his royal photographer, Joseph Albert, to take a set of photographs of the performers in their costumes on set.[3] These are staged photographs, and to contemporary eyes, they look rather stiff, even if they do provide a useful record of the costumes and set of these mid-century performances. What is more important, however, is that these photographs were published and distributed widely, spreading the Passion's fame far beyond those who had previously made the journey to Oberammergau.

And finally, the railroad network around Europe and southern Germany greatly developed at the end of the nineteenth century. Munich had become within easy reach of other European cities by rail by the latter part of the century, and a train line to Oberammergau itself was in place in time for the performance in 1900. The arduous voyage that earlier visitors described in getting to Oberammergau in 1850 or 1860, then, was much easier. This ease came from the general development of transport links across the continent, not simply the rail line to Oberammergau. This relative ease of travel meant that, at least for those who could afford it, Oberammergau offered a unique, famous, and exotic experience that was both enticingly rare yet still accessible enough to be a reasonable part of a Grand Tour or a summer's voyage to the Continent.

Aside from these technological developments, we should also recognize a cultural one: that the turn of the twentieth century was the waning days of English Romanticism. The appeal of a small Alpine village maintaining a medieval performance tradition in pure sincerity with no care for the modern world was, for some, irresistibly alluring. Such an appeal was not universal or unequivocal—Alpine pastoral romanticism was not to everyone's taste by 1890—but it did attract a certain sort of cultural seeker to the Passion.

There was, however, one major disincentive. The devout Catholicism of the Oberammergauers was not appealing to the rationalist, Protestant English visitors. American visitors more influenced by Emersonian Transcendentalism may have been more willing to embrace the Passion as simply a spiritual experience, but the Passion was not such an amorphously spiritual creation. It was concrete, and that was the problem. The Catholic doctrine and imagery that so pervade the Passion—its Marian devotion, its typological reading of Old Testament narratives, and its enthusiastic embrace of a visual and tactile New Testament narrative with a maximum of sensory detail and a minimum of metaphorical gloss—were not aspects that the cultured English visitors could valorize or affirm. Passion Plays themselves, of course, had a history in medieval England, but it was seen as a crude and somewhat barbarous old tradition that the educated modern Englishman would wish to distance himself from. If the attractive and admirable qualities of the Oberammergau Passion—that which was worth taking home with them—was to be understood as religious or spiritual, then it needed to be extracted out of the embarrassing and inappropriate Catholic package in which it came.

The solution to this puzzle was to treat Oberammergau anthropologically, not theologically. The particular doctrines and narratives of the Passion were less important than the simple, sincere, and almost primitive faith that it exemplified. Oberammergau became the place that the modern world, with its interests and troubles, had overlooked. In particular, English visitors were keen to emphasize that whatever else it was, the Oberammergau Passion was not a capitalist venture. Any income it happened to generate was nearly an accident and certainly not the purpose of the whole affair.

This nostalgic opposition to capitalist modernity is, of course, an ideological self-positioning that requires an understanding of modernity to assert. Oberammergau may have been a village, but the villagers understood the world around them, they were able to effectively navigate the world of princes and priests, railmen and restaurateurs, and businessmen of all sorts. They were far from naïve peasants whom the world just happened to discover. Ironically, the Oberammergau Passion was only possible as an international pilgrimage because of the very technological, capitalist system that its visitors so longed to escape.

* * *

While a very few English visitors were present in earlier years,[4] the first wave of correspondents arrived in Oberammergau for the 1871 performance, and their narratives they sent back were formative in shaping views of the Passion in England. A number of periodicals ran reviews; most expressed surprise that such crude peasants could make so compelling a performance. The *Times* ran a review from the Rev. Malcolm MacColl, the Anglican rector of St George's Church in Bloomsbury, London. His amazement was palpable:

> I went to see it with very mixed feelings. From what I had heard and read, I was prepared for a striking exhibition, but also half prepared for some rude shocks to one's natural sense of religious propriety. So impossible did it seem to represent on a public stage and in a worthy manner the sublime story of Gethsemane and Calvary. Well, I have seen it, and I shall go home with the conviction that the thing is not impossible where a vivid faith and an intense devotion are combined in the representation. I have never seen so affecting a spectacle, or one more calculated to draw out the best and purest feelings of the heart.[5]

Note that he does not mention theological precision or artistic skill alongside faith and devotion. The affective power came not from the quality or accuracy of the performance, but from the sincerity of the performers. And the Play's power was not in what it depicted, but in how the audience responded to it (the "drawing out"). The trope of the Oberammergau Passion as a surprisingly compelling diamond in the rough was echoed by another reviewer, who called himself simply "An Oxonian," who was struck by the quaintness and "simplicity" of the performance:

> All through the Play, I kept repeating to myself, "This is a primitive mediaeval, half-civilized peasantry, still sunk in the trammels of priestcraft; it has never known what it is to have an open Bible, and a free press; it is deprived of the blessings of the Electric Telegraph, and is about 800 years behind the present age." But it would not do. I would not but confess that I was witnessing, not only a beautiful, but a most subtle and delicate and thoughtful rendering of the Gospel history.[6]

We should not, perhaps, take these expressions of surprise too literally. The trope of the world-weary urban sophisticate who travels to a place that time has forgotten and discovers the noble simplicity and grace of untrammeled natural man is an old one, and these writers were reenacting it in their prose. It is noteworthy that few of these reviews describe the performance in much detail, but rather, focus on their journey and their delight at what they found. It made for punchy journalism and piqued English interest in Oberammergau. But it was not enough to sustain a relationship with the play.

In order to make Oberammergau into not just a romantic surprise but a repeatable reality, this initial attraction needed to be given substance through more than the occasional pamphlet, review and literary journal. This mix of sentiment, nostalgia and devotion needed to be packaged and sold to the British public. It would be unwise to underestimate the role in this of Thomas Cook and Son, the pioneering travel agents and expedition planners who introduced several generations of well-to-do Britons to the luxuries and excitements of international travel. Thomas, the founder, was a Baptist with a strong pro-temperance position, and his son was equally staunch in his nonconformist Protestantism. They were in no way sympathetic to the Catholic demonstrativeness of the Passion. And yet, they were businessmen and knew an opportunity when they saw one. In preparation for the 1880 production, which was one of the earliest to attract a large international audience, the Cooks put aside their personal distaste for the Passion and "felt compelled to take such steps as we considered necessary to secure the best possible arrangement and the greatest comforts we could for the large number of comparatively wealthy and well-educated English speaking travelers, whom we knew would wish to travel under our arrangements to Ammergau."[7] The company opened a temporary office in Oberammergau in 1879, which would become permanent in 1930 and remain open into the twenty-first century. However, in promoting Oberammergau, the company took pains to separate its own cosmopolitan, commercial aims from those of the village in order to appear to be appropriately respectful of the simplicity and certainly not motivated by profit:

> We gave instruction to our representatives specially to avoid entering into any arrangements which could possibly offend the susceptible villagers, or be looked upon by any one as combining pleasure or money-making with religious object, and in that spirit we declined proposals made to us by speculators who wanted the use of our name to support them in announcements.... [We did this all] without charging the traveler a single penny for our services.[8]

The Passion may not have been religiously supportable for the Baptist Cook, but it—and the villagers who put it on—did have a sort of fragile innocence that was "susceptible" to contamination and thus ruination from the influence of the modern (and commercial) world. (Exactly how Thomas Cook expected to bring 6000 well-off British tourists to a rural Bavarian village without introducing more than a bit of modern influence is another matter.[9]) The Cooks refer to the villagers' religion as a sign of their faith and purity, but they are not themselves making a religious appeal. Twenty years later, in promoting tours to the 1900 production, the Cook advertisement was even more explicit about this distinction. In particular, it was important that the performance was so without artifice that it was not only non-commercial, it was in fact not a piece of theatre:

> Oberammergau ... as an embodiment of simple old-world faith and piety is without parallel in our day.... The scenery surrounding this picturesque Bavarian village speaks to the traveler of peace and simplicity, idylls and pastorals—of anything, in short, rather than a great theatrical exhibition. And indeed it is due to the villagers to state that they do not consider the taking a part in the Passion Play a dramatic performance, but an act of worship. It is this important fact that elevates the representation above all other spectacles and renders it so profoundly impressive to the beholder.[10]

What was being sold in Oberammergau, then, was not the quality of the performance or even value of the spiritual instruction it could offer, but rather the sincerity and authenticity of the performers. This could be "profoundly impressive" even to the most skeptical of Englishmen. By treating the Oberammergauers as stalwart guardians of an ancient mindset and tradition, it was not necessary to admire the content or form of the performance to admire that they were doing it.

* * *

This admiration seems to have been necessary, because for many visitors, the performance did not meet particularly high standards of artistic quality or theatrical taste. Fairly typical was Benno Rauchenegger's description in *Bruckmann's Illustrated Guides* from 1900:

> Simplicity and naturalness, supported by a certain religious enthusiasm, lend to the homely gifts of the country actors a consecrated dignity that cannot fail to make an impression on the spectator and to put to silence every critical analysis. In consequence of the great success obtained by the people of Oberammergau, there has been no lack of attempts to alter the present form of the Passion Play, and to propose changes in accordance with views on modern art, but these endeavors have met with no acquiescence on the part of the conservative population, and we shall not be going far wrong, if we approve of their persisting in this line of action. Not that the Play is incapable of improvement, nay rather that it is in need of it—but whether the improvements could be just as well mastered by the performers, is a question difficult to answer.[11]

For others, of course, this pastoral dignity was not enough to overcome the Passion's weaknesses. Henry Gideon wrote that only "a religious devotion which condones every shortcoming, will obliterate the memory of the wretchedness of the musical performance of the musical performance which accompanied the Passionspiel of 1910. No intelligent tourist who possesses an iota of the critical faculty can take exception to this statement."[12] Gideon's view may stand on the more polite end of the mockery of the Oberammergauer's peasant ways, and other voices defended them from this mockery. Hermine Diemer prefaced her 1900 account of the play with the claim that "the Ammergauers are a people which [sic] deserve to be taken earnestly and to be treated earnestly, and that neither they nor their Play deserve the assault and ridicule which is hurled upon them from certain quarters."[13] This tension between those who thought that the villagers' sincerity and simplicity excused all artistic shortcomings and those who did not can be seen in the differing responses of the explorer Richard Burton and his wife Isabel Burton to the performance. Richard found the performance dull, poorly done, and uninteresting. But for Isabel, the experience was one of transformation. Yes, she admitted, quoting approvingly from MacColl and the Oxonian, there may be a "shortcoming here and there," but "it seemed not a play, but as if we were carried back eighteen hundred and forty-seven years ago, and that all was real, and we were talking part in it."[14] This denial that there was any artifice in what, for any of its faults, was clearly a consciously staged production extended to a denial that it was done for the audience's benefit. "They are unconscious of us," she wrote. "They did not ask us to come, they cannot hinder us in coming."[15] This frankly ridiculous fiction—that the villagers simply are acting naturally, that Oberammergau in fact *is* some sort of religious otherworld with an appropriate disdain connection for the economics of this massive audience—is one the Oberammergauers were not above promoting themselves. The published script of the 1922 Passion includes this in its preface:

> We are often reproached that the spirit of the vow is extinct, and that the Play is a matter is a mere matter of speculation [i.e., business]. If that were so, we should surely not have taken the important step of resuming the matter, which brings us uncertainty and which might be our ruin. We have brought many sacrifices for our object, the Community is striving to produce the Play in a worthy manner, and to offer a pleasant home to their guests, but we do not expect great profit or riches. We cling to our tradition with faithfulness, in remembrance of our forefathers, and hope to be remembered in the same way.[16]

One does not have to accuse the villagers of insincerity to say that they had done the math and knew the enormous economic impact that the Passion had on the town. That they felt the need to include this in the Preface—in English, notably—does indicate that they knew how important it was that the outside world saw them that as disinterested in their own performance as anything but devoted, faithful service. Note, however, the slight equivocation here: the faithfulness shown is to the vow, to tradition, and to the forefathers, but not to God or the Church, as would have been the case a century earlier. Tradition has replaced religion as the focal point of the Oberammergauer's simple sincerity. This position was, of course, far less taxing for Protestant tourists, and did not require one to actually change the performance, only the way it was publicized.

This tendency to treat the Passion as a natural outpouring of the character of the village itself was perhaps encouraged by the normal mode of housing for visitors to the productions through at least 1900. As a rule, the performances would begin early in the morning, pause around noon for lunch, and finish in the late afternoon.[17] This made arriving on the day of the performance impractical. Therefore, most visitors arrived the evening before. Lacking adequate hotels, guests would stay overnight in the home of villagers, have breakfast with them in the morning, see the performance, and leave in the late afternoon. The experience of the arriving in a strange village and sharing room and board with a local—who may very well be seen a few hours later on stage—was part of the charm. An illustrated travelogue for children titled *Zigzagging Amongst Dolomoites* (unsigned, but authored by Elizabeth Tuckett) which tells the story of a family's travels around Europe, describes staying "in the house of 'Nathaniel'"—which may be the name of her host or his role, or a deliberate elision of the two—in the same sentence as describing the lingering music and "bright-robed chorus."[18] For some, these were simply substandard accommodations. "Much has been said of the poor accommodation and scarcity of food," wrote A.W. Buckland in 1872,[19] but for many, this simply added to the excitement of living amongst people who "seem to belong more to the past than the present"[20] and were not so much performing the Passion as living it.

One of the consequences of this identification of the play with the people of Oberammergau was the frequent idea amongst supporters of the Passion that it would be wholly inappropriate for it to tour outside of the village, or for it to lead to a surge of staging of passion plays by others elsewhere. In Oberammergau, the character of the village and the isolation and infrequency of the event made the Passion possible and noble. Elsewhere, or by others, it would be corrupted by the profit motive or cynically manipulated by modernity, becoming blasphemous, crude or simply inappropriate. George Molloy, who was especially impressed with his visit to the Passion in 1871, was nevertheless clear that it ought not to be brought back to England:

> The peculiar combination of circumstances which, in the course of many generations, has brought it to its present perfection in this mountain hamlet, could not, I think, be found elsewhere in the world; nor could they long subsist, even here, without the protection which is afforded by its rare recurrence. The curiosity of visitors would easily degenerate into irreverence, and the simple piety of the people would inevitably suffer from frequent contact with an ever-changing concourse of tourists.[21]

As early as 1860, one correspondent who was quite impressed with the Passion thought it wholly inappropriate for "the natural reserve and delicacy of a more northern and more civilized people.... This, beyond all dispute, is an institution which cannot be transplanted without provoking sentiments the exact opposite of those which it excites in its own locality."[22]

The view had not changed much twenty years later: in 1890, the Irish priest P.J. O'Reilly visited in 1890 and reported back that "one place alone exists where any effort to represent Christ's Passion in a drama would not be either artistically weak and ineffective, and consequently disedifying and repulsive or on the part of some of those engaged be mercenary, and therefore blasphemous and sacrilegious. That place is Ober-Ammergau."[23] Part of what these writers were reacting to was what they saw as the impressive stoicism, seriousness and closeness to the Gospel narrative the Oberammergau Passion, at least as it was staged in the late nineteenth century. (Earlier productions, as Shapiro notes, may have been quite different.[24]) The English tradition of mystery plays that they were more familiar with, in contrast, was (rightly) seen as one that was heavy on ribald (or "indecent") humor, larger-than-life characters, and broad comedy and melodrama, with only a thin link to biblical narratives. As a form of public religion, this raucous crowd-pleasing carnival was seen as backwards at best. A.W. Buckland wrote, "Now that we have attained to somewhat of light, let us know seek to go back into the darkness. If curiosity leads us to see a miracle play let us wait till 1880, and then visit Ober Ammergau, but let us not seek to re-introduce among us that which is so happily dead and buried."[25]

* * *

There is, after all, something dangerous about a Passion Play, and it has to do with the audience. All theatre audiences have the potential to become unruly mobs, and there have been a great many techniques that theatre and performance makers have used over the centuries to tame and control them.[26] For most contemporary thinkers, including Shapiro, the great danger of the tradition of the passion play tradition was its ability to provoke an audience into a hateful, violent mob, especially at the expense of the Jews. When the Gospel is presented in dramatic form, the dramaturgy of the event suggests that Jews—or at least the Temple Priesthood—make for the obvious and emotionally compelling villains. The nineteenth-century Oberammergau Passions certainly used this pattern: an 1860 review refers to the "forcible representation of the predominant guilt of the Jewish hierarchy," and quotes the (repeated) invocation of the trans-generational blood guilt of the Jewish people in calling for the crucifixion of Jesus ("His blood on us and on our children be/Yes! Upon you and on your children too.")[27] Shapiro quotes Alexander Sellar, who also attended the performance in 1860, on how this dramaturgical anti–Semitism could provoke an affect of range and hatred in the audience that could lead to mob violence:

> With strange emotions you gazed upon the executioners as upon wild beasts when they tore his mantle into shreds, and cast lots for his vesture; and the Jewish race appeared hateful in your eyes, as you watched them gathering round the cross, looking upon the man they had crucified, and railing at him, and taunting him with his powerlessness and his pain. Then for the first time you seemed to understand the significance of those ungovernable explosions that in the history of the middle ages ones reads of, when sudden outbursts of hatred against the Hebrew race had taken place, and have been followed by cruelties and barbarities unexampled in history. Just such a feeling seemed excited in this Ammergau audience by this representation.[28]

The early Oberammergau visitor most sensitive to issues of anti–Semitism was likely Joseph Krauskopf, rabbi at a reform synagogue in Philadelphia. He visited the Passion in 1900 and delivered a series of lectures on his experience from his pulpit, which were published the next year. He describes the performance in terms similar to others, but also points out the more subtle Jewish stereotypes being used, such as the portrayal of Judas as haggard, snake-like, and repulsive, especially in the betrayal scene, and how this character formed a model for the anti–Semitic images of the Middle Ages: "Everything that is vile in human nature is pressed into that one character of Judas Iscariot."[29] But his biggest concern was the effect of watching the portrayal of a band of Jews mocking and assaulting Jesus:

> I had heard of the emotional and hysterical outbreaks on the part of some of the spectators at the sight of the outrages perpetrated against the Jesus of the Passion Play; I had heard that some had been so wrought up by the play as to become temporarily insane, and run about town haunted by wildest hallucinations, and I could readily understand why; and I could also imagine the kind of feelings against Jews that hundreds and thousands of these spectators would take home with them to all parts of Europe, and to distant lands across the seas, as a souvenir of Oberammergau.[30]

Krauskopf's response—that these outrages did not in fact happen, and that the narrative of Jewish guilt is untrue—is both correct and irrelevant. The potency and danger of these representations was not that they convinced their audience that they were correct; everyone knew that this was a staging with actors portraying roles distinct from themselves. Rather, the power came from the affective appeal. And fictionality does not have much of a role in challenging that.

But did audiences in fact respond to incitement in this way? Neither Sellar nor Krauskopf in fact observe them doing so. In fact, both remark on how quiet the spectators were. Certainly, the argument can be made that the Passion helped to plant certain anti–Semitic seeds in German culture which, a half century later, would be harvested by Hitler, but they were hardly the only ones to do so, and these seeds do appear to be quite slow-growing. Though they saw clearly how the material of the play could provoke it, they did not actually observe that provocation in the theatre itself.

In fact, it is striking how seldom other audience members are mentioned in the travelers' accounts. Many of these narratives seem quite individual—the intrepid explorer discovering a foreign land and its culture alone. But with 4000 spectators a day arriving as early as 1900, the visitors likely outnumbered the locals for a long time. Oberammergau has never been easy or inexpensive to get to, and knowing who makes the effort to attend it can tell us a good bit about the character of the Passion, setting aside questions of anti–Semitism. It is also instructive to see how those audiences behave when they are there. We have a different set of behavioral expectations for audiences in the theatre than we do for audiences for stand-up comedy, or for congregants at a worship service. Importantly, some twentieth century theatre makers looked to religious worship as a model for how audiences could participate more as co-creators than as passive spectators. Because of the hybridity of the Passion, it makes an interesting test case for the appropriateness of these models.

When the audience is mentioned, there is a noticeable difference between the earlier accounts (until 1880 or 1890) and the later ones. Early accounts call the audience remarkably calm, peaceful, and silent, if emotionally touched, and sometimes refer to it as a "congregation."[31] As a rule, these accounts are those that are more unashamedly in awe of the noble simplicity of the Oberammergauers. The audience are taken to be villagers as well, though this may not in fact be the case, and thus the unique nature of Oberammergau requires them to be as pristine as the performers. Isabella Burton, perhaps the strongest voice for Oberammergau as a romantic otherworld, wrote: "No one ate and drank at the solemn parts of the Play. the spectators are too rapt, and I never saw a better-conducted audience in my life; and I am told it is always so."[32] But note the reference to food and drink here; no contemporary review of Hamlet would bother mentioning what the audience was not eating. Later accounts, as well as those which are a bit more skeptical, sometimes portray a somewhat rowdier audience, eating, drinking, shouting and talking. This is not a condemnation as such, but merely evidence that there was a difference between their understanding of this event and an Englishman's understanding of what it meant to go to the theatre or to church. Henry Blackburn, in 1890, described the behavior of the audience of "peasants":

> The peasants had more the attitude of being in a picture gallery; they were more or less impressed, but evidently under no particular restraint of conduct. Some were in tears, and one or two indeed hysterical towards the end; and some—let us be exact—took beer frequently through the day. They came and went as they pleased, they brought their little children, and old men were carried in and had every incident read to them from the book of the play.[33]

Blackburn does not particularly mind this; it was, he says, "a picture speaking to them in a language they could understand."[34] In a similar vein, he notes in passing that there were some scenes of "ludicrous incident" that it would be "unfair to write down."[35] It is not a problem that a performance designed for peasants presents itself in a way that is appealing to them. There are two problems with this. First, not all the audience were peasants, even in 1890. As the Passion grew, local audiences became a smaller and smaller part of those who attended. By the 1930s, the Oberammergau Passion would be turned into a symbol for all of Germany, which, even if it celebrated a pastoral ideal, spoke more to a national and international elite than to local woodcarvers and shepherds. And second, this image of the play as "picture gallery"— reminiscent of the notion of church art as the bible of the unlettered—will need to fall away once the audience becomes more educated and cosmopolitan. This wildness, of course, is just what put off a number of Englishman as insufficiently restrained. If the Passion does not make this transition, it will simply remain a local event for an increasingly small community. And it is worth noting that there is nothing in Blackburn's description that suggests that this increase in audience activity made them feel a higher level of responsibility for or participation in the Passion as an event.

When I saw the Passion in 2010, the audience was far from the peasantry. Tickets were expensive—about 150 euro, or two hundred dollars—and included an advertisement for BMW on their reverse side. Most guests seemed to be middle-class tourists of the sort who would attend other major cultural festivals such as Glyndebourne and Avignon, though it did appear to be an older group. The audience was quiet and well-behaved, with only the occasional whispering amongst themselves. A few brought snacks, but no more so than to a Broadway show. While the audience was attentive, I did not see any signs of religious passion: I heard no cries or tears, even at the crucifixion scene. I did not have the sense of participating in the performance, as opposed to watching it. Of course, unlike in 1900, the contemporary Passion begins at two p.m. and, after a dinner break, concludes in the evening. This means that, as the play builds to a dramatic climax, night has fallen and we can no longer see our fellow audience members. The stage is illuminated, but we are not, creating the more traditional individualized theatre audience that most of us are used to, where each individual spectator feels as if they are watching the performance for themselves alone. Whether they were silent and respectful or drunken and hysterical, this was certainly not an experience that nineteenth-century Oberammergau audiences could have shared.

* * *

We have one further clue as to what brought visitors to Oberammergau at the turn of the twentieth century. Souvenirs of the visit were popular then, as now, and some remain. In particular, we have a set of picture postcards of the 1890 and 1900 performances, which, if they do not give us a perfect indication of what these performances looked like, do give some indication of it as well as a sense of how audience members choose to remember them.

The Oberammergau Passion has been photographed since 1850,[36] and by 1870, the year Ludwig II commissioned photographs of his own, there was a "brisk traffic" in these images, spreading the Passion's fame.[37] Like the photographs in the decades that follow, they come in one of two types. They either show a close-up of an individual actor in costume and character, particularly the more famous actors, or a wide-shot spanning the width of the stage, displaying one of the Passion's crowded, picturesque, opulent scenes. Referring back to Blackburn's idea image of the audiences as visitors to a visual art gallery, these images seem to suggest a performance that is built on relatively static, large scenes with little movement, which give the audience time to contemplate the picture in front of them as the dialogue proceeds. The play also makes use between scenes of a series of *Lebedene Bilder*—"living images" or *tableau vivants*—a series of stylized, static depiction of scenes framed by

Spiritual Voyeurism and Cultural Nostalgia (Edelman) 79

the white-robed chorus explaining in song how they prefigure the events of the Gospels. But this preference for pictorial grandeur over movement seems to apply to the rest of the Passion as well. Of course, when one has over a hundred people on stage, a still staging is far easier than a moving one, but this is also an aesthetic choice which facilitates a contemplative, meditative relationship between the spectator and the performance.

Figures 4 and 5 are two official photographs from the production in 1900 and 1890, respectively.[38] The first is an official postcard from the 1900 production showing Christ before Caiaphas and the Sanhedrin. Note the grand opulence of the set which, while perhaps evoking the empires of Venice or Austria-Hungary, makes no real effort to evoke the aesthetics of first-century Jerusalem. The priests' outfits are ornate, luxurious and (likely) vividly colored, as opposed to the more simple flowing garments worn by Christ on the image's right. Caiaphas and the other high priest (in black on the left) wear headdresses with two round horns, a common depiction of Jews in Christian art since medieval times. The shape, garment, and formality of gestures refer more to the tradition of Biblical scenes depicted in oil on canvas than a stage tradition of medieval carnival. This image could be contemplated, as a Book of Hours used to be, after it was sent as a postcard across the world. The second figure shows an equally painterly image of Anton Lang as Jesus, in the pose of Ecce Homo. This figure includes all the

Figure 4. Official postcard from the 1900 production showing Christ before Caiaphas and the Sanhedrin.

iconography expected for such a scene—the crown of thorns, the spear, the bound hands, the downturned face—but isolates them from the rest of the scene as it would have been depicted in the performance. As was the fashion of the time, his body remains clean and unmarred by wounds; the suffering that the viewer is asked to contemplate is expressed only in the face.

The stillness and pictorial majesty of these images do seem to suggest that at least part of the audience had the calm, devout attitude that Burton and other visitors observed. But this need not be the case. These guides and postcards were created more for tourists than for locals, who would have had no need to send a card home. And they bear the official stamp of the Oberammergau community, meaning that they were part of the maintenance of the attitude of pious simplicity which was so attractive to outsiders. This was certainly one way of perceiving Oberammergau, but we should not conclude that it was the only way. I see no reason to assume, as Burton does, that the audience responded as a single unit. Audiences rarely do, and large and diverse audience are even less likely to do so. The hybridity of the Passion as a spectacle, as a practice, and as an event may have been every bit as present in 1900 as it was in 2010, if under a different guise.

Figure 5. Anton Lang as Christ—*Ecce Homo*.

* * *

With this reception history in mind, then, I return to my initial struggle to make sense of what sort of event the Passion was in 2010. Was this a religious pilgrimage, a piece of theatre, a nostalgic reenactment, or a celebration of Bavarian culture, or a tourist trap? How was I, as an audience member, being asked to engage with it?

At the most concrete level, I felt a sense of awe at the monumental scope and weight of the performance. The enormous stage is at times filled with a cast of several hundred, and those who cannot fit crowd onto the roof. There are live animals on stage—horses, donkeys, and of course camels. The pacing is often quite deliberate, heavy, even ponderous, so that the minutes add up to hours. There are many long speeches, little stage movement, and a great deal of narration. And the large choruses of supernumeraries—hundreds of people at once—can take considerable time to get on and off the stage. The *Lebedenes Bilder*, with the static images in shockingly bright colors at the back of the stage framed by the white-clad chorus, was the clearest presentation I have ever seen of the theological concept of typology. The two testaments were explicitly tied together but never confused; the static Old was framed as an illustration of the living New. The production felt didactic, stodgy, old-fashioned and proudly so; it wore its tradition as a badge of pride.

The music which is used in every *Lebedenes Bilder* and in much of the rest of the production—largely still that composed by Rochus Dedler for the 1820 production—had a heavy formality and pre–Romantic stiffness. For the audience, this omnipresent music had the effect of placing the performance within a secular artistic tradition, that of classical German-language opera from Gluck to Mozart and Beethoven and Weber. While this music is obviously pre–Wagnerian, Oberammergau's place in this operatic tradition connects it to German festival opera, the modern apex of which is, of course, Bayreuth. (In fact, in a 1960 photo essay, *Life* magazine mentioned Oberammergau as a destination for opera-loving American tourists in Europe alongside Glyndebourne, Salzburg and Aix-en-Provence.[39]) Such festivals are very high in cultural capital, in Pierre Bourdieu's sense—but they also represent high cultural nationalism, both German and specifically Bavarian. These national and cultural capitals are more visible in Oberammergau than its religious value. While I saw exactly one nun, and no obvious priests or monks, I saw several dozen people in lederhosen or dirndln, traditional Bavarian costume. In the shops around the show, I saw no rosaries or small devotional items, but there were many tourist souvenirs: T-shirts, caps, tote bags, as well as cultural artifacts like scripts, books and CDs. Visitors can also buy the handcarved wood sculptures that are the traditional crafts of the area. While many of them are statues of saints or angels, these tend to be the larger and more expensive pieces: the majority (and certainly the most purchased) are of secular subjects and seem to be intended for decoration rather than devotion.

And yet, while I don't think we can understand Oberammergau without placing it in the frame of Bavarian high cultural tourism, it does not fit wholly into that category either. Even for an audience that may not be as religious as that of centuries past, it is clearly constructed for an emotional, and even spiritual, appeal. The play is performed in German without benefit of subtitles or translation, yes, but the language it is performed in is Hochdeutsch, high or standard German, very much not the local dialect. And quite a few American and British church groups were there, trying desperately to follow with their nose in the English translation. And, while long, this was well-crafted performance, a compelling piece of dramatic art that used standard and effective theatrical techniques to evoke empathy and pathos. Though it was hardly naturalistic, the 2010 version was far less stuffy and stylized than Passions past. Whereas in past performances there was an attempt to treat Jesus and his followers like a king and their court, this year, the disciples' costumes were simple and iconic. The Roman Empire and the Temple Priesthood still wore extravagant frocks, but they seemed like a dazzlingly beautiful swirling storm with Jesus as its eye. In fact, it was notable, even surprising, how seldom Jesus spoke. Frequently, other characters would speak around him, about him, while he maintained a calm, simple, but compelling central presence. Our eyes were caught by the spectacle, but they kept being drawn back to him no matter how little he did. That he spoke so little added to the sense of mystery surrounding this central character.

One could see, however, the ghost of another audience at this production, that may not even have been in the theatre with us on that August day. This was the battalion of Catholic theologians and Jewish rabbis who, since the 1970s, have been following the lead of the Second Vatican Council in purging the Oberammergau Passion Play of its anti–Semitic content, as Shapiro describes so usefully. The production in 2010 seemed to go out of its way to show a highly Jewish Jesus, who prays in Hebrew with his disciples, holds up a Torah scroll to the assembled masses, and speaks with great respect toward the Law and the Prophets. These developments are to be welcomed, surely, but they seemed out of place, as if they were added separately to appeal to yet another audience: those who visited Oberammergau to check it for anti–Semitism. In fact, the only words spoken that are not in German are in Hebrew. It is one thing to add an operatically sung version of the Shema (the Jewish prayer of God's unity), which, while probably not a known or comprehensible text for the bulk of the audience, will serve for those who know it to emphasize the Disciples' membership in the Jewish tradition. It is another entirely when, at the Last Supper, Jesus quotes from twentieth-century Hebrew poet (and Zionist heroine) Hannah Senesh without naming her. While non–Jews might appreciate the beauty of this one line ("Blessed is the match consumed in the kindling of flame") it is highly unlikely that it would be more memorable than the spectacle surrounding it. It functioned as a particularly targeted hail, in the terms of performance theory: a call-out from the performance to acknowledge and affirm the identity of a small but essential subset of the audience. In this, it functioned differently than the overt "Jewish content" (the Torah scroll, the Hebrew prayers): the Senesh was an appeal to the small audience that would go unrecognized by the rest, while the more overt content was legible to all. Whether it was helpful in recasting the traditional antagonistic relationship between Christ and the Jews that Passion

Plays traditionally convey, or if it was simply an awkward fit with the traditional spectacle of the piece and thus hard to relate to, is hard for me to judge.

For most of us, though, who were neither monastically devout Christians or politically conscious Jews but simply compelled audience members, we were faced with the question of what, exactly, this spectacle was *for*? Why take the trouble to put on such an enormous show?

The two possible answers mark out the tension between an Oberammergau as a devotional event and as a piece of cultural tourism. First, the spectacle reflects the value of tradition. This is true in the (crude) causal and economic senses—the play has grown larger and more spectacular over the centuries in that its tradition has been monetized—but also in a (more relevant) justificatory one. This play is spectacular as a *statement* about its importance in the culture of Bavaria, Germany, Catholic Christendom, and the town of Oberammergau. This need not be a mode of cynical commerce; the staging of the play is itself a devotional act, as the opening song reminds us, done in fulfillment of a vow by the grandchildren of those whom God has spared. In this reading, our responsibility as audience members is to notarize and witness to that devotion. We are *not* its addressees, as much we may be moved by it. By this view, the audience genuinely are tourists, though not in any derogatory sense of that term: they are there to witness something strange and exotic from their own life. The profound *otherness* of that spectacle is what makes it powerful. This is a Levinasian notion of otherness, not a Kristevan one: the other in its specificity does not *become* us but, in its alterity, compels our response.

The second option is that the spectacle is there for the purposes of the story—that is, to heighten the power of the drama. And in this, it is very effective. The Passion, of course, centers around that simple, quiet, enigmatic and charismatic figure of Jesus. It is a standard director's trick to increase a character's social status by having others talk them up, and to increase the audience's sympathy for them by contrasting them with others who are less sympathetic. That is what the spectacle of the Passion does. It focuses our attention on the figure of the incarnated Christ and how radically unlike the world around him he and his ministry were. But as Jesus speaks so seldom—because he is performed as a relative blank—the audience is asked to discover his character for themselves. And that contemplation is a devotional act that the audience *themselves* are given space to do, not as observers but as thoughtful contributors.

Inevitably, both modes of audiencing are present; the spectacle makes us both witnesses and devotees. But I want to point out that there is not as much space between them as it might seem. Both models begin with contemplative observation of that which is going on front of us. Both follow the phenomenological model of the audience's relationship to performance exemplified by the work of the great Bert States.[40] We are not participants in what is going on. We watch it and think and respond. And that watching may be devotional or purely aesthetic, but the fourth wall separating the audience from the stage is never breached. And that, to me, was a disappointment.

Let me explain by describing the play's final scene, the resurrection. By now, the sun has set and the theatre is quite dark. In half-light, we make out the women by the tomb. They discover that Jesus is risen, and they run, joyously, to spread the good news. A child enters from upstage, singing, carrying a small lit candle. The chorus has entered in two long rows, and the child turns to the two nearest him and lights the candles they hold. They turn to light the next, and so on, and so on, and from this one small flame, a cascade of light grows and spills downstage toward us until we are looking at a sea of candlelight. But this is where it stops. The cast turn their backs to us and leave the stage, singing, bringing their light with them.

It would not have been unreasonably difficult or expensive to give us candles, too, and to let the light flow from the tomb of the risen Jesus, on to the cast, and on to us, so that we can bring the light out into the dark Bavarian night. But they chose not to. It was not our job to be involved. Artistically, culturally, or devotionally, we were asked to participate in this Passion through spectation, reflection and contemplation alone. All three of these are imaginative actions, and our audiencing was not certainly passive. But they are all private and individual pursuits, like books of hours or shopping. And my disappointment comes from the way in which the spectacle did not allow us to overcome that individuality and do something *together* as a single audience, a community of witnesses for this extraordinary performance.

Part of theatre's power is that it is always and thoroughly collaborative. As the audience play a key role in that collaboration, the questioning of their role is necessary. In Oberammergau in 2010, we were asked to watch, listen, feel, and think. This was extraordinarily powerful, but the logic of the Christian message, as well as the logic of the performative event, both imply a necessary concept of a community of reception, not just individual receivers. That this logic was not meaningfully applied to Oberammergau in 2010 gives the sense that it was first and foremost a touristic and cultural spectacle, reenacting and addressing a past that now had more value as history than as an address to a present public. Asking the motley bunch of tourists, critics, pilgrims, and fans that make up the contemporary Passion audience to all particulate in a single community may simply be impossible. The hybrid performance has fractured, and forcing it into a single mode of address for this diverse audience would be too violent, too disrespectful, and too rash a revision of what the Passion has become.

NOTES

1. This idea of iterated performance that establishes a convention resembles Judith Butler's arguments on the performativity of gender. Each iteration of a performance

of gender further establishes the seeming 'naturalness' of the convention, but each act of re-performance can also be different than its predecessors, modifying the convention in intended or unintended ways. Oberammergau is performed far less frequently than gendered acts, of course, and with far more conscious planning. The Oberammergau Passion may then develop more consciously than gender, but the principle of their development is the same. See Judith Butler, *Gender Trouble* (London: Routledge, 1990).

 2. James Shapiro, *Oberammergau: The Troubling Story of the World's Most Famous Passion Play* (London: Little, Brown, 2000), 68.

 3. John P. Jackson [author, with photographs from Joseph Albert], *Album of the Passion-Play at Ober-Ammergau* (Munich: Joseph Albert, 1873).

 4. The earliest report appears to be that of Anna Mary Howitt, in her two-volume text *An Art-Student in Munich,* published in London in 1853, in which she mentions her 1840 trip to Oberammergau. The 1850 performance featured in the novel *Quits* by the Barones Tautphoeus (London: Richard Bentley, 1857). At least two writers seem to have been present in 1860: Dean Stanley and Alexander Craig Sellar. The former wrote about his experience anonymously (as 'A Spectator') in *Macmillan's Magazine* of October of 1860 under the heading "The Ammergau Mystery, or Sacred Drama of 1860" (vol. 2, pp. 463–477) while the latter waited a decade to publish "The Passion-Play in the Highlands of Bavaria," *Blackwood's Magazine*, vol. 107, pp. 381–96, in 1870.

 5. I quote from a version of MacColl's review expanded into a much-reprinted pamphlet, "The Ober-ammergau Passion Play, with some Introductory Remarks on the Origin and Development of Miracle Plays" (London: Rivingtons, 1890, seventh edition).

 6. An Oxonian, *Impressions of the Ammergau Passion-Play* (London: J.T. Hayes, 1870), 25. A similar sentiment was expressed by the Rev. George Molloy, "The Passion Play at Ober-Ammergau in the Summer of 1871" (London: Burns, Oates and Co, 1872): "But no sooner had the Play commenced than my prejudices were dispelled" (n.p.).

 7. *Cooks Excursionist and Tourist Advertiser* (20 May 1880), 3. Brackets mine. This, and all Thomas Cook material, comes from the Thomas Cook Archives in Peterborough, England. My thanks to archivist Paul Smith for his assistance.

 8. *Cooks Excursionist and Tourist Advertiser* (20 May 1880), 3.

 9. The estimate of 6000 British tourists visiting Oberammergau under the Cooks' arrangements in 1880 comes from a 1990 Thomas Cook brochure for Oberammergau.

 10. *Cooks Excursionist and Home and Foreign Tourist Advertiser* (1 February 1900), 1. This issue of the *Excursionist,* as all other editions from that date through to the summer, carried a full set of details of the travel arrangements available for Oberammergau.

 11. Benno Rauchenegger, *Oberammergau,* Bruckmann's Illustrated Guides vol. 109 (Munich: A. Bruckmann, 1900), 39.

 12. Henry Gideon, "The Music of the Passion Play at Oberammergau," *The Forum* vol. 44, no. 6 (1910), 737.

 13. Hermine Diemer, *Oberammergau and Its Passion Play* (Munich: Card Aug. Seyfried and Co, 1900), v.

 14. Isabel Burton, *The Passion-Play at Ober-Ammergau* (London: Hutchinson, 1900), 194, 121. It is likely that the Burtons visited the 1880 production, as she gives the program for that year's performance.

15. Burton, 205.

16. Community of Oberammergau and J.A. Daisenberger, *The Passion Play in Oberammergau* (München: Jos. C. Huber, 1922), 11.

17. Joseph Krauskopf, *A Rabbi's Impressions of the Oberammergau Passion Play* (Philadelphia: Edwards Stern & Co, 1901), 28, says that the first act began at 8 a.m., the internal ran from noon to 1:30 p.m., and the performance ended about 5:30 p.m. P.J. O'Reilly, "At Ober-ammerga in 1890, a Reminiscence of The Passion Play" (London: Catholic Truth Society, 1890), 23, reports being woken at 4:30 a.m.—perhaps an hour before sunrise—by a gunshot, followed by another at 5 and a brass band at 5:30, all to wake the visitors up for an 8 a.m. start to the performance, and perhaps to go to church before.

18. [Elizabeth Tuckett], *Zigzagging Amongst Dolomites* (London: Longmans, Green, Reader & Dyer, 1871), 37.

19. A. W. Buckland, "Ober Ammergau and its People, in Connection with the Passion Play and Miracle Plays in General" ("A paper read before the Bath Literary and Philosophical Association, January 12th 1872") (London: Simpkin, Marshall and Co., 1872), 13.

20. Krauskopf, 23.

21. Molloy, 120.

22. Stanley, 477.

23. O'Reilly, 111.

24. The Passion has had a number of texts over the centuries, of course. Shapiro offers a particularly interesting description of the '*passio nova*' written by the Benedictine monk Ferdinand Rosner and introduced in 1750. It was enormous—8500 lines—had a "Baroque, Jesuit-influenced, operatic style" and retained quite a bit of medieval content, including plenty of devils. An attempt to reintroduce this text in 1960 went nowhere (Shapiro, 61–63).

25. Buckland, 31.

26. One of the most interesting contemporary sources on this process of audience-taming is Dennis Kennedy, *The Spectator and the Spectacle: Audiences in Modernity and Postmodernity* (Cambridge: Cambridge University Press, 2011).

27. Stanley, 476, 474.

28. Sellar, 392, also quoted in Shapiro, 77. Sellar uses the second person in this quote in order to place the reader squarely in the audience watching the performance, and as a part of this potential mob.

29. Krauskopf, 77.

30. Krauskopf, 33–34.

31. This is the case, for instance, in Molloy, Stanley, Tuckett, and Sellar, all.

32. Burton, 189. Recall that though this text is from 1900, it describes the 1880 performance.

33. Blackburn, 141.

34. Blackburn, 142.

35. Blackburn, 154.

36. Eduard Devrient, *Das Passionsschauspiel in Oberammergau und seine Bedeutung für die neue Zeit* (Leipzig: J.J. Weber, 1851).

37. Shapiro, 188.

38. These images come from William Stead, *The Passion Play at Ober Ammergau 1900* (London: Review of Reviews, 1900, third edition). 'Stead's Guide,' as it was often known, was published decennially from 1890 until 1930, even after Stead himself died at the sinking of the *RMS Titanic*. It included the full text of the play as well as a large

number of photographs. (The postcard, along with five others, was found in the copy of this guide in Trinity College Library, Dublin; it is not clear if these were placed there by the publishers or a later reader.) The financial control that the Oberammergau community asserted over the play can be seen in his frustrations in acquiring the 1900 text and photographs for publication: "This year, when I sent to Ober Ammergau to obtain the official version, now at last permitted to be published, I was confronted by what were virtually prohibitive charges for the copyright. Finding that the differences between my text and that of the official version were practically of no importance, I decided to republished the version of 1890. I was then informed that my text so closely resembled the authentic version that no permission would be given to republish it except as a copyright work, chargeable with payment of author's fees" (vii). The 1900 edition contains photographs from 1890 for the same reason.

39. "Music in the Air of Europe: Tourists Swarm to the Festivals," *Life* vol. 29, no. 3, 1 August 1960.

40. See his *Great Reckonings in Little Rooms: On the Phenomenology of Theatre* (Berkeley: University of California Press, 1985).

Atemporality in the Heidelberg Passion Play, the Passion Play of Oberammergau and Sarah Ruhl's *Passion Play: A Cycle*

JUTTA EMING

Die Große Passion, a three-hour-long documentary released in German theatres in 2011 about the making of the 2010 Oberammergau Passion Play, features encounters between members of the directorial team and representatives from the American Anti-Defamation League (ADL) and the American Jewish Committee (AJC).[1] The representatives of these organizations have come to personally observe the preparations for the Passion Play in Oberammergau, and to discuss some aspects of the representation of Jews in scenic design and script. The guests are also shown costumes for the so-called *Lebende Bilder* (tableaux vivants, or "living pictures"). The costumes hang in an adjacent space, which is partitioned off with a cord. This spatial segregation, as it turns out, is symptomatic: as the Oberammergau dramaturg, Otto Huber, explains to the visitors, an intentional effort is made to present the living pictures as separate from the actual plot of the Passion Play.[2]

The point of the tableaux vivants is to prompt viewers to recall well known stories from the Old Testament by depicting key scenes: the expulsion of Adam and Eve from the Garden of Eden, Daniel in the lion's den, Moses and the burning bush, etc. A bit later, the film audience sees Huber in front of a model of the tableaux, explaining to the representatives from the Jewish institutions that the play's organizers consider Moses to be the central figure of the Jewish religion, and that they have therefore made a special effort to

Figure 6. Tableau vivant: The expulsion of Adam and Eve from the Garden of Eden (Passionsspiele Oberammergau 2010, photograph by Brigitte Maria Mayer).

do justice to this in the tableaux. The foreign guests are very interested, and why wouldn't they be: the living pictures continuously reference the corpus of biblical books that constitute the basis of not only the Christian, but also the Jewish faith. The question of how this common inheritance is scenically dealt with leads us, of course, to an extremely sensitive point, which, given not only the historical relationship between the two religions, but also that of German society and Jewish culture, is of eminent importance. As the dramaturg further explains, the Oberammergau play attempts to make the relationship of the tableaux vivants to the Christian story of the Passion clear despite their separate presentation. The foreign guests do not seem to have any fundamental objection to this technique of distanced reference. At least it does not appear from further discussions, witnessed by the viewer in the course of passion play preparations, that the tableaux are found to be problematic. Nonetheless, the typological tradition underlying the tableaux vivants, "a way of juxtaposing Jewish and Christian texts that inevitably showed how the former were fulfilled and superseded by the latter," had been a point of contention during preparations for earlier stagings.[3]

However, at one point the dramaturg reports that there were misgivings about some dark, knit cloth costumes because these could, depending on the visitor's perspective, convey a negative image of Jews; in the end, these misgivings had been able to be dispelled. This little incident illustrates—as consistently emerges from the film—that the sensitivities on the side of the Jewish reviewers are high and that the play's organizers take pains to accommodate them as far as possible. This reaches a certain comic climax at a later point in the documentary. The viewer listens in on a telephone conversation in which Otto Huber explains to an American on the other end of the line in a slightly resigned, but also determined voice that the organizers will do their best to take Jewish interests into account, but that they cannot change the fact that (and I quote) "Jesus simply did not die in bed." Indeed, he explains, they would have preferred it if the Austrians had killed him (instead of, as is implied, the Romans in combination with the Jews). The interactions leading up to this moment of comic exasperation give the impression that these misgivings could perhaps still be allayed, but in the end the situation was unfortunately irreconcilable. The homepages of both institutions state categorically that they have not endorsed or approved the 2010 German production.

The tableaux vivants of the Oberammergau Passion Play, as mentioned above, follow a hermeneutic Christian tradition in which episodes from the Old Testament are understood as harbingers—prefigurations—of New Testament events, particularly the Passion of Christ. This treatment is also referred to as typology. In this scheme, the figure of the New Testament is understood as a "fulfillment," that is as a resumption on a higher level and at the same time the completion of the Old Testament precursor. Alexander Nagel and Christopher S. Wood describe it as follows: "The theology of typology identified formal rhymes between historical events that revealed the pattern imposed on reality by divinity. One event was the shadow, the image, the figure of another."[4] This relationship was picked up and played out in countless permutations in medieval theology, art and literature. Typological allusions are an integral component of the iconographic inventory of premodern religious art. One such typological reference, for example, is the obligatory skull under the cross of Christ in depictions of Calvary, which indicates that Christ has come to the people as a "new Adam."

Medieval religious plays integrate allusions to the prophecy and prefiguration of the Old Testament in many ways. The fact that the Oberammergau play adheres to typological references and, consequently, depicts Jewish teachings exclusively as an imperfect "predecessor" of Christian doctrine has plagued the relationship between the organizers and the Jewish organizations in recent years. The Oberammergau production of 2000 had already made significant changes in the tableaux for this reason.[5]

The staging of the Oberammergau Passion Play is notable for the freezing of prefigurations into static tableaux. It is, as a glance at the medieval tradition shows, a possible, but not the only acceptable way to reference the Old

Testament by theatrical means. Furthermore, typologies are not the only way with which medieval and early modern religious plays bring together different time and historical levels. It should not be forgotten, however, that there is no direct link between the Oberammergau play tradition and the medieval passion play.[6] The medieval tradition dies out in the course of the Reformation, and only occasional aspects survive in new European play traditions, such as Jesuit or Baroque drama.[7] Whether its "export" to the New World has retained some of the original theatrical practice (see below), seems questionable.

My analysis focuses on "atemporality," the tendency of religious plays to connect different levels of time, including references to the present, with another. Atemporality can be understood as an artistic method that avoids a strictly chronological narrative and portrayal. Anachronisms are therefore tolerated or, as will be explained later, not viewed as such. As the examples drawn from typological hermeneutics have already demonstrated, atemporalities and anachronisms are clearly integral components of historical and historicizing religious plays. Interestingly enough, however, atemporality also appears in a new American project, which adapts the genre of the passion play for the contemporary stage: Sarah Ruhl's *Passion Play: A Cycle* (2005).[8]

In the following, I focus on atemporal structures in three passion play traditions: the historical late medieval passion plays, the 2010 Oberammergau production, and Sarah Ruhl's modern piece. In each case, the dramatic realization of the life and suffering of Jesus in various historical periods is furnished with new meaning. Central to my analysis are, on the one hand, the plays' relationship to the Old Testament or, more generally, to the handling of the Jewish legacy and, on the other hand, the plays' connection to the present.

After an introductory discussion of the concept of atemporality, I will draw on the 1517 Heidelberg Passion Play as my first example, analyzing its typological approach and then profiling its differences to the 2010 production in Oberammergau. I will then take up Ruhl's dramatization of passion plays, whose aesthetic structure, as I shall show, poses a question that with an eye toward the Oberammergau staging, has less to do with the production itself than with the accompanying documentary film: what does it mean to make the story of the passion relevant for a modern audience? Since the third act of Ruhl's cycle is set in Oberammergau in the year 1934, this allows a transition to the Oberammergau staging of 2010, whose treatment of history and present I shall describe in closing.

Given the chapter's focus on the organization of temporality and historicity, questions of the sometimes extremely anti–Jewish tendencies in late medieval passion plays, the anti–Jewish elements of the Oberammergau Passion Play text, and its relationship with German Anti-Semitism receive only marginal treatment in the following. In German-language passion play research, there is currently a well-established discussion regarding this problem. James Shapiro's book demonstrates just how strongly the problem is inscribed in the history of the Oberammergau staging tradition. These anti–Jewish tendencies are without a question a burden of history with which the passion plays must come to terms. In the following, I am particularly interested in this aspect with regard to the question of how it affects the historicity and authenticity of re-stagings of such plays.

Atemporality, Anachronism and Achronicity

The methodological potential of terms like "atemporality," "achronicity," and, in particular, "anachronism" have recently come under discussion in literary and cultural studies. While "achronicity" and "atemporality" are neologisms, "anachronism" is an established and well-known term. However, it is currently undergoing a resignification (in Butler's sense).[9] An array of publications came out between 2007 and 2010 in which the term and its traditional implications are critically examined. In the following passage, Margrete de Grazia reminds us of the negative assessment of "anachronism," particularly in literary and cultural studies:

> In the field of literary studies, as presently historicized, nothing could be worse than to be accused of anachronism.... The unpardonable sin occurs when a present way of thinking is imposed upon the past.... Indeed the failure to differentiate the world of the present-subject from that of the past-object is a violation of the basic principle of epistemology: the viewing subject must remain distinct from the viewed subject. When one collapses into the other, knowledge cannot take place.[10]

De Grazia points out that while chronology is often approached as an "absolute" form of historiography, it is actually a relative concept with its own history. "Chronologia," according to de Grazia, is originally bound up with the thought of narration, the recounting of temporalities.[11] It was closely associated with rhetoric as well as narratological terms, which included anachronisms as a matter of course.[12] Only when this association with narration and rhetoric was broken—around the seventeenth century—does "chronologia" become an "absolute" category.[13] But since the Renaissance the ability to identify anachronisms has served as proof of historical consciousness.[14] It has even been granted the status of a distinguishing epochal feature.

Nagel and Wood also deal critically with the apparent self-evidential nature of chronological time in their 2010 art historical book *Anachronic Renaissance*. They write, "Chronological time, flowing steadily from before to after, is an effect of its figurations: annals, chronicles, calendars, clocks.... This is not an obvious concept."[15] The authors point emphatically to the ability of art to set various levels of time into motion, writing, "'Art' is the name of the possibility of a conversation across time … by complicating time, by reactivating prestigious forebears, by comparing events across time, by fabricating memories."[16] In the Renaissance this possibility of artwork was not "discovered," but rather integrated as a self-referential element for the first time.

Carolyn Dinshaw's studies on the English mystic Margery Kempe have argued that it is essentially possible to apply this potential to earlier artworks as well. Dinshaw invites us to think of time as multiple, as something that might be experienced in different ways simultaneously and not simply in terms of clearly delineated borders between which time flows inexorably forward in one direction only. Invoking a famous phrase of the German philosopher Ernst Bloch, she calls for paying attention to the issue of "asynchronous temporalities."[17]

Indeed, my following thoughts on passion play traditions attempt to demonstrate that the employment of multiple and various levels of time constitutes both medieval art as well as the occupation with the Middle Ages, i.e., medievalism. As Nagel and Wood describe it, "the ability of the work of art to hold incompatible models in suspension without deciding is the key to art's anachronic quality, its ability really to 'fetch' a past, create a past, perhaps even fetch the future."[18] Questions that follow from this line of thinking include, for example: "How can anachronism be strategically deployed to highlight problematic aspects of temporality? How can anachronism be used to signify competing temporal frames? and How does anachronism contribute to expressing complex schemes of history, e.g. by linking the eschatological to everyday experience?"[19]

"The fulfilled present" in the Heidelberg Passion Play

The Heidelberg Passion Play is conceived, like all religious medieval dramas, as an interaction of "multiple temporalities." Medieval theology and the medieval understanding of history, i.e., "salvific history" (*Heilsgeschichte*), are reflected in various aesthetic forms: Christ's present is fulfilled historical past and points simultaneously toward the future end of times. In some dramatic genres, particularly the *Weltgerichtspiel* (Last Judgment Play), the end of days is even staged in the form of the Last Judgment, allowing the audience an opportunity to play through a catastrophe, which is interesting not least from a psychological perspective.[20] In the passion plays, additional temporal levels join typological and eschatological references. The theatrical realization of the life and suffering of Christ has a historical dimension insofar as it occurs via a series of experiences that are to have historically happened in Israel.[21] Finally, various references to the current present of the audience are constructed, whether in the form of contemporary urban realities or in the simulation of the direct presence of salvation events.[22] Often misunderstood as proof of the naiveté of medieval audiences, this organization of time is complex, forcing the spectators to continuously differentiate between different levels of representation, or, what's even more difficult, their concurrence. In general, this organization of time is a central theatrical means to create an atmosphere of religious truth and to involve spectators. The convention of addressing the audience in pre-modern drama—a technique that is often compared with Brecht's epic theater—is no coincidence.[23]

Living pictures or tableaux vivants as employed in the Oberammergau Passion Play were included most often in Corpus Christi Plays (Fronleichnamsspiele).[24] However, all religious plays establish multiple references to well-known stories and prophecies from the Old Testament. A common method is the integration of Old Testament figures, often prophets, who open or close a scene with an explication of its significance for salvation history; some of the plays also employ prefigurations. However, only the Heidelberg Passion Play of 1514 contains 13 Old Testament scenes that are interspersed among Holy Week events (rather than staging them as a group before the stations of the New Testament, as in the Lucerne Passion Play).[25] The prefigurations of the Heidelberg Passion Play and the forms of their correspondence to the Passion of Christ are particularly multifaceted. The instances of foreshadowing demonstrate some general characteristics: they are of varying length (some of them quite long), and appear more and more frequently as the Passion proceeds. Unlike the Oberammergau Passion Play, there is no continuous symmetrical contrast between Old and New Testament events. Of even more consequence: the spatial isolation of the Old Testament scenes in the Oberammergau version—their clear decoupling from the theatrical representation of Holy Week events—is not present in the late medieval play.

In the Heidelberg Passion Play, the Old Testament scenes are part of the theatrical plot itself. This is designed in such a way that an Old Testament episode "takes over" the stage and presents the event in question as mimetic play. At the end of each episode, a prophet comes forward and explains to the audience where the scene they have just seen appears in the Bible and how it is related to the episode of Jesus's life that directly follows. This creates a transition to the events of the Passion, which then begins again.

In the Heidelberg play, scenes from the Old and New Testament are presented on the same theatrical and medial levels as regards body, language, and plot. This has the important consequence that the events in the Old Testament suggest the same present time, and have basically the same standing as those in the New Testament. A comparison with the prefigurative tableaux vivants in the Oberammergau Passion Play makes this clear: there the prefigurations dialectically convert their segregated stage space into a distant temporality. In addition to the immobilization of the action, the spatial separation of the scenes renders them irreal and temporally distanced, transforming them into an image worthy of veneration. This is further supported by their differing medialities, in particular the simultaneous employment of sacred music. The Heidelberg Passion Play, on the other hand, brings the scenes as close as possible to the time-space present of the audience. Past events are literally brought to life.

The attempt to produce a proximity to passion events and the reality of the audience via the Old Testament prefigurations is also evident in the selection of the Old Testament scenes. Several particularly well-known biblical episodes that are also taken up by the Oberammergau Passion Play, for example the Expulsion from the Garden of Eden, the Exodus out of Egypt, or the Desperation of Cain, do not appear in the Heidelberg Passion Play. Instead episodes out of the canonical and apocryphal books of the Old Testament appear, which were among the most popular themes in sixteenth-century dramatic literature.[26] Among the popular stories in circulation in the sixteenth-century theatrical repertoire are those of Joseph and Susanna, both of which receive lengthy and complex treatments in the Heidelberg Passion Play.[27] A more concise episode, on the other hand, is the story of Rebecca's courtship, the first prefiguration that occurs in the Heidelberg Passion Play. This scene exemplifies the method of weaving together disparate temporal reference points employed in the Heidelberg Passion Play.

In the episode, Abraham instructs his servant to seek a wife for his son Isaac in his homeland. The servant resolves to decide for the woman who provides him a drink of water at the well:

> Rebecca komptt hubsch vnnd woll gezyrtt zcu dem bron vnnd hoitt einn krug vff yre schulder vnnd schefft wasser vnnd will widder vmb ghenn. So spricht der knechtt:
>> "*Pauxillum aque michj ad bibendum prebe de idria tua.*
>> Iunckfrauw zcartt, rein vnnd klug,
>> gieb mir drinckenn vß deinem krugh."
>
> Rebecca beudtt dem knecht baltt denn krug vnd sprichtt:
>> "*Bibe, mj domine.*
>> Lieber her, drinck einn guttenn drunck,
>> wann ich hann des wassers gnugk" [V. 1401–1404].
>
> Rebecca, well-mannered and prettily attired, comes to the well. She carries a jug on her shoulder, adles water, and wants to go back. Then the laborer says, "*Pauxillum aque michj ad bibendum prebe de idria tua.* Fine maiden, give me something out of your jug to drink." Rebecca immediately offers him the jug and says, "*Bibe, mj domine.* Dear sir, take a good mouthful as I have enough water."

The passage is short and relatively unspectacular, but it illustrates several typical conventions of late medieval passion plays as well as their arrangement in manuscripts. This includes play instructions in the vernacular, a type of stage direction from which the scene arrangements can be gleaned. The passage in question is very revealing: Rebecca should appear as a pretty young woman, capable of attracting the attention of the servant—and with him, that of the audience. As a result, the arrangement of the scene is slightly reminiscent of a "boy meets girl" structure, presumably a concession to the previously mentioned tastes of the contemporary audience. The use of Latin to anticipate the initial line of vernacular text follows a tradition—the content is redundant, but it assumes an important communicative function by connecting the play back to Latinate rituals and addresses educated listeners.

Although religiously educated viewers can likely effortlessly recognize the typological content of the scene, the prophet Jesaja nonetheless highlights it once again at the end of the sequence (excerpt):

> also wirtt auch Ihesus ghann
> vnnd einn weyll bey einem bron stann.
> dann wirtt komen einn freylein clug
> vnnd schepffenn wasser in einen krug.
> zcu der wirtt sprechenn Ihesu crist:
> "weyp, gieb mir drincken zcu diesser frist" [V. 1471–1476].

In just this way, Jesus will also go and stand beside a well for a while, and then a cultured maiden will come and ladle water into a jug. To her Jesus Christ will say, "Woman, give me something to drink."

What follows, as part of the Passion Play proper, is the story of Jesus and the Good Samaritan.

Passages like the one above in which characters in the play, to speak metaphorically, "break through the fourth wall" (which at that time did not yet exist as a convention) have probably contributed to the long-held perception of passion plays as a medieval "mass media," which religiously indoctrinated people on a large scale.[28] In her sophisticated analysis of city history, Dorothea Freise counters that the plays are founded upon a heterogeneously constituted "Spielträgerschaft" (play sponsorship) which differs from city to city, and which in no way can be identified with "the" Christian church.[29] The quoted passage from the Heidelberg Passion Play makes it moreover clear that the direct addressing of the audience also takes on aesthetic functions insofar as it assists in the orientation of spectators between the temporal levels of the play, makes its typological structures transparent, and creates transitions between scenes.

The structure of Sarah Ruhl's *Passion Play: A Cycle* (2005) is also based on the aesthetic decision to conceptionally couple a passion play with the present timeframe of the viewer. The ways in which this is realized differ in many fundamental ways from those in the late medieval tradition, but are likewise based on the linking together of disparate temporal levels. It is no coincidence that the Oberammergau play tradition constitutes the core of Ruhl's cycle.

Sarah Ruhl's Passion Play: A Cycle: *Passion Plays Through the Ages*

Why does a famous contemporary American playwright take recourse to the medieval tradition of passion plays? It is far from obvious that American audiences might have an interest in religious drama. Historically, these plays come from a Catholic tradition, and they are very much linked to the now extinct life style of late medieval European cities. And while they were present everywhere in Europe during the late Middle Ages they went into decline at just about the time many New World cities were first being founded. Claire Sponsler's book *Ritual Imports* helps to understand how passion plays made the leap across the cultural gap from Europe to the United States.[30] Apparently, these dramas were supposed to provide spiritual nourishment for American communities, as well as support their identification with European roots.

In a certain way, Sarah Ruhl's piece takes up the whole tradition of the decline of the plays in the Old World and their re-adaptation in Oberammergau and in the New World.[31] However, her cycle of plays does not try to mimetically re-enact the historic tradition. Instead, she includes personalities involved in the performance of passion play productions in three different time periods. Part I is situated in England in 1575, at a time when Elizabeth I is about to abolish all Catholic traditions. Part II is set in Oberammergau in 1934 and features a surprise visit by Hitler. Finally, Part III brings us to Spearfish, South Dakota, U.S.A. in the 1960s and up to the present. Until its recent closing in 2008, the Spearfish production was "the oldest and most famous of the tourist-attraction passion plays in the United States."[32] As Sponsler shows, the success story of the Black Hills Passion Play in Spearfish has to do with the idea that a small-town community could be committed to keeping a religious tradition alive. Likewise, descriptions of Oberammergau performances in American magazines underpinned this impression, projecting the irresistible idea of quaint life in a traditional Bavarian village, with simple people living in cute houses, being morally transformed by watching the spectacle of Christ's passion. In the second half of the nineteenth century Oberammergau became a popular tourist destination every ten years when the Passion Play was staged—particularly for American tourists.[33] Ruhl, in her playwright's note, is quite explicit about her intentions, writing, "I realized that little is more American than the nexus of religious rhetoric, politics and theatricality. Especially at the present moment, when it seems as if we are in the midst of an unacknowledged holy war, conducted by a man who feels himself to be appointed by God.... Never have the medieval world and the digital age seemed so oddly conjoined.... Whatever happened to the founding father's rationale for separating church and state?"[34]

In this respect, I could not agree less with her. Historically, passion plays were primarily intended as an attempt to bring Christ's body in the flesh to an audience, this being a significant break from earlier symbolic representations of Christ in the liturgy. Their involvement in political questions was an important, but secondary development.[35] It is, however, legitimate to look at intersections of political and religious theatricality, as Ruhl does. Her interest is obviously stimulated by a contemporary conflict which was, first and foremost, wrapped up in American interests even though it was detrimental to U.S. relations with political allies as well as its reputation in the world: the so-called "war on terror," initiated by former president George W. Bush, who himself is known as a deeply-religious man and who employed crusade metaphors for the public and media legitimation of his cause.

All three plays deal with the problem from different angles and in complex ways. Each can stand alone as an autonomous theater piece, but they are also strongly interconnected, ultimately creating a dramatic trilogy, which is indeed something more than the sum of its parts. In all three parts we watch the actors not only rehearsing different scenes of the passion play, but also continually questioning what impact this has on their lives. To their great misfortune, they have difficulties keeping their stage lives and their real lives separate. This is most obvious in Part I, where the actress Mary is obsessed with the idea that in order to play the virgin she has to lead a chaste life. This proves impossible when she becomes pregnant with the child of one of the other actors. Seeing no way out of the predicament, she ultimately chooses suicide.

Unfortunately, Ruhl could not resist including some clichés from the recent social and cultural history of the U.S. In Part III, the small-town community has surfaced in the somewhat empty and depressing context of Spearfish, South Dakota, where the telephone poles reach toward an endless horizon. Not only do they seem to symbolize the relentless stream of crucifixion scenes the town has already witnessed, and is doomed to witness in the future, they also remind us of the opportunities for a better life that are missing from that same horizon. But whichever way they prepare their performances, nothing prepares them for the crisis that evolves in their community. It begins when the actor "P," as he is called, returns from Vietnam and tries to resume his former life. Here Ruhl is clearly employing obligatory motifs made famous by Hollywood: the experience in Vietnam has traumatized the actor to a degree that he can't find his way back to "normal." This time the play deals with the question of whether or not embodying a character in a religious drama can provide an identity that helps in times of personal

Figure 7. Sarah Ruhl's *Passion Play*: Spearfish, South Dakota, where the telephone poles reach toward an endless horizon (used by permission of Bill C. Ray).

crisis. The answer is clearly no. Rehearsals degenerate into a repetitive argument about the meaning of lines.

The middle act of the cycle is set in Oberammergau in 1934. This time the villagers are lead to illusions about even bigger achievements, what makes them susceptible to a political ideology whose dangerous consequences they ignore. Arena stage's 2005 production in Washington, D.C., captured the spirit of the peculiar American fascination with Oberammergau. At the same time

Figure 8. Sarah Ruhl's *Passion Play* at Oberammergau, 1934 (used by permission of Bill C. Ray).

the production created the uncanny atmosphere of a false idyll, in the middle of which persecution and death lurk. The artfully carved wooden trees seem to stem directly from a Grimm's fairy tale. They complement the equally picturesque Lederhosen and the director's alpine hat. It is no coincidence that in one of the most memorable scenes Violet, a Jewish girl who prefers to stay under the table during dinner and who in contrast to the actors knows all of the lines perfectly, turns the fairy tale of Hansel and Gretel into a horrible vision of the deportation to Auschwitz and the looming danger of the "oven." It is also one of the rare scenes in the cycle when we actually get a glimpse of the performance of the play itself where the rehearsal for once is neither interrupted nor fails, but rather becomes an event in its own right and creates an impression of how the "actual" production might have appeared. Interestingly, the magic of this moment is indicated in the production by the actors freezing into tableaux vivants of well-known motifs, such as the Last Supper. When the Passion Play is successfully realized, it suggests, the viewer is carried off together with the performers and takes part in their transcendence. Then, however, every critical dialog with the play is also cut off.

This is the strength of Ruhl's interpretation: posing the question of what it means to put on a passion play and where its points of contact with the present lie. That is why during most of the three parts we just see bits and pieces of rehearsals. The audience is disabused of the illusion that a "genuine" passion play is being presented. Ruhl's cycle is concentrated substantially on the personal and political consequences associated with the performance of such a play. This decision by the playwright is one of many, which I would sum up as a choice not to attempt to reconstruct or re-stage the past. Instead, *Passion Play: A Cycle* involves us in a dialogue with the ultimate goal of better understanding our present.

The appearance of "Hitler" in Oberammergau,[36] who enters the set to watch the rehearsal, is remarkably staged in this context. His arrival goes unnoticed by the actors. The first words he speaks are "Do you know who I am?" As Ruhl's stage directions note, he delivers the line "to the audience, a private moment."[37] In this way he directly challenges the viewers to engage critically with him and his appearance on the set. His question has further implications, like, for example, "Do you know why I, as a politician who is not particularly religious, am watching a passion play?" or "What is the motivation to watch a passion play?" His interest in the Passion Play is focused on the depiction of violence and the staging of the denunciation of the Jews: "never has the menace of the Jews been so convincingly portrayed as in this presentation of what happened in the times of the Romans."[38] In this, his appearance has a different motivation than that of Elizabeth I in the first act and of Ronald Reagan in the second. All three political leaders, however, are not only fascinated by theatricality in others, but their own use of drama far exceeds that of the passion play performers. In contrast to the performers, the political leaders we encounter throughout Ruhl's cycle are also completely secure about the roles they assume.

Sarah Ruhl's *Passion Play: A Cycle* is thus not some sort of archival reproduction of a passion play. It is an unmistakably modern piece of theater that references this long lost historical tradition. It is very much about acting, simulating, and pretending—about illusions, misinterpretations of religious signs and symbols, and the loss of reality. While those political leaders actually appear to be devoid of any genuine religious feeling, the small-town actors portrayed in the piece are driven to extremes by their religious involvement. Ruhl is clearly using these troubled lives as metaphors for the consequences of interpreting reality too narrowly through a religious framework. In watching the characters stumbling through their rehearsals and struggling with their own personal lives, we begin to understand that the historical productions must have involved communities and individuals in significantly different ways. What's more, *Passion Play: A Cycle* assumes a very important function which medieval dramas also performed: that of being a medium for reflecting contemporary political questions. So paradoxically, in keeping history at a distance, Ruhl has taken exactly the right direction. In any case, Ruhl's play has shown that the historical decision to separate religion and state was a wise one that should not be reversed.

History and Connections to the Present in the Oberammergau Passion Play

Tableaux vivants were first introduced "between the acts" in an Oberammergau staging in 1750. They were part of a whole suite of theatrical revisions undertaken by the Benedictine monk Ferdinand Rosner, swelling the length of the play from 4900 to 8500 verses.[39]

As the example of the Heidelberg Passion Play has vividly shown, a distanced approach to the Old Testament is atypical for the historical play tradition. In this case, based on typological thinking, the point is to stress the relevance, or the literally "bodily" presence of scenes featuring Abraham, Moses and many others.[40] In the Heidelberg Passion Play the theatrical realization of scenes out of the Old Testament leads to a veritable suggestion of their contemporaneity. This does not mean, as also became clear, that the ways in which medieval passion plays approach the media of time and space are comparable with the techniques of illusion employed in bourgeois theater, such as the unity of plot, time and space. Quite the opposite—different levels of time are linked together and in part arranged simultaneously, but are also always marked in their difference and asynchrony by techniques that are most comparable with Brecht's critical theatre.

Sarah Ruhl's approach to the European and American Passion Play tradition is nothing short of distanced and anachronistic—in the best sense. In three separate epochs, albeit in differing historical contexts, she recognizes analogous attempts to misuse religious theatre in the interest of politics. Actually, the conclusion that emerges from her cycle is that it is impossible to stage passion plays today—a statement that nicely puts every production in performative self-contradiction and thereby creates a productive tension.

A third way of dealing with time and history, which exhibits both historicizing and sacralizing tendencies without thematizing the present, is apparent in the contrast between the tableaux vivants and passion events in the Oberammergau production of 2010. I have already discussed the spatial and temporal isolation of the images "between the acts." This isolation is heightened by the fact that the movement is suspended. Beyond this, the bright, almost garish color scheme, whose base tone changes from picture to picture—green to yellow to blue—but is consistently acutely luminous, is also of note. Apparently this opulence of color is meant to act as a foil to the increasingly sinister hues and appropriately darker staging of the passion itself, thereby advancing the optimistic perspective of the Christian message of redemption. This strong contrast is in principle a contradiction insofar as the production simultaneously attempts to clearly exhibit the Jewish roots of Christ's ministry: Jesus is consistently staged as a Jew. For example, he is addressed as "Rabbi" throughout.

The tableaux vivants not only frame the subsequent stage action and charge it with meaning, they also produce on a basic level a sense of eternity and unquestionable authority while transmitting an aura of holiness. The solemn Baroque music here—as in many other scenes of the Oberammergau Passion Play—does the rest. From a historic perspective, the tableaux vivants assumedly also took on the function of creating devotional moments,[41] but as such they were still integrated into the play. They are the sign of the medieval play's status between ritual and theatricality, of which no trace remains in the modern Oberammergau stagings.

As the study by James Shapiro shows, Oberammergau staging conventions, particularly the script, had become untenable during the 1960s, not least due to public protests from various groups, and were considered in need of revision. The Oberammergau Council, which maintained a strict control over the play, could only partially understand the call for change. A tense, long-term tug-of-war concerning the proper balance between tradition and innovation ensued. The efforts of the ADL and the AJC, who examine the Passion Play productions critically with an eye toward controlling anti–Jewish and anti–Semitic tendencies, are historically understandable and also appropriate. The reduction of anti–Jewish elements indeed means that the play has lost what was for centuries a component part, yet one which was traditionally balanced out, at least partially, through the portrayal of other adversaries of Christ. The revisions undertaken at the beginning of the nineteenth century by the Benedictine monk Otmar Weis, particularly the deletion of scenes featuring the devil, subsequently highlighted Jewish roles.[42] Leaving that element out today is historically defensible: it is hard to imagine that after 1945 the often extremely defaming anti–Jewish rhetoric of the historical plays should be given a voice. The plays lose no authenticity when the script is expunged of this rhetoric. Quite the opposite: constant modification is a part of the cultural approximation. As Shapiro clearly demonstrates, that doesn't mean that it is as simple as putting a menorah on the table at the last supper: for Christians to misappropriate Jesus as a Jew just raises the problem to another level.[43]

The filmic documentation of the preparation of the Passion Play is at least as interesting as the performance itself, if not more so. It offers—in this it is very similar to Ruhl's concept—deep insights into the difficulties faced by a civic community to put on such a production as a community effort, as well as the struggles to learn roles and make effective use of the stage. In this, the actors' respect for the roles—in particular the double-cast role of Jesus—appears completely authentic. Efforts to historicize the staging through an obligatory study trip to Israel for the central Oberammergau cast and through shopping trips to India, where fine fabrics for the costumes are purchased, are contrasted unproblematically with promotional appearances on American television, designed to insure against the feared drop in American ticket sales, which still make up the lion's share of the financing for the production. All of this seems neither cynical nor materialistic. The director is passionate about the production and develops a magnetic charisma during rehearsals that pulls others along in the wake of his infectious enthusiasm.

It appears more problematic that the third level, namely the connection to present time in addition to the Old Testament and historical perspectives, is banned from his production. What the Heidelberg Passion Play and Ruhl's modern drama integrate into their aesthetic structure in various ways is outsourced to the medium of film documentary. In the play itself, the Old Testament prefigurations seem static, transformed by the tableaux into an unquestionable past. This might be explained by the clearly deep-seated Oberammergau conviction that the action presented onstage recounts a "true story," not an interpretation. This precludes the possibility that it could have ended differently and thus would invite the discussion of alternative interpretations. The organizers of the 2010 Oberammergau Passion Play trust that

Figure 9. Director Christian Stückl (left) with actor Frederick Mayet playing Christ.

their radically historicizing approach, the historical acts of Christ themselves, will speak directly to the viewers. However, the entire staging seems strangely distant from the audience.

Perhaps this explains why one sees the actor who plays Jesus alongside the director during intermission—apparently on the way, like the 3000 spectators, to a nourishing meal—who has stopped in shorts on his bike to converse with several guests. The opportunity to "meet Jesus on the street," not to mention other members of the cast, is an integral part of the Oberammergau myth—in particular for British and American attendees. Frederik Mayet and Christoph Stückl, actor and director respectively, do not appear, however, as if they are preening for their audience. Rather, it seems as if in this manner they are grabbing a bit of the ingredient that every passion play so desperately needs: contact with the viewer's reality.

Notes

1. Jörg Adolph, *Die große Passion. Hinter den Kulissen von Oberammergau*, DVD, directed by Jörg Adolph (2011; Distributor: if ... cinema), DVD 2012.
2. James Shapiro, *Oberammergau: The Troubling Story of the World's Most Famous Passion Play* (New York: Pantheon Books, 2012), 3ff. Shapiro's book reveals that Otto Huber has a good deal of experience in this debate, since he took part in the preparation of the millennium performance under the direction of Christian Stückl. In this context he had hoped to communicate his text revisions to representatives of the Jewish institutions, partially while travelling in the United States. This proved to be exceptionally difficult.
3. Shapiro, 24.
4. Alexander Nagel and Christopher S. Wood, *Anachronic Renaissance* (New York: Zone Books, 2010), 10f.
5. Shapiro, 94–99.
6. See also Shapiro, chapter two for a history of the text.
7. See also Ursula Schulze, *Geistliche Spiele im Mittelalter und in der Frühen Neuzeit. Von der liturgischen Feier zum Schauspiel. Eine Einführung* (Berlin: Erich Schmidt Verlag, 2012). Regarding the Oberammergau tradition, see Schulze, 225–230.
8. Sarah Ruhl, *Passion Play: A Cycle* (New York: Broadway Play Publishing, 2005).
9. Judith Butler, *Excitable Speech: A Politics of the Performative* (New York: Routledge, 1997).
10. Margreta de Grazia, "Anachronism," in *Cultural Reformations: Medieval and Renaissance in Literary History*, eds. Brian Cummings, James Simpson (Oxford: Oxford University Press, 2010), 15.
11. de Grazia, 15.
12. de Grazia, 15.
13. de Grazia, 16.
14. de Grazia, 26–30.
15. Nagel and Wood, 9.
16. Nagel and Wood, 18.
17. Carolyn Dinshaw, "Temporalities," in *Middle English*, ed. Paul Strohm (Oxford: Oxford University Press, 2007), 120.
18. Nagel and Wood, 18.

19. These questions were addressed at a conference on "Anachronism/Achronicity" held at the University of North Carolina at Chapel Hill in the spring of 2013.

20. Compare Elke Koch, "Endzeit als Ereignis. Zur Performativität von Drohung und Verheißung im deutschen Weltgerichtsspiel des späten Mittelalters," in *Drohung und Verheißung. Mikroprozesse in Verhältnissen von Macht und Subjekt*, eds. Evamaria Heisler, Elke Koch, Thomas Scheffer (Freiburg: Rombach, 2007).

21. See Jutta Eming, "Simultaneität und Verdoppelung. Motivationsstrukturen im geistlichen Spiel," in *Transformationen des Religiösen. Performativität und Textualität im geistlichen Spiel*, eds. Ingrid Kasten, Erika Fischer-Lichte (Berlin: De Gruyter, 2007); Dorothea Freise, *Geistliche Spiele in der Stadt des ausgehenden Mittelalters* (Göttingen: Vandenhoeck & Ruprecht, 2002) 482–499. It was attempted to bring this historical level into play by way of "historical," Biblically-based, repertoire of props and costumes, which certainly had a symbolic nature. The repertoire was, however, limited.

22. See Hansjürgen Linke, "Unstimmige Opposition. 'Geistlich' und 'weltlich' als Ordnungskategorien der mittelalterlichen Dramatik," *Leuvense bijdragen* no. 90 (2001); Christoph Petersen, "Imaginierte Präsenz. Der Körper Christi und die Theatralität des geistlichen Spiels," in *Das Theater des Mittelalters und der frühen Neuzeit als Ort und Medium sozialer und symbolischer Kommunikation*, eds. Christel Meier, Heinz Meyer, Claudia Spanily (Münster: Rhema, 2004).

23. Werner Röcke, "Protestantismus und 'episches Theater': Jörg Wickrams biblisches Drama *Tobias*," in *Vergessene Texte—Verstellte Blicke: Neue Perspektiven der Wickram-Forschung*, eds. Maria E. Müller, Michael Mecklenburg (Frankfurt a. M.: Peter Lang 2007).

24. Glenn Ehrstine, "Das figurierte Gedächtnis: *Figura*, Memoria und die Simultanbühne des deutschen Mittelalters," in *Text und Kultur: mittelalterliche Kultur 1150–1450*, ed. Ursula Peters (Stuttgart: Metzler 2001). These are some of the "figures" [figurae] with which religious plays work on various levels.

25. Elisabeth Meyer, "Zur Überlieferungsfunktion des Heidelberger Passionsspiels: Von einer Spielvorlage zur erbaulichen Lektüre?" *Leuvense Bijdragen* no. 90 (2001). It is debated if the Heidelberg Passion Play was ever produced.

26. Erika Kartschoke, "Eine feine liebliche gottselige Comedie. Ehelehre in Tobias-Dramen des 16. Jahrhunderts," in *Eheglück und Liebesjoch: Bilder von Liebe, Ehe und Familie in der Literatur des 15. und 16. Jahrhunderts*, ed. Maria E. Müller (Weinheim: Beltz 1988), 79.

27. Kartschoke, 79.

28. Compare Rainer H. Schmid, *Raum, Zeit und Publikum des geistlichen Spiels. Aussage und Absicht eines mittelalterlichen Massenmediums* (München: Tuduv Buch, 1975); Thomas Cramer, *Geschichte der deutschen Literatur im späten Mittelalter* (München: dtv, 1990), 219.

29. Freise, *Geistliche Spiele*, 31–36; 81–334.

30. Claire Sponsler, *Ritual Imports. Performing Medieval Drama in America* (Ithaca: Cornell University Press, 2004).

31. Ruhl, *Passion Play: A Cycle*.

32. Sponsler, *Ritual Imports*,124.

33. Shapiro, *Oberammergau*, 11; 38. The documentation also shows, however, that there were fears during the preparations of the Passion of 2010 that this interest had dropped not only due to the financial crisis, which could have led to considerable financial losses. In this context, there was also talk that American interest had generally dropped. In the end Frederick Mayet, one of the two actors playing Jesus who

was also working in the public relations section travelled with another actress through the United States in order to promote the production. They did American television spots. Shapiro claims that the 1990s saw a decline in American interest in the Oberammergau Plays (38), on the other hand, he also notes that the organizers could easily have sold four to five times more tickets at the 2000 production than they did (11).

34. Ruhl, *Passion Play*, without page numbers.

35. Compare, for example, Schulze, *Geistliche Spiele im Mittelalter*, Jan-Dirk Müller, "Mittelalterliches Theater: Geistliches Spiel," in *Theater im Aufbruch. Das europäische Drama der Frühen Neuzeit*, eds. Roger Lüdecke, Virginia Richter (Tübingen: Max Niemeyer, 2008).

36. Shapiro, *Oberammergau*, 137–186. See Shapiro for historical information regarding Hitler's presence in Oberammergau in 1930 and 1934 and the misuse of the plays for propagandistic purposes.

37. Ruhl, *Passion Play*, 76.

38. Ruhl, *Passion Play*, 77. Ruhl notes that this line, as well as the rest of the monologue on this page, "is a quotation from Hitler's remarks." *Ibid*. The passage is also discussed by Shapiro, 167. Compare also Shapiro, 165: "Probably nothing has damaged Oberammergau's international reputation more than Hitler's enthusiasm for their play."

39. Sponsler, *Ritual Imports*, 127. See also Shapiro, 61f. Shapiro's analysis shows that Rosner's adaptation was composed of a hybrid construction of Baroque elements including the introduction of verse and music, and Medieval elements including *Marienklagen* and appearances of the devil, which was received well by the audience.

40. Ehrstine, "Das figurierte Gedächtnis," 429.

41. Compare Ehrstine, "Das figurierte Gedächtnis."

42. Shapiro, 69f.

43. Shapiro, 31.

Tableaus and Selves in Vrindavan and Oberammergau

DAVID MASON

Plato wanted to exile poets (who included, at that time, dramatists) on account of his fear that the essentially representational nature of their work threatened public order. Not only do acts of *mimesis* lie to us, in the sense that an imitation can never *be* what it imitates, but an act of *mimesis* undermines reality by introducing to reality things that are not, in themselves, real, or, worse, are unnatural combinations of things that do not, naturally, go together. Aristotle rescued theatre and laid the foundation for Western dramatic theory by arguing that imitation teaches us. From our earliest ages, we learn how to be human by imitating the other humans around us; hence, theatre, by its imitation of humans around us, teaches us how to be (properly) human. We in the Western world have, thanks to Aristotle, happily carried on our theatrical imitations in spite of Plato.

On the other hand, Aristotle's acceptance of the Platonic premise that theatre is essentially imitation locked the West into a theatrical concept against which it has been struggling for more than two millennia. From Horace to Diderot to Schiller to Brecht, Boal, and Grotowski, we have thanked Aristotle for justifying the art while searching for ways to reject the imposition of the Aristotelean framework that relies on the Platonic notion that theatre is, in essence, a mimetic activity, and which "works," therefore, only upon principles that ensure a particular fidelity of imitation. Rather than persisting in the often frustrating project of legitimizing theatrical art by recapitulating Aristotelean principles, we might intervene between Plato and Aristotle to interrogate Aristotle's strategy.

A pre–Aristotelean response to Plato might challenge the idea that theatre only re-presents, since, if theatre is not a merely derivative activity, it need not be said that it lies to us nor contributes to confusion about what is real. In the sixteenth century, Sidney tried this response by arguing that the "poet is the least liar," though Sidney only justified this assertion with the claim that the poet never pretends to tell the truth.[1] In radical contrast, the madman Antonin Artaud tried to articulate a kind of theatre that did not imitate anything, but was, itself, a pure reality of its own. Artaud's vision has never been realized, least of all by Artaud himself.[2] The post-modern revision of the moves to recover a non–Aristotelean justification of theatre has been to challenge the idea that there is anything real for theatre to imitate. Where Sidney excuses the poet's lie as that which never claims to be anything else, Derrida, et al., excuse the poet for not lying any more than anything else.

The curiosity that is the Oberammergau *Passionsspiele* is a continuous theatrical exercise that has spanned nearly five centuries of dramatic theory. When Sidney was struggling to explain why poets need not tell us the whole truth, the Passionsspiele was first composing itself as a great truth couched in a decidedly duplicitous, theatrical form.[3] In the almost post-postmodern twenty-first century, where we no longer trouble ourselves with the idea of Truth, the Passionsspiele openly confesses its fabrication and yet will not relinquish a claim to truth. Consequently, the Passionsspiele recommends itself as an antidote to Western theatre's chief ailment. The Passion Play is a theatrical production that affirms its legitimacy not by way of mimetic accomplishment, but on account of not imitating nor re-presenting.

Which is not to say that *mimesis* is not happening at Oberammergau. In fact, most of the six-hour production is presented in a rather stale, if colossal, naturalism.[4] In the 2010 production, Frederik Mayet and Andreas Richter, on alternating schedules, certainly imitated Jesus, and the action of the production certainly imitated the arrest, trial, and execution of Jesus. The production trotted out all sorts of mimetic devices to impress on its audience its representational nature, including a horde of children (because the streets of 30 CE Jerusalem, would certainly have been clogged with children), terrific beards (because the men of 30 CE Jerusalem would certainly have worn terrific beards), and camels (*real* camels, because Herod's wife in 30 CE Jerusalem, would certainly would not have ridden a fake camel). The production, in most respects, fastidiously offers a fantastical representation of Jesus's Jerusalem.

On the other hand, the production also includes thirteen *lebende bilder*—tableaus, or living pictures—that seem very out-of-character with the pseudo-historical naturalism of the rest of the show. Thirteen times across the play's six hours, the plodding, costume drama comes to an almost complete halt in deference to a still image composed of the very living bodies of the Oberammergau cast, disclosed inside the frame of the looming, upstage scene house in a very stylized, unnatural manner. At the tableau moments, the chorus of more than sixty solemn voices parts like a curtain to reveal, in the manner of a priest revealing a piece of the true cross, a frozen scene from the Christian Old Testament—Adam's and Eve's expulsion, Moses's descent from Sinai, Daniel in the lion's den, etc.—done up in brilliant colors and formal poses not at all asserting themselves as representations of a historical Israel. Of course, that these scenes each have titles shows that the scenes are representational of *something*, even if it isn't an imagined history. The tableaus are arresting, and strange in other ways, but they don't leap radically out of the mimetic matrix in which theatre is embedded.

Nevertheless, Oberammergau's tableaus are a hint, at least, of a non-mimetic theatre that was once in operation in the West, in spite of Plato, Aristotle, and the rest of the theorists for whom representation and re-presentation have been theatre's *sine qua non*. It may be true that staged action cannot not be representational. Even if one's reading of theatre is primarily phenomenological, the chair on stage may be something other than the chair on the stage, as Bert States reminds us, but, nevertheless, the chair that *is* on the stage signifies whatever that other chair may be.[5] But staged action is not all that occurs in a theatre. The refusal of the Oberammergau tableaus to represent action (by remaining still) draws attention to that other *sine qua non* of theatre. Oberammergau's *audience* is the object of the *Passionsspiele*'s peculiar device. The production's tableaus occur not only on the village's century-old stage, but also in the experience of the enormous audience and in the unique experience of each individual audience member, and what happens in *that* event may not be mimetic, at all. The imaginative effort that the tableaus require of audience members contributes actively to the meaning of the play that audience members construe. Furthermore, that imaginative effort and the meaning it engenders contributes dramatically to the identities that audience members are always in the process of forging. Those identities partake of the tableaus, and, in a very real way, they live in the tableaus' dramatic world, and the play in which they take part is not representational, or, at least, not merely representational. My starting point is a pair of complimentary theoretical foundations: role theory and reader-response theory. The first of these is a theory of identity, from which much of the postmodern sense of identity has derived. The second is an approach to understanding art, especially literature. Together, the two theories offer a picture of the self as a thing in development, a thing *in play*, in fact, that does not come into forever-fixed existence, but does, really, exist in a flux of activity that we may as well call acting. After a brief examination of the implications of reader-response theory and role theory, I will go to Vrindavan, India, for an explicit model of the non-mimetic theatre I am identifying. I will then come back around to the Passionsspiele as a model in which this kind of theatre is implicit. I will also suggest that Oberammergau is continuing a tradition of

Figure 10. *Lebendes Bild* from the 2010 *Passionsspiele*, "The Ten Commandments and the Dance Around the Golden Calf." Designed by Stefan Hageneier (image courtesy Oberammergau Passionsspiele 2010 Office of Public Relations).

non-mimetic theatre that was explicit in the late middle ages, but which has sequestered itself under the demands of the modern age.

Self and Reader

The "role theory" of the social sciences has a distinct predilection for theatrical metaphors, as it posits that personal identity is not an individual's essential, irreducible quality, but that identity develops from the part the individual plays in a society. By entering into socially constructed functions—father, friend, citizen, and so forth—and by adopting the characteristics those functions require—maturity, authority, insight, and so forth—we reinforce the legitimacy of the conditions that construct those roles and also impress upon us a sense of our selves as intimately composed of these functions and characteristics. From George Herbert Mead to Erving Goffman, the basic premise of role theory asserts that we are not selves, but we play them on TV. The theory partly derives from the semiotics of the early part of the nineteen hundreds, which, by identifying the socially-constructed relationships between signifying elements and their referents in the world we encounter, undermined the concept of a unified, autonomous self that encounters the world and projects itself into the world. After semiotics, a happy "hello" and a wave of the hand were no longer the genuine expression of an essentially well-intentioned soul, but the adoption of a socially-determined signal in a specific social context. Role theory follows to suggest that the "hello" and the wave of the hand proceed from a cultural complex to shape the individual who employs them, to lend an identity to the hello-ing and waving person. Indeed, for Mead, the mind, that feature of selfhood that our Western tradition has most closely associated with an essential, irreducible self-hood, and which we have imagined produces behavior, is, on the contrary, the product of socially-conditioned behavior. The very words we speak, the very gestures we employ, are features of roles we act out. And every actor who has worked in the Stanislavskian tradition, at least, knows that acting a role can mean experiencing the role as a "'self.'"[6]

By the nineteen-sixties, Erving Goffman had made the idea of acting (in the theatrical sense) as a fundamental feature of identity one of the most popular concepts of twentieth-century academia. About this time, Swedish psychologist Hjalmar Sundén adapted role theory to rationalize religious experience. Not only do we play roles that cause us to experience ourselves as identities, reasoned Sundén, but we play particular roles that cause us to experience ourselves as particular identities. The adoption of religiously-constructed roles fosters in individuals the experience of religiously-determined selves. According to Sundén's role theory of religious experience, the way in which religious individuals adopt and play religious roles structures their perception of their own identities and of the reality they inhabit. Sundén saw that among social mechanisms, religion tends to provide more fully realized roles in the form of characters sanctified and promoted by tradition as exemplary models of living. Religious scripture, as well as spiritual tradition that glorifies saints and sages, offer individuals roles with whole backstories and mostly complete endings—with *purpose* that lends the individual a ready-made, ready-to-go self.

A person's behavior, says role theory, makes the person's self. A person's religious behavior makes the person's self religious. Sundén's use of role theory here anticipates the way the social sciences adapted literary theory in the late nineteen sixties. Structuralist theories of narrative led to Frank Kermode's *The Sense of an Ending* in 1967, which proposed that, in literature, endings constitute meaning.[7] "Once a plot is initiated," writes Dan McAdams in his explanation of the way personal narratives shape human psychology, "the action assumes a teleological orientation and the listener comes to expect that he or she will eventually encounter an 'ending' that resolves the problems and tensions that got the story going in the first place."[8] That is, the story leads the reader to expect a resolution. For Sundén, the structured narratives of scriptural literature from which religious individuals adopt roles engender a literary anticipation that the individual's life will resolve in the same way that the story of the scriptural role with which the individual has identified.

Reader-response theory steps in here to suggest that if the story which has promised an ending does not provide an ending, the reader will work very hard to supply it. The active reader that the principal theorists of this approach envision is not a slate on which an author imposes his or her text, but an artistic collaborator, who actively and creatively fills in what Wolfgang Iser calls "gaps." Where a story leaves gaps, which might be breaks in continuity or merely the consequences of the impossible project of comprehensively accounting for every element of a scene, the reader-writer inserts herself in an ever-oscillating project of perception and construction. "Indeed," writes Iser, "it is only through inevitable omissions that a story will gain its dynamism. Thus, whenever the flow is interrupted and we are led off in unexpected directions, the opportunity is given to us to bring into play our own faculty for establishing connections—for filling the gaps left by the text itself."[9] The text might very well initiate an expectation, but the text does not determine the realization of that expectation. Instead, the text's ending arises from the creative collaboration between itself and a reader.

Furthermore, that collaboration changes everything. The reading process reveals the text as a fluid, indeterminate entity. The reader, too, finds herself to be indeterminate, and the reading she does changes her. "Reading reflects ideas and attitudes that shape our own personality before we can experience the unfamiliar world of the literary text," Iser continues. "But during this process, something happens to us."[10] Iser's "something" is paradigmatically theatrical. Literature demands that we readers read as though we were someone else, and this playing facilitates an interaction with the world of a text. In effect, reading is *acting*, in the theatrical sense of the term, and every reader is an actor playing a role through which he accesses an author's asserted reality. Iser does not seem to realize the theatrical implications of reader-response theory—at least, he does not adopt theatrical terminology—but he quotes at length Georges Poulet's intentionally convoluted summary of the reading process that expresses a marvel at which the typical actor would only shrug a shoulder:

> Whatever I think is a part of *my* mental world. And yet here I am thinking a thought which manifestly belongs to another mental world, which is being thought in me just as though I did not exist. Already the notion is inconceivable and seems even more so if I reflect that, since every thought must have a subject to think it, this *thought* which is alien to me and yet in me, must also have in me a *subject* which is alien to me.... Whenever I read, I mentally pronounce an I, and yet the I which I pronounce is not myself.[11]

But the "I" that Poulet pronounces might *become* himself. Role theory returns here to suggest that the "something" that happens to us in the reading process is the transformation of our selves. By acting the role, by hosting the thoughts of an author and the presumptive interior worlds of characters and playing those thoughts and inclinations as our own, we initiate an anticipation that structures our perception. The consequence is a different self than we brought to the reading. "The production of the meaning of literary texts ... does not merely entail the discovery of the unformulated, which can then be taken over by the active imagination of the reader; it also entails the possibility that we may formulate ourselves..."[12]

Sundén's version of role theory sees the religious devotee as a reader who engages with the world as with a frequently blank and often cryptic text that demands the adoption and playing of a role. That role supplies the structure that fashions identity, so that the devotee-reader comes to perceive himself as a combination of the role and whatever the devotee-reader may have been prior to the advent of the role. The devotee-reader-role then comes to perceive reality as a combination of the role's reality and whatever reality was prior to the advent of the role.

The Judeo-Christian devotee, for instance, at a time of suffering may see in the Biblical Job a canonical model for dealing with suffering, and may initiate the Job narrative in his own life by internalizing the assumptions of the narrative—that the Devil caused this suffering, that God is conducting a test, that the test requires patience, etc. Stepping into this role and into this narrative, the devotee enters into an anticipatory register, a *play* register, in which the Biblical text and the devotee's material life blend and anticipate God's immanence. The role, then, gives a certain structure to the devotee's "view" (or perception) so that the devotee construes through the mechanism of the role the confirmations of the role's reality in the events and circumstances of the devotee's own life. In Nils G. Holm's summary of Sundén's theory, when a person takes the role of an agent in a narrative, the role "comes to structure his field of experience" so that he "experiences the external course of events as the actions of God."[13] That structured experience acts as a confirmation of the role, and contributes significantly to the ongoing formulation of the individual's self.

The Self in Play in Vrindavan

At least seven hours from Munich by plane, and then another difficult five-hour drive through flat farmland from Delhi to Vrindavan, religious devotees often gather for a much smaller theatrical spectacle than Oberammergau's, but one with no less significance. Using some devices that we find in Oberammergau, India's *râs lila* theatre dramatizes the many episodes of the Krishna story. Like the Jesus story, the Krishna story has pieces that are historical and also ongoing. Where Jesus was born, broke bread, and died in the vicinity of Jerusalem two thousand years ago, Krishna was born, stole bread, and died, in the vicinity of Vrindavan five thousand years ago.[14] Where Jesus entered into a heavenly exaltation and is ever-present through the Holy Spirit, the divine Krishna continues his divine dance in an unmanifest, transcendent condition. Where Jesus effected a salvation of which humanity may still, even nowadays, avail itself, Krishna permeates mundane reality and may be manifest to the sincere devotee.

The *râs lila* theatre purports to reveal the ever-present Krishna in the ongoing activity that is part of his story. While devotees might regard the stories of Krishna's bucolic childhood as historical, they think of those historical events merely as representations—a kind of theatre—of what the divine Krishna is always doing. The dramatizations of Krishna lore that take place in *râs lila* performances are representational, but no more so than the fact of Krishna's historical existence. Behind the material fact of history or theatrical production, the divine Krishna is always playing, and both history and theatre are a mechanism by which Krishna's real, supernal playing is revealed.

On any given day, pilgrims in Vrindavan, visiting from all quarters of India, largely outnumber residents, and many of the residents are residents on account of their devotional spirit.[15] Almost all activity in Vrindavan is directed toward revealing the *real* Vrindavan for the devotees who dominate the population. In spite of the farmland that surrounds it, the industry that sustains Vrindavan is religious tourism, every dimension of which is directed toward sustaining the sense that the town is only a proxy for Krishna's ineffable village. At even the most mundane levels, Vrindavan residents adopt behavior to remind themselves and visitors that something else is going on in Vrindavan. Expressions of greeting and farewell in Vrindavan, for instance, are conditioned by the language of Krishna worship.[16]

Because of its significance to the practice of Krishna worship, Vrindavan also harbors a dense assortment of temples, through which the perpetual stream of pilgrims flows from very early morning until very late at night. The primary activity occurring in these temples is *looking*. Pilgrims go to temples in Vrindavan to look at the images of Krishna installed there. Typically, these images are small statuettes of Krishna appearing as a young cowherd, one leg crossed over the other, playing a flute. Often, Krishna is represented in devotional images alongside Radha, his girlfriend. Temple priests keep the statues opulently dressed and ornamented. For Krishna devotees, temple worship consists of entering into the inner chamber of a temple to look at the temple's Krishna statue. Devotees' widely-attested experience of this kind of looking—known in India as *darshan*—is of the transcendent, divine Krishna himself, manifest in a real way through the statue.[17] The notion that god inhabits the temple image leads to the reverential deference devotees give the image, which is bathed, clothed, fed, entertained, and left alone for naps throughout the day. Devotees revere the temple statue, and similar statues in their own home shrines, as the material manifestation of something that, though real, would otherwise be entirely removed from experience.

These temple images are rarely naturalistic. Though great effort is sometimes invested in fashioning Krishna's temple images, they rarely have any convincing resemblance to any possible cowherd boy. Krishna images in Vrindavan are traditionally jet black, with delicate limbs, chubby faces, and arresting, oversized white eyes. More often than not, the eyes are separate pieces, affixed finally to the statues with beeswax, so that they stand apart from the rest of the figure and draw a viewer's gaze. Which is to say, Krishna's temple images are gaps in the flow of reality's narrative. They are blanks that demand that devotee-readers adopt new roles, since, for Wolfgang Iser and other reader-response theorists, "it is only by leaving behind the familiar world of his own experience that the reader can truly participate in the adventure the literary text offers him."[18] The encounter with the Krishna images gives the devotee an occasion for role-play that leads to transformative experience.

The actors of *râs lila* theatre operate in the same way and serve the same function as the temple image. Caparisoned with the same trappings as temple images, the actors playing Krishna and Radha become objects at which devotees can direct their devotional looking, and devotee audiences commonly attest that the Krishna and Radha actors in *râs lila* shows are, in fact, the divine Krishna and Radha.[19] There's no naturalism in *râs lila* actors, whose acting style is what one would expect of seven- and eight-year-old amateurs, embodied in wooden gestures and spoken in a highly artificial rhythm and semi-falsetto. Performances are characterized by dropped lines and confused choreography, gaudy costumes that commonly come apart on stage, and scenery—when there is scenery—in two, saturated dimensions. In spite of their non—naturalistic style—in fact, *because of it*—Krishna actors do manifest the divine Krishna, as is evident in the rapt and reverential faces of temple-goers and theatre-audiences alike. *Râs lila* actors and temple images, together, are referred to with the term *svârûp*, the pure or unmediated form of god. The unnatural-ness of *râs lila* performances provides in a particularly effective way for the acting of audience members. In fact, the theology of Krishna devotion has advocated devotional role-playing for half a millennium. The ideal devotee *must* assume a role, since he or she aspires to be like the young girls of the Vrindavan of Krishna's own mythic time. According to Krishna lore, the village girls exhibit the most pure, the most earnest devotion to Krishna, and Krishna particularly favors them, as a consequence. A distinctly aesthetic theology developed in Vrindavan in the sixteenth century that explicitly valued the imaginative imitation of the mythic village girls. In his definitive study of one religious authority's widely influential revision of Krishna devotion, David L. Haberman concludes that, in the sixteenth century, the objective of devotional activity is the manifestation of Krishna's eternal reality in the material substance of Vrindavan, and that the devotee who takes on the role of a village girl is "in the best position to enter and participate in [that] dramatic world..."[20] The aim of Krishna devotion, which is the unmediated encounter with Krishna, is closed except to those who have transformed their feelings, their sensibilities, their character, so that they coincide with the feelings, sensibilities, and character of the mythic, Vrindavan girls who cavort with Krishna at night. Consequently, role-play is an indispensable element of Krishna worship, and every Krishna devotee engages in it, to a lesser or greater extent.[21] In essence, Krishna devotion is acting.[22]

One of the reasons to visit a Krishna temple and to keep a Krishna image in one's own home shrine is to develop, by attending to the image, more purely realized devotional feelings, such as those harbored by the village girls of Krishna's Vrindavan. So, a person plays the part of one who cares for Krishna by providing care and comfort to the statue, at the temple and at home. In most activities in Vrindavan, devotees are living their roles. At home, devotees wake Krishna in the place of honor he occupies in their homes, they bathe him, dress him, feed him, entertain him, and see to his peaceful rest. The same activities occur in Vrindavan's temples, and devotees are privileged to enter the temples to see the attendant priests wake Krishna, bathe him, feed him, and so on. What the image is made of and what it looks like have little bearing on the devotee's experience, which depends much more on the degree to which the devotee has developed the sensitivity, the girl-like character, necessary to see Krishna (who transcends the material, anyway).[23]

The *rās lila* plays offer devotees another opportunity for devotional role-playing. *Rās lila* audiences attend performances in a role-playing attitude, eager to exploit the performance as a means of developing more village-girl-like sensibilities. The amateurish nature of the plays lends itself to this spiritual exercise, not only because polish and sophistication may only interfere with the childlike simplicity of feeling that devotees are trying to cultivate, but because the rough quality of the productions leaves great gaps for the audience's own playing.

One particular *rās lila* device is worth mentioning here, since it is a conspicuous counterpart to Oberammergau's tableaus. The paradigmatic moment of *rās lila* plays is the *jhānkî*. During some song and dance sequences with which *rās lila* performances are replete, the actors playing Krishna and Radha come center stage and freeze in intertwined poses. These still moments, when the stage is only a picture, most clearly associate *rās lila* performances with temple worship, because the poses precisely resemble the postures of Krishna and Radha in the statuary and paintings of Krishna temples. The *jhānkî* poses hold high religious significance as the moments in which the metaphysical Krishna may be most available to discerning eyes.[24] Combined with Radha's form, the artistry of Krishna's posture indicates his transcendent spiritual qualities of youth, beauty, joy, and love, hidden from all but "in character" onlookers. The *jhânkî* act as snapshots of Krishna's divine form as discernible to the eyesight of pure devotees.

As a model of the interaction of role theory and reader-response theory, the text—the highly stylized temple image or the *râs lila* actor's slapdash acting—provides plenty of space for the devotee-actor's acting. Accordingly, the Krishna devotee takes on the role of the village girl, a role provided by sacred texts and valorized by Vrindavan's religious tradition, which initiates an anticipation and provides structure for the devotee's field of perception as he proceeds toward realizing that anticipation. In the role, the devotee actively works (or plays) to perceive Vrindavan in the way a mythic village girl would perceive it. The role and his interaction with the *râs lila* performance text, conditions the devotee's identity; ultimately, the role becomes a part of that identity, so that the devotee emerges from the text as a different self. In this way, the *râs lila* is not mimetic theatre.[25] The trappings of representation are, indeed, to be found on Vrindavan's stages, but, in a process much like reader-response's combination of reader and text (though even more vividly) the *râs lila* performance joins performer and audience in the "presence of the fictional world" and in "the realities of the text."[26]

Figure 11. Râs Lila Jhânkî (courtesy David Mason).

Audience Selves in Oberammergau

The *Passionsspiele* asserts itself as a representation of the Jesus narrative, but like other theatrical representations, it becomes a peculiar combination of re-presentation and event, of icon and item. The *Passionsspiele*'s *lebende bilder* present the ongoing story of Christian salvation in the forms of Adam and Eve, Joseph, Moses, and so forth, and also present this ongoing story in the forms of the bodies on stage. Partly because they are such a strange, antiquated device, the play's tableaus are especially effective at forging a bond between what is represented and the what, itself.

The Passionsspiele's tableaus contravene Western convention, which, thanks to Aristotle, values action and lesson. Oberammergau's tableaus, in contrast, offer no action, and no lesson. As strange a stage device as ever there was, the tableaus arrest the forward movement of the Passionsspiele's action. Though the production's chorus supplies a text for the living images—and a rather didactic one at that, since the chorus's contribution is a typological interpretation of each image—the living images themselves say nothing about themselves, assert no interpretation, propose no particular reading. Consequently, the tableaus carry out a decidedly not–Aristotelean function. Furthermore, that function, is decidedly not Platonic (which is to say, not-mimetic), insofar as the tableaus exist in a world that their viewers experience as their own.

Like the images installed in Krishna temples, and like the *râs lila jhânkî*, the Oberammergau *lebende bilder* move deliberately away from naturalism. Not only do they interrupt the naturalistic action of the Passionsspiele, not only do they suspend the laws of expression that we typically expect from dramatic action and from life, the tableaus intentionally and to a high degree stylize their subjects. Stefan Hageneier's designs for the Passionsspiele's 2010 performances construct striking but stiff compositions, saturated with color, but devoid of emotional expression, much in the manner of late medieval/early renaissance painting. The effect is distinctly otherworldly scenes, perhaps with some relationship to reality but without any solid mooring in it. The tableaus, consequently, interrupt not only the play, but life, dropping into the lived experience of audience members as great, ambiguous gaps.

The ambiguity of these gaps, their irregularity, denies the expectations that the play has otherwise encouraged audience members to adopt. For Iser, this effect is crucial. Art must "shatter" the audience member's preconceptions, must introduce an element of indeterminacy, before the reader's imagination can be brought into play so as to foment an aesthetic experience.[27] So also for Sundén's role theory. The devotee takes up a role in order to cope with disruption in his or her expectation of life. The crisis, which cannot be met otherwise, demands new thinking, new playing, an approach in a new, better-suited identity.

The space in these *lebende bilder* gaps draws audience members into rationalizing efforts—sense-making schemes—that initiate expectations of the text and launch the roles the audience members themselves must play to realize the fulfillment of these expectations. Here, Christian typology lends a hand. The chorus's ideological explication of the scenes' symbolism provides a rubric within which certain roles can form.[28] The role in which the audience member sees (or plays) structures the manner in which the audience member sees. Because the tableaus have so disrupted the audience member's typical modes of seeing, the audience member has little choice but to see through the structure available in the role that the play offers, so that that structure—that way of seeing—becomes, indeed, the audience member's own manner of seeing. That is, the Oberammergau audience member sees the representational stage as a twenty-first-century audience member. The Oberammergau audience member also sees what happens in the Oberammergau theatre—especially the *lebende bilder*—as a Biblical witness.

The transformation of the audience member is not only possible, but inevitable, because identity resides in the complex of our social environment, and, hence, also changes in accordance with shifts in that environment. At least, this is the contention of Erving Goffman: "The self ... is not a property of the person to whom it is attributed, but dwells rather in the pattern of social control that is exerted in connection with the person by himself and those around him. This special kind of institutional arrangement does not so much support the self as constitute it."[29]

The Oberammergau audience member comes away from the six-hour production a self much different than went in. The process by which that self transforms involves the intentions of the performance itself—the demands it makes on the audience member and the room it provides her to build what the play calls for—and the active role-playing of the audience member, who comes to inhabit, and to live, a role.

The Medieval Player

No wonder that Oberammergau's tableaus may be the most historically authentic parts of the four-hundred-year-old tradition. The thirteen tableaus of the 2010 production survive from at least eighteen tableaus introduced to Oberammergau's stage with Ferdinand Rosner's highly allegorical version of the passion play in 1750.[30] Rosner's contribution to the Oberammergau tradition was radical, even in its own day, because of its formally poetic language and its vivaciously theatrical, even grotesque, embodiment of evil. Death, Sin, Avarice, Envy, among other disturbing characters, all appear in Rosner's very first scene. Subsequently, a cohort of named devils (none of whom appear as characters in any of the four Gospels), conspire with the character Despair at the site of Judas's suicide, and then tear Judas's suspended body apart, eat his innards, and fling his body into a burning pit that opens up in the stage. The demons then leap after it, triumphantly.[31] Rosner's tableaus contributed to a staged world that did not pretend to a mere representation of historical events, but worked in a non-representational vein to better manifest the Christian reality in which Good was always at war with Evil.[32] Although Oberammergauers jettisoned Rosner's play even before 1800, the tradition held onto his tableaus.

Versions of the play prior to Rosner's seem to have had a similar taste for grotesque theatrics. The earliest surviving script, which comes from the 1662 production, includes elements that inform Rosner's later version, such as a horde of demons that minces about the stage and dismembers and devours Judas. In James Shapiro's estimation, the seventeenth-century Passionsspiel was "rough-and-tumble" theatre, "noisier and less musical than subsequent versions," and including unabashed attempts at irreverent humor, as when the play's opening "is almost immediately undercut with the appearance of Satan reading aloud a letter from Lucifer that encourages the audience to ignore the Prologue, desecrate the play with laughter, and join him in Hell."[33] The earliest incarnation of Oberammergau's play seems to have been striving for engaging entertainment as much as for anything else. This era of the Passionsspiel was informed by at least two sixteenth century plays, both a Catholic play and a Protestant one—scripts that precede the fabled plague that leads to the institution of Oberammergau's decennial performances in 1634. These sources of the Oberammergau play, themselves, seem to have sampled from still other scripts reaching back another century, or two.

Which is to suggest that the most forceful elements of the tradition, those expressly theatrical features that imbue Oberammergau's Passionsspiele with a transformative quality, survive from that period of the middle ages in which theatricality was a highly valued mode of spirituality. Glynne Wickham notes that many of the events that historical documents of medieval, English villages call "church ales" were merely tableaus, "processed around the streets following a service and as a prelude to a banquet..."[34] The pageant wagons that became the hallmark of Corpus Christi processions in the fourteenth century featured Biblical tableaus that, together, acted as a rolling sequence of scenes typologically associated with the central Christian narrative by following the eucharist's own privileged scene at the head of the parade. The Corpus Christi tableaus, themselves, inherit an existing tradition developed for entry pageants at least as early as the thirteenth century. Lynette Muir notes an event in Paris in 1313, for which "two craft guilds... presented a long series of tableaux from Adam and Eve to the Judgement (including the Passion), in the streets through which Philip the Fair of France escorted the visiting Edward II of England and his French wife, Isabelle."[35] Rosner's script adapted a theatrical device that had been rather familiar and important to Christians of earlier centuries, and, centuries later, the modern Christianity that sustains the *Passionsspiele*'s popularity has sensed, perhaps in spite of itself, the special potential in the tableaus and held onto them.

Rosner's reintroduction of tableaus to the Biblical drama of his region may have recognized the peculiar value of tableaus that the Christian devotee of the high middle ages took for granted. Theological reforms that developed from the Eucharistic controversy of the eleventh and twelfth centuries invested theatrical representation with new value. As it became possible to understand the Eucharist symbolically (as opposed to understanding it as a literal manifestation of the body and blood of Jesus), it became possible in Western Christianity to regard representation in painting, sculpture, and glass as spiritually expressive in a similar (if not equivalent) way.[36] Theatrical representation, then, followed naturally as a means of manifesting the Christian reality. Only a generation before Corpus Christi processions and their tableaus took root in popular practice, the thirteenth century saw Saint Francis inspire a devotional fervor in European Christianity that was especially attached to realizing the humanity of Jesus by a variety of theatrical means. Francis's "invention" of the Christmas crèche is one of the early significant experiments with Biblical tableaus—the experiment that has had a remarkably long, continuous tradition.

The culture that engendered the passion plays from which Oberammergau's Passionsspiel derives appreciated how representation could also be manifestation. Writing of some of the earliest Christian art—catacomb painting in Rome—art historian John Dixon admits of a distinctly amateurish style, but asserts that this roughness of execution contributes to the works' real purpose, which as Dixon asserts, was not "any purpose belonging to the classical art we know."[37] Rather than reaching for any sort of naturalistic representation, the Christian artists of the Roman catacombs sought to facilitate the realization of an unmanifest reality. "It is not that they were making pictures of people praying, although there are many examples of exactly that," writes Dixon. "They were making prayer present and enduring on the wall."[38] Historian Gail McMurray Gibson sounds a similar note in her analysis of the significance of the rough "visitation" sculptures ubiquitous throughout medieval Europe, which depicted the meeting of Mary and Elizabeth while each were pregnant, the former with Jesus and the latter with John. "What has too often been confused with the naive and the childlike," Gibson writes of the style of the sculptures, which often depicted the Jesus and John lying in embryonic state in cut-away relief in their mothers' bellies, "was in fact a deliberate and conscious effort to objectify the spiritual even as the Incarnation itself had given spirit a concrete form."[39] Following Paul Tillich's conception of a "symbol" as a sign that "participates in the reality it symbolizes," Dixon construes the catacomb paintings as "symbolic acts" whose function is "to make the Christ present."[40] The most compelling piece of Dixon's argument is his assertion that the symbolic act does not impose the presence at which it aims on viewers, but requires the viewer to engage with the symbol, actively. "The observer, therefore, does not simply receive the work passively. He must constitute it by his own participation in it."[41] The beginnings of Christian iconography anticipate and even expect a degree of role-playing on the part of devotee patrons, just as the roots of Christian theology imagine redemption through the suffering Jesus as an always ongoing reality to which humankind might gain access.

Following Anselm's eleventh-century *Cur Deus Homo*, and, especially, Saint Francis's highly theatrical realization of the humanity of Jesus in the twelfth century, Western Christianity entered into a distinctly devotional mode that facilitated the materialization of the Christian reality not only in painting, but in human activity. The legend of Saint Francis's crèche describes what is, essentially, a tableau (complete with living, breathing animals—no camels, apparently, but certainly donkeys and oxen) before which the saint celebrates a Christmas mass. Francis's primary biographer, Thomas of Celano, circumspectly describes a miraculous moment in which an unidentified observer sees Francis lift from the crib a child who rouses in Francis's arms as though from sleep.[42]

After Francis, individuals across Europe took up the representational devices of theatre to facilitate particularly non-representational experiences. The well-documented shift in the depictions of Jesus on the cross, from wide-eyed, stoic model of divine transcendence to bent and suffering man, beginning with the thirteenth-century Cimabue crucifixes, is understood as the evidence of the pervasive influence of a Franciscan spirituality that not only valued the human suffering of Jesus, but valued *seeing* that human suffering. Devotional texts with a particularly Franciscan appreciation for meditative role-play, such as the *Meditationes Vitae Christi*, proliferated throughout Europe after the thirteenth century as aids to seeing the events of the Jesus myth. These devotional handbooks encouraged Christian devotees to dwell, meditatively, on scenes and scenarios associated with the life of Jesus, scenes that were both attested in scripture (the crucifixion, for instance), scenes that were implied by scripture (the swaddling of Jesus), and scenes that were entirely invented for purposes of meditation, such as a visit the resurrected Jesus makes to Mary, his mother, prior to appearing to Mary Magdalene. Readers of the *Meditationes* worked to *see* Mary swaddling Jesus, and other such scenarios, as individuals embedded in the ongoing, spiritual reality of the narrative.

In addition to encouraging an imaginative, but only imaginative, meditation, the enormously popular *Meditationes Vitae Christi*, its English translation

The Mirror of the Blessed Life of Jesus Christ, and other such books, inspired the acting out of the imagined roles of the Jesus story in ways that are distinctly suggestive of the role-playing activity that forms the core of Krishna devotion in Vrindavan. In fact, the *Meditationes* and its counterparts urged the Franciscan nuns for whom they seem to have been written to imagine themselves as Mary's attendants—observers, like Vrindavan's cowherd girls, of the sacred events, but observers also embedded in the events themselves. The imaginative role-playing that these devotional texts prescribed emerged as literal acting in the lives of several female devotees of which we have accounts. Gibson shows how much of the late-medieval pilgrim Margery Kemp's autobiography is modeled on the discipline of the *Meditationes*. Following "as literally as possible" the exercises of the *Meditationes*:

> Margery assumes roles of active handmaidenship, as, for example, in the vision in which she acts as comforter to the Virgin Mary, distraught with grief after the burial of her son. Margery does this, in her typical womanly way, by bringing Mary nourishing food. A delightful detail in her *Book*, it is not Margery's invention at all but a suggestion of the author of the *Meditationes*, who had urged the Franciscan nun meditating on Mary's sorrow to "serve, console and comfort so that she may eat a little." It is, however, a telling difference between Margery's thirteenth-century devotional model and her practical and concrete fifteenth-century East Anglian spirituality that Margery's account of her vision actually names the food that she prepares and brings to the Virgin Mary's sickbed—a "cawdel," or mixture of warm spiced wine, egg, and gruel. Indeed it would not be surprising if the fragmentary fifteenth-century recipe (ground sugar and cinnamon are among its ingredients) that appears on the verso of the last folio of the Kempe manuscript was intended to be the recipe for Margery's wine caudle, a kind of spiritual chicken soup.[43]

Margery's imaginative meditation develops, here, into role-playing, as she actively adopts the part of Mary's attendant that the trivial details that she contributes to the scene facilitate.

In the fourteenth century, the adoption of Jesus dolls became common, and devotees attended to their dolls as to real babies, dressing them, cuddling them, and speaking to them.[44] In the two centuries prior to the Reformation, the centuries that provide the theatrical template for the Passionsspiel at Oberammergau, a theatrical spirituality was rampant across Europe, a spirituality for which representational theatricality was not only essential, but in which spirituality was, itself, fundamentally theatrical. That is, in the high middle ages, theatricality was not merely mimetic. It was also revelatory.

The inclination toward role-play, and the anticipation that role-play will manifest a spiritual reality to the experience of the actor, formed the foundation of the Franciscan devotion of Europe's high middle ages, and of the Krishna devotion that continues from the sixteenth century. Which is to suggest that an essential aspect of religion is its use of role-play to vivify an immaterial reality. It is also to suggest that theatricality, as Artaud, perhaps, intimated, inevitably moves toward manifesting a reality behind reality, or some speech before words. Oberammergau's *Passionsspiele* inherits a distinctly Franciscan spirituality, in that Oberammergau sustains a devotional tradition of the high middle ages that regarded theatricality as a means of seeing what mortal eyes don't, necessarily see.

Conclusion

The Passionsspiele's tableaus, as strange a stage device as ever there was, by contravening Western convention estrange themselves from the typical mode of representation, so as to eschew signification. The consequence is a hole, a great, meaning-less gap in which the audience can move around—not in their accustomed identities, which remain in the auditorium's stadium chairs, but in roles that the exegetical choral interludes suggest: witnesses of the Christian event. As in Krishna devotion, in which roles are more real by remaining always apart from the contingencies of reality, the roles that move into the meaning-less space of the *lebende bilder* are not fictional identities re-presented by the bodies of the actors (who are, in this case, the audience members), but something more like what Julia Kristeva calls the "true-real," a valuing of that which cannot be symbolized.[45]

The playing of a role that theatrical performances demand—by the audience member—contributes to the reconfiguration of the audience member's identity, from postmodern non-entity to a categorical other, or (in more pedestrian terms) from something mundane to something trans-mundane. Hjalmar Sundén and role theory tell us that role-playing can radically alter the way a person perceives his or her identity and the reality in which it is embedded. Anticipation of the predetermined fulfillment of a narrative into which an individual has entered conditions the individual's cognition of self and environment. But performance theories of various sorts have recognized this mechanism in theatre since, perhaps, the time of Plato, who panicked over the possibility that acts of representation would turn people into things they hadn't been. Twenty-five hundred years later, the postmodern reiteration of Plato confirms that performing roles can turn people into things they hadn't been, but there is less panic in the postmodern condition that also asserts that people aren't anything in particular to begin with. "An examination of acting theory through the lens of deconstruction," writes Philip Auslander, "reveals that the self is not an autonomous foundation for acting, but is produced by the performance it supposedly grounds."[46] It is this postmodern concept of identity that lies at the foundation of the assertions that identity is something performed.[47]

Oberammergau's *lebende bilder* remain the most historically consistent element of the Passionsspiele production because the role-playing that they facilitate contributes to the construction of identities that many Oberammergau audience members long to inhabit. The production in which the tableaus are embedded may be merely a Christian fantasy, all unreal, even if affirming Christianity's premise. The determined naturalism the production inherits from Othmar Weis's and Joseph Alois Daisenberger's nineteenth-century script can only represent what it must characterize as a naturally historic event, and, consequently, like all other representations, the production can only tell the audience that what it means is somewhere, somewhen else.[48] But the tableaus themselves slip out of naturalism's trap. Although appearing to be the most representational elements of the play—they are pictures, after all—the tableaus are more insistent in their strangeness that all they are is not elsewhere, elsewhen, but there, on the stage, in the moment of their exposure, to be accessed by viewers in a way that stranges the viewers, as well. Where there was signification, the concourse between tableaus and audience engenders play that constitutes selves.

NOTES

1. Quoted in Bernard F. Dukore, *Dramatic Theory and Criticism: Greeks to Grotowski* (Boston: Heinle, 1974), 172.

2. In fact, Artaud would happily agree with Plato that theatre could undermine reality. Only, Artaud's non–Aristotelean response to Plato would be that we desperately need to undermine reality.

3. In fact, the *Passionspiele* seems to have reinvented itself in the early seventeenth century from a tradition of passion plays that persisted in southern Germany well into the sixteenth century.

4. A naturalistic style more-or-less required by the nineteenth-century script that Oberammergauers have repeatedly refused by public referendum to abandon.

5. Bert O. States, *Great Reckonings in Little Rooms: On the Phenomenology of Theatre* (Berkeley: University of California Press, 1987), 20.

6. Role theory intersects in a rough way with the existentialism that developed beside it in the mid–twentieth century that asserted that existence precedes essence. Sartre's contention that a person "appears on the scene and only afterwards defines himself" has abandoned the ideal of an identity that exists a priori in the individual (quoting from Jean-Paul Sartre, *Existentialism and Human Emotions*, Bernard Frechtman, trans. [New York: Citadel, 1987], 15). Simone de Beauvoir's, and, later, Judith Butler's, characterization of gender as something that is acted, rather than inherent, follow as much from role theory as from existentialism, and, perhaps, even more so from role theory than from Sartre, as Beauvoir and Butler both understand gender as social constructions that are thrust upon individuals as much as individuals might choose them.

7. For his part, Kermode is following after Husserl's assertion: "Every originally constructive process is inspired by pre-intentions, which construct and collect the seed of what is to come, as such, and bring it to fruition" (quoted in Wolfgang Iser, "The Reading Process: A Phenomenological Approach," *New Literary Theory* 3.2 [1972]: 282).

8. Dan P. McAdams, "Personal Narratives and the Life Story," in *Handbook of Personality: Theory and Research*, Lawrence A. Pervin and Oliver P. John, eds. (New York: Guilford Press, 1999), 480.
9. Iser, 284–5.
10. Iser, 296.
11. Iser, 297.
12. Iser, 299.
13. Nils G. Holm, "Sundén's Role Theory and Glossolalia." *Journal for the Scientific Study of Religion* 26.3 (1987): 384.
14. Krishna dies some distance from Vrindavan, at Dwaraka, which is thought to be in the region of modern-day Mumbai. But his youth, the portion of his life that is most important for Krishna devotion today, occurs exclusively around Vrindavan.
15. A mild surge of residential construction radiating around its western edge since 2002 may be shifting Vrindavan's ratio of pilgrims and residents.
16. "*Radhe, Radhe!*," an expression fraught with devotional implications, not only serves for "hello" and "goodbye" in Vrindavan, it also serves for "pardon me," "make way," and "watch out for the thieving monkeys."
17. For a very concise and accessible discussion of *darshan* in India, see Diana L. Eck, *Darshan* (New York: Columbia University Press, 1998).
18. Iser, 287.
19. Although the Radha character is female, she is always played by a young male actor. No women appear in Vrindavan's *râs lila* performances.
20. David L. Haberman, *Acting as a Way of Salvation: A Study of Râgânugâ Bhakti Sâdhana* (Oxford: Oxford University Press, 1988), 37.
21. The implicit role-play involved in day-to-day living in Vrindavan is the subject of chapter six of David V. Mason, *Theatre and Religion on Krishna's Stage: Performing in Vrindavan* (New York: Palgrave, 2009).
22. In a popular illustration of this principle, the divine Shiva hears of the wonder to be found in the nighttime dancing and frolicking of Krishna and the village girls, but he wanders and wanders in the forest without finding them. Finally, he stops and asks for directions. A brahmin tells him he's on a fool's quest. You have to be a girl, the brahmin says, to see Krishna dancing in the forest at night. Undaunted, Shiva turns himself into a girl and satisfies his curiosity. This story of Shiva's interest in Krishna comes from mythic lore, and is a common episode of *râs lila* performances.
23. The form of the image does, of course, make some difference. Vrindavan residents speak of particular statues as being "more beautiful" than others. These preferences do not indicate the degree to which naturalism, as a feature of an object, suits it to representing god, but indicate how aesthetic considerations (which are always conditioned by cultural and historical forces) facilitate the development of individual devotional responses.
24. *Râs lila* plays never include a curtain-speech forbidding the use of flash photography, and devotees eagerly snap up their own copies of these *jhânkhî* poses.
25. Of course, if one's definition of theatre insists on mimesis, then *râs lila* theatre is not theatre.
26. Iser, 291.
27. Iser, 288, 292.
28. The chorus's typology contributes greatly to what Hans Robert Jauss would call the tableaus' "horizon of expectations," or the cultural context within which possible readings can take place. See Hans Robert Jauss, "Literary History as a Challenge to Literary Theory," *New Literary History* 2.1 (1970): 7–37.

29. Quoted in Kurt A. Bruder, "Monastic Blessings: Deconstructing and Reconstructing the Self," *Symbolic Interaction* 21.1 (1998): 107.

30. Ferdinand Rosner, *Passio Nova: Revised for Oberammergau* by Alois Fink, anonymous translator. American Jewish Committee Archives, accessed February 6, 2012, www.ajcarchives.com. An English translation of the heavily edited Rosner script that was performed as a "trial" in Oberammergau in 1977, exists as an unattributed and unpublished manuscript in the American Jewish Committee archives. Relevant documents in the archives show that this translation was produced by a delegation from the American Jewish Committee that attended previews of the production. The delegation seems to have included Rabbi Marc H. Tanenbaum, Miles Jaffee, William Trosten, and, perhaps, Bert Gold. In letters to German hosts, Miles Jaffee concedes his inability to understand German. The translation, then, seems to have been the work of the other delegation members.

31. For a summary of the scene, see Saul S. Friedman, *The Oberammergau Passion Play: A Lance Against Civilization* (Carbondale: Southern Illinois University Press, 1984), 171–72.

32. One of the reasons that the American Jewish Committee and other Jewish groups supported Oberammergau's flirtation with resuscitating the Rosner script in the 1970's was the play's explicitly allegorical character. Rabbi Marc Tanenbaum, who led the AJC's delegation to Oberammergau in 1977, wrote in an official report that the Rosner script is preferred because it is "cast in metaphysical terms" so that the "role of the Sanhedrin and 'the Jews' tends to be less central..." (Marc H. Tanenbaum, "Report on the 1980 Oberammergau Passion Play," August 25, 1977).

33. James Shapiro, *Oberammergau: The Troubling Story of the World's Most Famous Passion Play* (New York: Pantheon, 2000), 60.

34. Glynne Wickham, *The Medieval Theatre* (Cambridge: Cambridge University Press, 1987), 96.

35. Lynette R. Muir, *The Biblical Drama of Medieval Europe* (Cambridge: Cambridge University Press, 1995), 40.

36. For an exhaustive treatment of this matter, see Michal Kobialka, *This Is My Body: Representational Practices in the Early Middle Ages* (Ann Arbor: University of Michigan Press, 2003).

37. John W. Dixon, Jr., *Art and the Theological Imagination* (New York: Seabury Press, 1978), 61.

38. Dixon, 61.

39. Gail McMurray Gibson, *The Theatre of Devotion: East Anglian Drama and Society in the Late Middle Ages* (Chicago: University of Chicago Press, 1989), 8.

40. Dixon, 64.

41. Dixon, 62.

42. Thomas of Celano, *The First Life of St Francis of Assisi*, Christopher Stace, trans. (London: Triangle, 2000), 84.

43. Gibson, 51.

44. Margery Kemp describes encountering a group of women on the pilgrimage trail who played with their Jesus dolls in the evening. As a more extreme example, in the mid–thirteen-hundreds, Margaret Ebner received a baby Jesus doll into her room in a convent in southern Germany. By her own account, the doll kicked in its cradle, spoke to her, insisted on sleeping with her, and even nursed from her at its own request.

45. Elin Diamond, "Mimesis, Mimicry, and the 'True-Real,'" *Modern Drama* 32.1 (1989): 68.

46. Philip Auslander, "'Just Be Your Self': Logocentrism and difference in Performance Theory," in *Acting (Re)Considered: Theories and Practices*, Phillip B. Zarrilli, ed. (New York: Routledge, 1995), 60.

47. Consider, for instance, the theories of Simone de Beauvoir and Judith Butler that aver that gender identity (at least) is something a person does rather than something a person *is*.

48. The play's naturalism sustains the Passionsspiele's ongoing struggle with its own anti–Semitic character, as the historical pretense of the production's style insists on "the way it happened."

Oberammergau in America/ America in Oberammergau

Kevin J. Wetmore, Jr.

In the film *Network* Diana Christensen (Faye Dunaway) watches audition tapes for a religious figure they can put on the air. At one point, after a particularly apocalyptic one rants about "the beast" opening "the seals," she shouts to her team, "If we wanted hellfire, we'd get Billy Graham. We don't want faith healers, evangelists or Oberammergau passion players!" For a film from 1976, this is a fascinatingly unique American reference and somewhat telling of how the Oberammergau Passion Play has been viewed in the United States. For much of America's history with Oberammergau, the production stood for simple, unsophisticated piety and anti–Semitism. The village performers are equated with faith healers and evangelists. "Oberammergau passion player" was shorthand for deeply religious, deeply provincial, simple folk dedicated to God. In a film about the television news industry in the seventies, it was intended as a put down, but for much of America's early understanding, the same term was intended as a recognition of the height of Oberammergau's collective piety. American Passion Plays vied for the title of "America's Oberammergau."

Since the late nineteenth century, and especially since the postwar period, the United States has played an increasingly important role in relationship to Oberammergau. The relationship, however, is not unidirectional, and the Oberammergau Passion Play has also had a tremendous influence on American passion plays. American interest in Oberammergau has caused a number of religious dramas in the United States to refer to themselves as "the American Oberammergau," partly in an attempt to capture some of the magic and partly as a means of providing a shorthand to identity. Since Oberammergau is known as the simple, pious Alpine village, whose simple, pious people perform the play as part of their faith and their community, the local

American play capitalizes on that reputation as well and avoids the connotations of the professional theatre (sinful) and community theatre (amateur and possibly also sinful).

Conversely, the United States, particularly after the occupation of German at the end of the Second World War, exerts an influence over Oberammergau and shapes the perception of the Passionspiele in multiple ways, and especially by advocating for change of anti–Jewish elements. Given that the majority of attendees of the Oberammergau Passion Play are from North America, and the United States in particular, the village at least pays attention when American groups speak out about the Passion Play.[1] The result is that the United States has cultural and economic influence over the Passion Play, especially in the years that lead up to the next production. While the villagers wish to remain faithful to the tradition, they also wish not to alienate a large potential audience. This tension is not felt from Europe, it is strictly an American-made phenomenon.

Further shaping the reception of the 2010 production was the release in 2004 of Mel Gibson's controversial film *The Passion of the Christ*. Many American critics cited the historical controversies over the Oberammergau play in terms of its representations of Jewish characters, its anti–Semitic elements and its focus on the bodily suffering of Christ instead of his teachings or resurrection to frame the same issues in Gibson's film. Subsequently, American critics then read the 2010 Oberammergau Passion Play in the wake of Gibson's film. Given the significant audience size from the United States, already cited many times in this volume, many who saw the play in 2010 had seen or had at least heard the criticisms of *The Passion of the Christ* and watched Oberammergau in that context.

In this essay, we shall consider the relationship between Oberammergau and the United States, look at how Oberammergau influenced American Passion Plays, consider the role of American organizations in critiquing the Oberammergau Passionspiele in such a manner that the village responds to those critiques and changes the play or defends the play in situ, observe the intertext formed by the Oberammergau Passion Play and *The Passion of the Christ* and then close by looking at the reception of the 2010 play by the popular and academic critics in the United States.

Oberammergau and America: A Twentieth-Century Evolution, 1880–1950

The Oberammergau Passion Play, an Edison Manufacturing Company Film completed in 1897 and released in 1898, was actually filmed on a rooftop in New York City. The previous Passion Play, in 1890, could not be filmed as the equipment had not yet been invented. So Edison's film is an American adaptation directed by Henry C. Vincent, an American stage director, to be screened first in Broadway theatres (since cinemas did not yet exist) and then at religious services. The producers had asked if the village would perform the play to be filmed, and they refused. So the American motion picture company simply filmed their own performance and called it "Oberammergau." We might read this as a metaphor for American appropriations of the Oberammergau Passion Play and the Oberammergau identity—claiming an Oberammergau connection when the thing in question is pure American-derived and only bears a tangential relationship to the German event.

Commercial, economic and technological shifts at the end of the eighteenth century resulted in Oberammergau becoming both more accessible to and more in the awareness of Americans. As Susan Spano reports, "In 1880 English tour company Thomas Cook added Oberammergau to its brochure, spurring the Passion's popularity among people from English-speaking countries, who still make up about 60% of the audience."[2] In 1899 a rail line was completed that connected the village of Oberammergau to nearby Munich and thus to the rest of Europe. Travel to the Bavarian village became much easier and more convenient.

For those unable to afford the trip to Germany, multiple venues presented information about Oberammergau to the American public. American magazines published accounts of travel to see the Passion Play in the nineteenth century.[3] Beginning in 1880, several individuals toured the country telling the story of Oberammergau. John L. Stoddard began offering lectures on the topic that year, as did many other platform lecturers, although within a decade the lecturer most identified with the German village was John J. Lewis.[4] The Central Lyceum Bureau offered a lecture and stereopticon presentation on "The Passion Play of Oberammergau" by Lewis, termed "the apostle of the passion play in America."[5] The promotional brochure for the lecture notes that just as the villagers of Oberammergau give their lives over to performing the Passion, "for years Mr. Lewis has identified himself so closely with the Passion Play that it has become his very life to give the story." Lewis became identified with the Passion and served as a model for the interpretation of Oberammergau in America. From 1890 to 1900, Lewis "gave the story of the Passion Play upwards of 2000 times to more than 2,000,000 people. This, we believe, is a record without parallel upon the lecture platform."[6] Those two million people learned about Lewis's Oberammergau—what he termed "The Only True Passion Play"—and saw images of the play as well as silent films of performances, none of which were actually from Oberammergau, which did not allow photography of the play. As with Vincent's film for Edison, the images Lewis claimed were from Oberammergau were not, in fact, genuine.[7] Lewis presented images of simple, pious villagers presenting a play that reflected Christian values shared by all Americans. As a result, as Claire Sponsler observes, Oberammergau is "for most Americans, the iconic Passion Play."[8]

These early presentations of Oberammergau were, as Sponsler states, "uncritical."[9] As Rick Altman surmises, "Turn-of-the-century Americans were a pious people," and they wanted to see in Oberammergau a response to modernity in the form of faith.[10] The citizens of the United States attending the lectures of Stoddard, Lewis and the others wanted to see "that old time religion" fighting back against the forces of modernity, and the Oberammergau Passion Play, at least as presented in America, offered precisely that. American audiences wanted to see Oberammergau "as a relic of an earlier era of innocent Christian piety."[11]

Germany and all things German were anathema during the Second World War, but between the wars there was a fascination with the Passion Play. Sonja E. Spear reports, "American interest in Oberammergau peaked in the interwar years, just as liberal Protestants struggled to come to terms with turn-of-the-century immigration of Catholics and Jews."[12] It was global conflict that actually brought the most Americans to Oberammergau in two waves in the twentieth century. Americans occupied Germany after the First World War, learning about the Passionspiel. In 1930, fifty thousand Americans attended the passion play that year, making them the largest national contingent out of the three hundred thousand to see the drama.[13] Inflation in the Weimar Republic was already spiraling out of control, but allowed for inexpensive travel. American soldiers and those traveling to Europe on business were able to attend the play and report back first hand to the folks back home.

The desire to get Oberammergau on film also increased. Several American film companies wanted to film the Passion Play in exchange for a fee, but the villagers still declined. Anton Lang said that to do so would be "a desecration. It would destroy all the influence for good which the Passion Play has done for the world."[14] Hollywood wanted to bring Oberammergau's Passion Play to America via film, and the village refused. As noted above, however, this did not stop the circulation of numerous spurious travel films claiming to be images of the Oberammergau Passionspiele, often film of other Passion Plays combined with travel footage of Germany and Switzerland.[15]

Instead of allowing footage of the actual Passion Play to be taken and circulated in the United States, a fourteen-person delegation led by Anton Lang, who had played Jesus in 1922 and would play the Prologue in 1930, had a six month tour in 1923–1924 of the United States to promote tourism to the village. They went to Washington, D.C., met with President Coolidge, brought examples of the village's woodcarving, and were frequently asked for their opinions on matters of the day, especially religious ones.[16] Sonja E. Spear reports that when Lang and his cohort arrived in New York City on December 13, 1923, Lang posed on the deck of the ship for reporters: "his Christ-like flowing locks blowing in the breeze.... Always partly in character, Lang delivered a Christ-like message of peace and goodwill."[17] Lang was always publically identified with Christ, with a role that he played on stage. The irony is that Lang's perceived authenticity is rooted in the idea that he is *not* an actor, but a simple village woodcarver for whom playing the Christ is a religious duty, but his entire tour of the United States was nothing but a performance.

Sonja E. Spear recounts the need for Americans to believe in the piety and lack of professionalism of the villagers. *The Indiana Farmer's Guide*, she reports, "praised the actors in these terms: 'These people are not artists. They are sincere men and women who do this work as a means of worship and not for the honor that ordinary actresses and actors seek.'"[18] The first statement is of significance. Although their acting is what brought them to the United States, for let us be honest—simple woodcarvers from Bavaria would never be invited to meet the president and share their insights on the issues of the day, but world-renowned Passion Play performers would be—these people were artists. That was the whole reason they were in the United States in the first place. The narrative of the simple piety of Oberammergau was part of the sales pitch of the villagers to the United States. However, just as visitors to the village today are the ones pushing the myths of Oberammergau while the villagers are rather honest about the origins and purpose of the play, Americans needed Lang and his companions not to be artists. They simply went along with the narrative.

Lang himself reported in his autobiography *Aus Meinen Leben* (From My Life, 1930) that he met with Thomas Edison, who told Lang he had seen the play in 1890.[19] He seems impressed with the famous people he met who had already seen him act. (Indeed, later Henry Ford saw the play in 1930, as did William Randolph Hearst in 1934. It was a journey for many to take during the years between the wars.) Lang also viewed his role as Christ on stage as giving him a unique opportunity to comment on American society, something that would be granted to an artist who had played Christ, but not to a simple German woodcarver.

In a report in *Literary Digest*, Lang took the United States to task for religious discrimination, holding Oberammergau up as an example:

> "At Oberammergau we have all kinds. There is a Catholic church, and a chapel that is used by the Protestants—Baptists, Methodists, Episcopalians, and all kinds. But that isn't what counts, it is how one lives that makes one good or bad; and Jesus, I believe, will take us all to heaven according to our virtues. There are no religious quarrels in Oberammergau..." [Lang said].
>
> "And the Jews?" a reporter asked. Lang smiled again, and replied: "Yes, I think the Jews, too, will go to heaven."[20]

While Oberammergau was known for the anti–Semitism of its drama, praised by Hitler in 1930 and 1934, and not removing the "Blood Libel" from the script until half a century after the fall of the Nazis as detailed in chapter two, Lang in 1923 displayed a remarkable ecumenism for the time. This claim serves Lang's purpose in representing Oberammergau as a simple, pious place where theological differences between denominations are not as important as simple faith and devotion to God. As part of that narrative, Jews are also welcome in the kingdom of God as well as the Bavarian village.

The American context also matters here: "Lang addressed a nation in which Catholics and Jews were pushing back against the cultural and political hegemony of the Protestant majority even as they sought to ally themselves with liberal Protestants against reactionary nativism. American responses to Lang's tour—Protestant, Catholic and Jewish—arose from this context."[21] When considering the context of the Oberammergau visit, we must remember the United States' own anti–Catholic, anti–Semitic culture of the time. Lang, a lifelong Catholic, downplayed his own Catholicism in place of a universal Christianity. In turn, Americans perceived Lang as a representative not of a Catholic culture, but a pious Christian one, regardless of denomination. One must remember that American engagement with Oberammergau is always in a larger context.

Indeed, the fear of immigrants of different religious persuasions that dominated American culture at the turn of the century was often times reversed when dealing with the Oberammergau contingent. The fear was that American modernity might somehow corrupt and pollute the purity of the Oberammergauers. "But the *Portland Oregonian* regrets their coming, fearing the 'commercial conversion of the simple villagers, whose lives have heretofore been devoted to the service of an ideal,' and that 'much of their charm of character and sincerity of purpose will seem distorted in a land other than their own.'"[22]

Oberammergau was often presented in the American media and popular imagination as a kind of Christian Brigadoon, appearing once every ten years to perform a play honoring the Passion of Jesus Christ, untouched by the modern world.

Americans especially demand both authenticity and confirmation of the truth of the myths and history. Even to this day, the villagers themselves readily tell the true story of their town; they say it is the tourists who want Oberammergau to be a moment frozen in time. The American perception of Oberammergau, rather than the reality of Oberammergau, became the standard by which "authentic" passion plays would be measured.

As a result, when American tourists travelled to Oberammergau, they expected the myth, not the reality. A religious experience unencumbered by modernity was assumed: "Tourist-pilgrims particularly demand an aesthetic experience of authenticity in which the commercial does not appear to taint the spiritual."[23] For the performances in 1930 and 1934, tainted as they were by the rise of the Nazi party in Bavaria and the rise of Hitler to power, were well attended by Americans in the wake of Lang's tour, seeing Oberammergau as a pious alternative to the corruption of Weimar Germany.

In the wake of the Second World War, again the United States occupied Germany. Oberammergau returned to American imagination and popular attention. In 1950 the high Commissioner John J. McClay approved the resumption of the Passion Play which had been cancelled in 1940 because of the war: "The Americans believed the resumption of the Oberammergau Passion Play would help restore a sense of stability to defeated Germany," reports A. James Rudin.[24] McClay himself attended the opening performance on May 18, 1950.[25] Many American servicemen also attended the play that year. Originally only thirty-three performances had been scheduled, but the play proved so popular that the run was extended to a total of eighty-seven performances to accommodate demand.

In addition, an American appeared on stage for the first (and last) time. *Stars and Stripes*, the military newspaper reported the day after the premiere: "Johnny McMahon, 6, son of the executive officer of the MP detachment at the USAREUR Intelligence School here, joined his German classmates of the local grammar school to play the part of children called for in the script. Johnny, who said he was 'thrilled to death,' is, according to his father, Maj. John A. McMahon, of Boise, Ida., the only American child attending a German school in the village and is the first American of any age to take part in the play."[26] The review is positive, noting that the clouds that threatened to rain parted and allowed Anton Preisinger as Christ to lead the company of 1600 Oberamergauers to perform the drama in front of an audience of 5600 dignitaries and servicemen, not to mention officials from the postwar German government.

The article celebrates how American servicemen contributed to the smooth-running of the pageant: "Fifteen U.S. military policemen, of the 521st MP Sv Plat at Garmisch, commander by Maj Allen C. Schuler, and nearly 100 specially trained German policemen, acting with outstanding courtesy and efficiency, kept thousands of cars flowing smoothly through the narrow streets of the town."[27] While American primacy is clear, the article also plainly demonstrates the postwar collaboration between the German and American officials. Oberammergau becomes a symbol of postwar cooperation between two Christian nations, the larger subtext being that Germany was an ally in the new cold war against the Godless communists. Indeed, postwar prosperity is also prominently on display in the review: "Gaily decorated and brilliantly illuminated shops and restaurants sharply pointed up the postwar recovery of Western Germany."[28]

The United States in 1950 unmistakably saw the Passion Play as a means to an end, specifically its political ends, not an act of devotion or identity in and of itself, although it was happy to continue the narrative of simple, pious village folk performing a play out of religious devotion. The narrative, however, reflected the new political reality. The Soviet Union was now the enemy, postwar West Germany could point to Oberammergau as an example of Christian religious devotion, economic triumph and international cooperation. Oberammergau was good for business, good for America and good for Germany.

Oberammergau's Influence on American Passion Plays

As Oberammergau was the iconic Passion Play in the United States from the end of the nineteenth century through the present, numberless are the Passion Plays performed in the United States that dub themselves, or are dubbed by others "The American Oberammergau." We might observe both the actual influence of Oberammergau in the staging of the Passion in the United States and the creation of community identity through the promotion of a play as an "American Oberammergau." Not only do the local promoters seek to exploit the reputation of Oberammergau, they hope to frame their own production and their own community through the same lenses: simple, pious people on a mission from God, presenting an artless yet meaningful public performance that might inspire. Often present in these local American Oberammergaus is an overlay of nationalism, sometimes accompanied by anti–Catholicism. Oberammergau may be iconic, but it is German and Catholic. The local Passion Plays are superior, therefore, because American is better (and this version is not Catholic, except when it is).

This list of productions is neither encyclopedic nor comprehensive. Rather, it is a survey of specific plays that were influenced by Oberammergau and that call themselves "America's Oberammergau."

The Holy Night—Pomfret, Connecticut (1913)

One of the first plays to be dubbed "America's Oberammergau" was not, in in fact, a Passion Play, but rather a nativity play performed at Christmas in New England. Pomfret, Connecticut, was called "America's Connecticut Oberammergau" in the press in 1913 for their production of *The Holy Night*, not least of which because the play's creators acknowledged the influence of Oberammergau in the planning of the show.[29] The play was subtitled "As in the Passion at Oberammergau, Working Men, Women and Children of Pomfret, Conn., Regardless of Creed, Enact Scenes from Our Saviour's Life, and Establish an Annual Nativity Performance."[30] The play was presented on Christmas Eve—three scenes performed on a stage in a large converted barn. The entire village of Pomfret, regardless of religious affiliation, were allegedly involved in the performance. In the play, the Nativity was re-enacted. A good deal of Christmas music was also performed as part of the event.

In "'The Holy Night' Solemnly Played by New England Village" the *Spokesman-Review* of Spokane, Washington, on the other side of the nation, provided an analysis of the second annual performance. The reviewer compared the hills of Northeastern Connecticut with the Bavarian Alps and Pomfret with Oberammergau, noting similar geographies, sizes, and pieties: "For more than half a century the peasants and artisans of Oberammergau have enacted 'The Passion Play,' which latterly has drawn visitors from all over the world."[31] While the reviewer got the duration of the Passion Play tradition wrong by a few centuries, we might note that Oberammergau had recently come to American attention for its peculiar tradition and thus "Oberammergau" was the comparator for local Passion Plays. Those who perform the play in Germany were "peasants and artisans," so in order for the Connecticut production to be the American equivalent of Oberammergau, the simple nature of the village, the pious nature of the endeavor and the non-denominational nature of the production are featured:

> Recognition of no special act of providence actuated the people of Pomfret to enact the drama of the Nativity as a mark of their thankfulness—as the people of Oberammergau in a similar way celebrated their escape from the plague. It was the desire of these New England villagers simply to celebrate in an appropriate manner and with reverential feeling, that event of nineteen hundred and thirteen years ago which was to cast the grateful spell of Christianity over the peoples of all lands.[32]

What is remarkable about this assessment is both the favorable comparison with the German production, but also a claim of American superiority: the Bavarians did it to escape the plague, the New Englanders did it because they are simply a faithful people devoted to God who required no additional impetus. This assessment would become standard with "American Oberammergaus"—the American version is just like the German production, but better in some way because it does not have some flaw attributed to the Oberammergau play. Similarly, the Pomfret production would be carried out annually, as opposed to the once-a-decade approach of the Germans.

The reviewer similarly pointed out the erasure of doctrinal (and even ethnic) difference: Congregationalists, Episcopalians and Roman Catholics all helped organize the play, and performers included "native Puritans" as well as "Irish, Swedish, English and Scotch, Italian, Portuguese, Canadians, negroes and a few Swiss,"[33] all of whom were of "humble" background: the three wise men were played by "a plumber, a day laborer and the village postmaster." The important point was that, like Oberammergau, this was as much a civic event as a religious one and that all in Pomfret were welcome to attend.

While the Pomfret Nativity play ceased its run before the Second World War, it was frequently celebrated as the embodiment of civic religious performance in early twentieth-century America. While clearly inspired, influenced and shaped by Oberammergau, the production also established its own identity, sometimes in direct contrast to the German play, with reviewers emphasizing that the American play celebrated the birth of Christ, as opposed to the German one, focused on the Passion. What is also clear is that none of the reviewers or writers about *The Holy Night* had actually been to Oberammergau or seen the Passionspiele. Instead, the very word "Oberammergau" had now become shorthand for pious communal performance.

The Passion Play—Union City, New Jersey (1915)

The Passion Play of Union City, New Jersey, "bills itself as 'America's Oberammergau, the oldest Passion Play in America.'"[34] Much of the Union City area was populated by German Catholic immigrants, including a significant number of Bavarians. Two Catholic parishes had been established in the community to serve the German-speaking part of the community: Holy Family in 1887 and St. Joseph's shortly after. By 1915, both were offering competing local Passion Play performances.

St. Joseph's presented *Veronica's Veil* from 1915 to 1999, a play based on the legend of Saint Veronica, who wiped the face of Jesus as he carried the cross to Golgotha. Her veil displayed the face of Christ from that moment forward. In what became an alleged friendly rivalry, Holy Family began performing *The Passion Play* in the church. The play was first produced in 1915, dubbing itself "the American Oberammergau" at least in part for its inspiration, as well as for the promotional effect. The Archdiocese of Newark originally built the Park Theater in 1931 as part of the Holy Family Church complex. Construction and planning was overseen by Monsignor Joseph Grieff, a priest who believed in the power of theatre and who had been directly inspired by the Oberammergau Passion Play.[35] Grieff hired a Broadway architect to design the theatre with *The Passion Play* specifically in mind.[36]

The generic title reflects the focus of the play—to present the story of the trial, suffering and death of Christ. It matches the same time frame as the Oberammergau narrative. Father Grieff sought to create a permanent theatre in which the community Passion Play would be performed annually, both for the parish but also forming a place of pilgrimage easier to reach than Southern Germany. The origins of this drama are also rooted in the specific German immigrant community that created it. Holy Family created a

Passion Play for individuals who may have seen the Oberammergau production, and certainly had grown up hearing about it.

Like Oberammergau, the content of the drama was accused of being anti–Semitic. Unlike Oberammergau, however, the diocese of Newark and Holy Family Parish responded more quickly. In the 1980s the script was updated to remove "any material that might be considered offensive to the Jewish community."[37] The bigger challenge facing The Passion Play in its current incarnation are the challenges facing Oberammergau—decreasing attendance and a graying population both on stage and in the audience.

The National Pilgrimage Play—
Los Angeles, California (1920)

In 1920 Christine Wetherhill Stevenson organized the "National Pilgrimage Play" in Los Angeles, "transcribed from the scriptures by Mrs. W. Yorke Stevenson" and presented in fourteen scenes with a prologue and epilogue in two acts. The play was performed annually in an outdoor amphitheater in the Cahuenga Pass in Los Angeles from 1920 to 1929, when the theatre burned down, then again in 1931 to the mid-forties, and then finally from 1955 to 1961 when the city announced no money from public funds could be used to support religious drama.

The *Los Angeles Times* reported in 1920 that "it is simply an effort to establish in America in Los Angeles a play which we and many ministers of all denominations believe will be greater than the Passion Play of Oberammergau.... The Oberammergau play presents only the last week of Christ's life, but this one will present the whole story of his life."[38] World War I had just ended, so there is a good deal of nationalism behind these statements: American Passion Plays are superior to German Passion Plays, in this case especially because of the scope of the production, presenting the entire life of Christ. But the statements also bear witness to Oberammergau as the early standard by which American Passion Plays were measured.

We might also note the commitment to "all denominations," reflecting the ecumenicist approach of the production, as well as the name of the show: "The National Pilgrimage Play." Stevenson and those working with her sought to make the production in Los Angeles a destination for religious travel, like Oberammergau. Los Angeles was a very different city in 1920 than in later years, so Stevenson could still construct it as a smaller municipality, whose simple, pious folk were putting on a Passion Play to which people could travel from all over the nation. The American separation of church and state, however, made it increasingly untenable to promote an obviously religious play as a civic event with public support.

The American Passion Play— Bloomington, Illinois (1924)

Delmar Duane Darrah (1868–1945), a professor of oration, elocution and drama at Illinois Wesleyan University and active Free Mason, "envisioned his own version of Christ's story in 1915, based on several European models," especially Oberammergau.[39] He finally realized his vision in 1924 with "The Easter Pageant," presented five times that year. Two years later, the play was renamed *The American Passion Play*. The Masons built a temple containing a theatre specifically for Darrah's production, the Scottish Rites Temple, which was renovated and renamed the Bloomington Center for the Performing Arts in 2006.[40]

The name reflects the identity of the drama: it is the "American" Passion Play. National identity is aligned with religious identity. Those associated with the *American Passion Play* link it to Oberammergau. For example, the book *The American Passion Play: A Study and a History* by Louis L. Williams opens with a chapter on Passion Plays in general. Chapter two is a history of the Oberammergau Passion Play.[41] The only reason to include Oberammergau in a book about a Passion Play in Bloomington, Illinois, is for a sort of genealogy. The American Passion Play is the descendant and heir to Oberammergau, but is superior to its ancestor as it is both American and Protestant.

Williams reports a letter sent to Darrah:

> Dozens of visitors to the *American Passion Play*, who have also seen the Oberammergau Play, usually echo the words of B.J. Palmer of Daveport, Iowa, who wrote Delmar D. Darrah a letter dated June 18, 1934, in which he said: "I promised you I would write you my opinion of the Oberammergau Passion Play as it compared with the American Passion Play of yours given at Bloomington, Illinois. I have been removed ten days from Oberammergau and have had time for a more matured reflection. Let me say to you: I have seen all the main and important Passion Plays of the world and the one in Bloomington by the Consistory players of which you are the director is by far the best."[42]

Williams outlines the reasons for the superiority of Bloomington to Oberammergau. First, "the intimacy of the theatre"—the *American Passion Play* is performed inside to an audience of 1400. In contrast, Oberammergau's auditorium presents the play in a semi-outdoor setting to 5000. This intimacy leads "to a finer shade of acting and stronger character delineation."[43] Second, the *American Passion Play* is presented as a more modern play: "*The American Passion Play* is written in this century for the people of now; not many decades ago for a less sophisticated audience than the theatre-goer of today. The *American Passion Play* is suited to the time and place."[44] Given the American drive to, as Ezra Pound put it, "make it new," Williams posits the superiority of the American play because the German one is medieval and the American one is modern. He may as well say it is also more American. These accounts demonstrate the same tension I have been outlining here. Namely, that American Passion Plays wish to connect their identity to Oberammergau while simultaneously asserting their superiority to their role model.

"Oklahoma's Oberammergau":
The Prince of Peace Passion Play at The Holy City of the Wichitas—Lawton, Oklahoma (1926)

Founded by Austrian minister, the Rev. Anthony Mark Wallock (1890–1948), who emigrated with his parents in 1892 at the age of two, attended Barret Biblical Institute, and preached throughout the central United States until settling in Lawton, Oklahoma, as the reverend at First Congregational Church, the *Prince of Peace Passion Play* began as a simple Easter Sunday event in 1926, a single scene concerning the disciples at the empty tomb.[45] In 1926 the Reverend Wallock took his Sunday School class up a mountain at Easter to put on a pageant. The following year, when a second performance was planned, the *Lawton Constitution*, the local paper, dubbed it "Oklahoma's Oberammergau."

By 1930 the audience had swelled to over 6000. As with Oberammergau, Wallock was able to transform his production into both a religious and civic event, securing government support for the performances. Funded by the WPA and Federal Grants, the theatre was built as part of "The Holy City of the Wichitas," a recreation of Jerusalem in the Wichita Mountains, approximately eighty miles south of Oklahoma City.[46] Wallock planned a pilgrimage site.

The passion play continued to expand. In 1931, the cast grew to one hundred and fifty local performers. By 1935 the cast was twelve hundred. At that point the production began to stabilize in terms of size and scope, and then shrink to a more manageable size, and the annual performances continue to this day. Like Oberammergau, the cast and crew are all local volunteers, non-denominational. Currently Protestants and Mormons dominate the cast, but all are welcome to audition.[47] The 2010 performance, the same year as the most recent Oberammergau, featured 350 local performers and was performed twice on Easter weekend.[48]

The Zion Passion Play—Zion, Illinois (1935)[49]

The Mesa East Pageant, also known as *Jesus the Christ*, which began as an Easter morning sunrise service in 1928 outside of Mesa, Arizona, and is one of the largest pageants of Church of Jesus Christ of Latter Day Saints (LDS/Mormon church), and like Oberammergau requires performers "to maintain strict standards of dress, character, and conduct and obtain a signed ecclesiastical endorsement."[50] The play's promotional material cites Oberammergau as an inspiration for the LDS play.

Black Hills Passion Play—
Spearfish, South Dakota (1939)

The *Black Hills Passion Play* "was first performed by a German company in 1932 and encouraged association with the (Catholic) Oberammergau Passion Play in Germany."[51]

Louis L. Williams observes that it "might be considered a shortened, Americanized version of Oberammergau, and as such for American audiences, that would constitute an improvement in execution."[52] In other words, as with all other productions in this list, the American play was shaped and influenced by Oberammergau, but based on American aesthetics, values, and nationalism is superior to the original.

The other inspiration for Sarah Ruhl's play, the *Black Hills Passion Play* of Spearfish, South Dakota, officially began in May 1939. The founder and lead actor, the first one to play Christ, was German-American Josef Meier. It was performed three nights each week; in summer it was performed in the outdoor Spearfish Amphitheatre and toured in Fall and Winter, developing a Florida performance home and featured professional actors and some local residents who served as extras in the crowd scenes. Meier retired in 1991 after fifty-two years of performing and his daughter Johanna Meier took over as Artistic Director.

Sadly, the production fell victim to the cultural and economic forces that have challenged numerous Passion Plays since the first decade of the twenty-first century and closed on August 31, 2008. Johanna Meier wrote the "Images of America" series volume on the *Black Hills Passion Play*, published the year the play folded. The introduction cites Oberammergau as "the best known" Passion Play, and implies that the Black Hills Passion Play is the American equivalent, "through its long history of production, its nationwide tours and its spectacular outdoor setting."[53] Yet another American play claims the legacy of Oberammergau.

The Great Passion Play—
Eureka Springs, Arkansas (1968)

Although one of the most recent to be developed, *The Great Passion Play* is arguably the most famous of those considered here and one of the few to still be performed annually. Gerald L.K. Smith, who first organized the construction of the Christ of the Ozarks statue in Eureka Springs, Arkansas, was inspired for his following project to create a Passion Play modeled on the Bavarian village. According to Smith himself, "He remembered that the tiny Bavarian village of Oberammergau had been staging a Passion Play at ten year intervals since being spared from famine in 1634 [sic]."[54] Jill Stevenson cites the program book for the *Great Passion Play*, which states the play "is modeled 'in form and function' after the famous Passion Play in Oberammergau, Germany, 'to involve the local community to glorify God.'"[55]

Not only did Smith model the Bavarian play and experience for his drama, he sought to connect *The Great Passion Play* with the German original, renaming Magnetic Mountain "Mount Oberammergau."[56] In doing so he forever linked the two plays in identity and devotion. Oberammergau had been evoked from the beginning of the project. When construction began on the natural amphitheater near the statue of Jesus Smith first erected on the spot, a sign was placed on the site:

> New Under Construction
> Scenic Staging Facilities
> For presentation of
> Oberammergau Passion Play
> Beginning Early Summer 1968[57]

The Great Passion Play was not the first nor the last American play to claim to be a direct adaptation of the Oberammergau Play. Oberammergau's name lends credibility to performances. The village itself, however, had nothing to do with the production. To this day, American Passion Plays are mentioned in Oberammergau to the folks who perform the plays, who report they know nothing about these productions. A.J. Goldmann reports that while he was speaking with director Christian Stückl, Americans approached and talked with him. He also relates of meeting a woman from Arkansas in Oberammergau who told him about the Eureka Springs passion play.[58]

The Oberammergau Passion Play: Original American Version—Strasburg, Virginia, 1973

The Strasburg, Virginia, *Passion Play*, which ran from 1973 to 1986, was also called "The Oberammergau Passion Play: Original American Version." Produced by Val Balfour, the profession production was presented in the Hendersonville High School Auditorium. Balfour played Jesus in the initial performances, but subsequently hired other performers to play the role in later years. "The Val Balfour production of the Passion Play received its inspiration from the German Oberammergau Passion Play," the local press reported.[59] Again, the name is the indicator of the intention—this is an "American Original" that is also somehow the Oberammergau Passion Play. Oddly, the play was not presented at Easter, but like Oberammergau ran for the summer, early July through Labor Day each year.

There are many more American Passion Plays than the ones listed here that also trace lineage and influence to Oberammergau. "Oberammergau" has more or less become shorthand for "Passion Play" in contemporary American theatre. Sarah Ruhl's *Passion Play* relies upon Oberammergau and the Black Hills Passion Play to frame her exploration of faith in art and on stage (see Jill Stevenson's interview and Jutta Eming's essay in this volume).

Oberammergau is thought of in the popular imagination as the essential religious and devotional drama. Suzan-Lori Parks referred to her play *365 Days/365 Plays*, a multiple, simultaneous theatrical event that lasted a year and took place in over sixteen cities as "a new kind of community pageant. It's that Oberammergau thing.... And the violence sometimes in my work, sure like in every good religious pageant there's blood. And passion. And a miracle, maybe. But mostly there is an invitation for the community to come together and put on a show. Sure, it's very much an Oberammergau thing."[60] Parks, unprompted, saw the pageantry of Oberammergau as a model for communal theatre production. Parks herself is a Catholic whose military family lived in Germany in the late seventies and who attended a German junior high school, leaving her with an awareness of Oberammergau. But it is her work as a theatre artist that makes her look at it as a model for modern American production. She has consistently referred to Oberammergau in interviews as a model for understanding her work.[61]

American Evaluations and Critiques of the Passion Play Script

After 1950 and the celebratory attitude toward the remounting of the Passion Play after sixteen years, a new critique of the village and its play began to emerge. In the wake of the Holocaust, the anti–Semitism in the play was untenable for many Americans. American organizations, particularly Jewish ones, began to become vocal in their opposition to the representation of Judaism in the play. "'What's a nice Jewish boy like you doing in a Catholic play like this?' Oberammergau 2010 and Religious Identity" examined some of these critiques in detail. These groups and others like them continued and continue to critique the Oberammergau Passion Play through 2010 and beyond.

The Secretariat for Catholic-Jewish Relations of the National Conference of Catholic Bishops (1968–1970), the "Ad Hoc Committee Report on the 2010 Oberammergau Passion Play" as disseminated by the Council of Centers on Jewish-Christian Relations, and a number of public pronouncements from the Anti-Defamation League, all American groups, have made pronouncements about Oberammergau's script and performances and all have publicly demanded changes from the village. I note, non-critically, that these American groups are self-appointed. They reach out to Oberammergau in the attempt to combat anti-Semitism. In other words, American groups want a say in how a German village performs an almost four-century-old play.

The committee which prepared the *Ad Hoc Committee Report on the 2010 Oberammergau Passion Play Script* consisted of nine individuals, all American.[62] According to the report, the Council of Centers on Jewish-Christian Relations (CCJR) proposed "that an ad hoc scholarly team of CCJR members study the English translation of the 2010 script of the decennial Oberammergau Passion Play."[63] The report then states the committee's approach:

> With the agreement of the producers, Professor Ingrid Shafer, of the University of Science and Arts of Oklahoma, the official translator of the revised Passion Play text into English, provided the ADL and the ad hoc scholars' committee the 2010 script in both German and English. Each member then prepared individual observations of the script, with particular attention to the English version. The coordinators edited the observations into a report and executive summary, which all the committee members reviewed and approved.[64]

CCJR is full of cautious praise and also recommendations for future "reform." They single out a number of features in the 2010 script that are improvements from previous years, but still find problems in the representation of Jews and Judaism in the play.

Fascinatingly, their final suggestion is not one for the play but for the German Catholic Church:

> A final suggestion might be offered to Catholic ecclesiastical authorities. Although numerous official Vatican documents bear on dramatic presentations of Jesus' passion, none in Germany has the level of detail found in the [U.S.] Bishops' Committee on Ecumenical and Interreligious Affairs' 1988, *Criteria for the Evaluation of Dramatizations of the Passion*. The composition of a cognate document by the German Conference of Catholic Bishops would be a valuable contribution in preparation for the 2020 Oberammergau play, which is, after all, a production with significant catechetical dimensions and which involves so many Catholics both as performers and viewers in its dramatization of Gospel texts.[65]

What is remarkable about this suggestion is that it proposes the German bishops look to the United States Catholic Church as a model for evaluating and transforming their own dramatizations of the Passion.

One of the reasons the Ad Hoc committee did this was because the American bishops had responded to accusations of anti-Semitism in American Passion Plays (with the concern about Oberammergau always lurking in the background) by tasking the Bishops' Committee for Ecumenical and Interreligious Affairs National Conference of Catholic Bishops with developing guidelines for the dramatization of the Passion in response to the charges in *Nostra Aetate*. Accusations of anti–Semitism began to occur in the media toward a number of Passion Plays in the 1980s. Most notably, Union City, New Jersey, saw a number of protests to the two Passion Plays there, and the response was to remove the anti–Jewish elements of the plays.

Thus the NCCB composed the Criteria for the Evaluation of Dramatizations of the Passion.[66] The document first outlines the mystery of the Passion and argues the theological reasons for the crucifixion was the sinfulness of all humankind. The guidelines then argue against "Caricatures and False Oppositions," noting a dozen ways in which Jesus and the Jews must and must not be represented, all of which, it should be noted, were also issues with the Oberammergau script.

The challenge, according to the bishops, is that once the Passion is put on stage, a number of other factors come into play that are not present when one simply reads the scriptures:

> It is all the more important, then, that extraliturgical depictions of the sacred mysteries conform to the highest possible standards of biblical interpretation and theological sensitivity. What is true of Catholic teaching in general is even more crucial with regard to depictions of Jesus' passion. In the words of Pope John Paul II as cited at the beginning of the Notes: "We should aim, in this field, that Catholic teaching at its different levels ... presents Jews and Judaism, not only in an honest and objective manner, free from prejudices and without any offenses, but also with full awareness of the heritage common [to Jews and Christians]."[67]

In short, the bishops advocate for virtually the same things that Jewish advocacy groups and the rabbis discussed in chapter two advocate for. The Ad Hoc Committee Report asks the German church to do the same and issue guidelines, which presumably would mandate the changes for Oberammergau as well. The Ad Hoc Committee sees the American approach as one Germany should follow.

The Anti-Defamation League, however, struck a very different tone. Despite an early posting on the ADL webpage about Oberammergau 2010, noting, "The script for the 2010 production has been significantly changed over the last ten years to try and avoid anti–Judaism. The director and producers are to be congratulated for their efforts and constant cooperation with ADL,"[68] the ADL found the 2010 production to remain highly problematic and highly anti–Semitic.

The report on the 2010 Oberammergau Play concludes:

> What is of serious concern in the 2010 production is that it continues to transmit— in word and image—noxious and hostile anti–Judaism and anti–Semitism. The Jewish High Priest Caiaphas is portrayed as a vicious bloodthirsty leader who oversees a hostile Jewish mob in repeatedly calling demanding the crucifixion of Jesus. Stage sets can be seen as insulting to the Hebrew Bible.
>
> The 2010 play continues to feature anti–Jewish theological concepts that have been the basis for religious persecution of Jews by Christians for two thousand years. One

such concept is known as supersessionism: "the centuries old Christian belief that Christianity has replaced the Jewish people as God's chosen community and that God's covenant with Jews is obsolete. Since the mid-20th Century some Christian churches have repudiated supersessionism as being inconsistent with Scripture."[69]

It is further noted, "The 2010 production has the distinction of being the only one in history that will have been presented during the papacy of a German native of the region who personally witnessed the Holocaust—Pope Benedict XVI."[70] No slight criticism there.

These statements note three areas of concern. The first is "word and image." While I am not sure what they mean by "Stage sets can be seen as insulting to the Hebrew Bible" (perhaps a reference to the tableau?), there is a definite concern that in the script, in the performances and in the designs there is an inherent anti-Semitic bias. The visual and textual negative stereotypes and connotations must be fully removed. The second, is the theology, in particular the blood libel and supersessionism. Third, and finally is the allegation of Pope Benedict and Oberammergau and the Nazis being linked. The implication is that Benedict, as a German native, a witness to the Holocaust and (although not noted here, widely reported when he became pope), a member of the Hitler Youth, has a special obligation to ensure the anti-Jewish elements of Oberammergau are removed and replaced.

The ADL issued subsequent reports, the titles of which clearly state the ADL's position on Oberammergau 2010: "American Jewish Groups: We Have Not Approved 2010 Production of Oberammergau Passion Play" and "Despite Changes, Oberammergau Continues to Transmit Negative Stereotypes of Jews."[71] These reports imply that Oberammergau 2010 is still stereotyping, despite efforts not to do so. It still makes theologically unsupportable statements about Judaism and the relationship between Christianity and Judaism. Some of the issues that the ADL has with Oberammergau are not specific to Oberammergau, but rather endemic to Christianity itself (let us remember the "blood libel" appears first in the gospel of Matthew, one of the foundational texts of Christianity). Lastly, the ADL wished to make clear that they did not accept the 2010 script as an improvement nor that they had given any kind of approval, which begs the question if such approval was required, sought after or necessary. The ADL would say yes, Oberammergauers might not agree. It is, however, a point upon which the United States and Oberammergau continue to explore.

Oberammergau and The Passion of the Christ

The American reception of the 2010 Oberammergau Passion Play was shaped by several things: the anticipation and perception of the upcoming production as shaped by such texts as James Shapiro's *Oberammergau: The Troubling Story of the World's Most Famous Passion Play*, published in 2000, and the previously discussed *Ad Hoc Committee Report on the 2010 Oberammergau Passion Play* as disseminated by the Council of Centers on Jewish–Christian Relations, not to mention reports by the Anti-Defamation League, Mel Gibson's film *The Passion of the Christ*, and the presentation of the play in the international media. Further shaping the perception of the production was the global financial crisis (leaving the dollar and pound weaker than the euro) as well as numerous scandals within the Roman Catholic Church.

Mel Gibson's *The Passion of the Christ* (2004) also shaped reception of the 2010 production, even as the history of Oberammergau shaped reception of Gibson's film. Initially, after the hoopla over Gibson's film died down, a number of critics saw it as not having much of a cultural influence. "If debate over Mel Gibson's film *The Passion* has temporarily overshadowed that over Oberammergau," wrote Jeremy Cohen in 2007, "I predict the spotlight will return to Oberammergau well in advance of its 2010 production and that the public will rapidly forget the Gibson movie."[72] Cohen was wrong in the sense that the public did not forget it, but rather often compared the two, both before and after 2010. Indeed, the two cultural phenomena formed an intertext, with each being interpreted through the other, numerous scholars comparing Gibson's film to the production at Oberammergau.

"Both the Passionsspiel at Oberammergau and Gibson's film are, as stated, veritable Rorschach tests for critics with strongly held religious views," assessed Page R. Laws.[73] What one sees in either text is determined by one's own faith, religious background and culture. Evangelical Christians praise both for being historically and scripturally accurate. Liberal Christians and non–Christians have found both to be anti–Semitic (as this volume has abundantly shown), scripturally selective, and historically heterogeneous, blending medieval, biblical and modern elements and theologies.

Robert A. Faggen, in a devastating critique of Gibson's film (he began the essay by stating "Mel Gibson has embarrassed the twenty-first century," observed that *The Passion of the Christ* "has been regarded as crude and irresponsible populist effort, analogous to the most crude and inflammatory Passion plays, such as the Oberammergau Passion play [sic]."[74] While the scholars represented in this volume, present author included, would take exception to calling the Oberammergau Passion Play "most crude and inflammatory," the construction of the film as analogous to the play provides an interesting insight into the perception of both. For critics like Faggen, comparing Gibson to Oberammergau is a complement to neither, as Oberammergau is viewed as a medieval throwback, an embarrassing part of the history of Christianity; Gibson's film harkens more to the past than to a contemporary understanding of the Christ event. Ironically, Faggen condemns Gibson as being the same as Oberammergau at a time when Oberammergau was working to transcend the historic accusations leveled against it and present a Passion Play for the twenty-first century, the same century Gibson was apparently embarrassing.

Marvin Perry and Frederick M. Schweitzer locate *The Passion of the Christ* as the latest episode in "an uninterrupted flow of contempt and vilification of Jews," of which Oberammergau is one of the most prominent examples.[75] They further state, "No wonder Jews are distressed by Mel Gibson's *The Passion of the Christ*."[76] They argue that Gibson repeats medieval imagery of Jews and Judaism, vilifying the Jews as "Christ killers":

> What do viewers of *Passion of the Christ* learn about Jews? Do they acquire insight into Jesus's Jewishness—his Jewish upbringing and his commitment to his ancestral faith? [No.]
>
> Instead, viewers see a blood thirsty and jeering Jewish mob, incited by ghoulish, cruel, vengeful, scheming priests crying out for more lashes and more blood—a combination of medieval images and Nazi caricature.[77]

This accusation can be (and was) leveled at Oberammergau before 2010. In 2010, however, as noted in chapter two, a large number of Jewish elements—prayers in Hebrew, a Passover Seder for the Last Supper, a Torah and Menorah on stage—illuminated the Jewishness of Jesus. What do viewers of Oberammergau in 2010 learn about Jews? Far more than they did viewing *Passion of the Christ*.

Even though Oberammergau 2010 was, in the end, a very different Passion Play than the ones that had been presented before, when Gibson's film was released those changes were still in the future, so the play formed a model through which Gibson's dramatization of the Passion might be comparatively understood. Oberammergau was presented by critics *as The Passion of the Christ*'s older, less technologically sophisticated sibling through which Gibson learned how to present the trial, torture and execution of Jesus. Laws sees Gibson's film as a controversial, dramatic, multisensory experience that allows Christians to actively observe the crucifixion with little to no attention paid to the resurrection, a charge also leveled against Oberammergau: a great deal of time is spent on the physical agony and death of Christ, a few minutes are spent on the resurrection.[78] Laws further observes, "Consciously or not, Gibson has borrowed several techniques from Oberammergau and the larger passion play tradition."[79] These techniques include the use of primarily unknown performers, linking the Old Testament to the New, primarily through visual references (for example, Oberammergau's tableaux), and a focus on the pain and torture of the body of the wounded Jesus.[80] In other words, Oberammergau was seen as the model for Gibson and his film can be (and was) read through the German Passion Play tradition.

We might further note that both *The Passion of the Christ* and the Oberammergau Passion Play are Catholic in origin, yet appeal widely to Protestant

Christians. Catholics often focus on the physicality of the cross and the body of the man hanging on it. As James Martin, S.J. indicates, Catholic churches often feature a large crucifix, presenting the body of the crucified Christ, whereas the Protestant tradition offers an empty cross—emblematic of the resurrection.[81] Like the German play, Gibson spends 95 percent of his narrative on the events up to and including the crucifixion with the resurrection as a sort of epilogue to both.

In his analysis of the film, Stephen Prothero calls it "unapologetically Catholic," arguing that from Oberammergau, "Gibson borrowed his blood-and-guts sacramentalism and the tradition of cranking up Jewish culpability for dramatic effect."[82] He further posits, "Gibson also borrowed from Oberammergau and its European and American imitators the tradition of tableau vivant."[83] *The Passion of the Christ*, like the Oberammergau Passion Play, maintains a tension between being a faith experience (and thus theology) and claims that it is an historic recreation (and thus history). Historical accuracy was a main selling point of Gibson's film. William Fulco, S.J. translated the script into Biblically accurate Aramaic and the publicity for the film repeatedly promised the amount of research that informed every aspect of the film.

All of these critical assertions about *The Passion of the Christ* being linked historically, structurally, theologically, thematically and visually with Oberammergau resulted in both texts being read in comparison with one another. Just as Oberammergau framed *The Passion of the Christ*, so too did *The Passion of the Christ* frame the 2010 production of the *Oberammergau Passion Play*. Given all of the changes to the script and production of the Passion Play, especially as related to the representation of Jews, the first framing was one of the similarities, the second framing could not escape the differences. If Gibson's film was indeed an embarrassment for the twenty-first century, Oberammergau 2010 was an entrance into it and an apology for the previous forty performances.

American Reception of Oberammergau

When 2010 finally arrived, the reviews were mostly mixed. The focus of the reviews was on past controversies, how the economics of the global recession would affect attendance, perpetuating the myth of Oberammergau as a simple village filled with simple people fulfilling their religious vows and how much the play had changed in its representation of Jews. Yet the shifts in the play and in the village as outlined in this volume also appeared in the more scholarly reviews of the production. Elizabeth Johann Montgomery, writing in *Theatre Journal*, saw the piece as less emblematic of religion than of coming to terms with changing demographics, arguing the production, "was inextricably and uniquely linked to a collective performance of the town's identity."[84] She saw the play as reflected the struggle within Judaism, rather than the birth of a new faith: "Mayet's Jesus was played with quiet conviction as a reformer fighting against corrupt politicians."[85] In the end, Montgomery concludes that "the Oberammergau Passion Play 2010 was more about Oberammergau than about Christ's passion—and that Oberammergau is increasingly becoming more secular, even as it searches to maintain the relevance of the town's religious showpiece."[86]

"Relevance" might be the wrong word here. While the individual village citizens and the town itself might be becoming increasingly secular, the play was still very well attended both by people of deep faith and people of different faiths and people of no faith. The term "religious showpiece" also seems a bit reductive, as the play has become, as Montgomery herself notes, more than the religious story it tells. It has become a story about the story—village identity is now about the production of the play far more than the filling of a religious vow. While those who come to the play out of faith are welcomed and receive what they came for, the play is now framed in such a manner that it is as much civic event and historical recreation, not of the Passion itself but of the historic Passion Play.

Oana Lungescu, reporting for the BBC, also focused on the village itself. As with so many of the reviews, she presents the behind-the-scenes events of Oberammergau, introducing Andreas Richter as a child psychologist before mentioning he plays Christ.[87] Also as with many of the reviews, Lungescu sites the performance in the changing nature of the village and the challenges to the Catholic Church as well as from the financial crisis: "This year about half of the village's 5,000 in habitants are taking part, despite recent scandals that have rocked the Catholic Church in Germany. But the play, which runs from May until October and attracts visitors from round the world, has been plagued by the financial crisis."[88] And, accordingly, perhaps the biggest challenge facing the American presence at Oberammergau 2010 was simply the realities of the global financial markets that year. Over half a million attended the 2000 production, but that figure was reduced by over 20 percent in 2010, with most of the blame going to the economy: "The mayor blames the unfavourable dollar and pound exchange against the euro. Travel agents also point out that ticket prices have doubled since 2000 and that hotels in the village have become so expensive that many prefer to stay in nearby towns or over the border in Austria."[89] Oberammergau relies not only on the income from play tickets but from the lodging, food, souvenirs and other services purchased in the village. The result is an audience base that is more elite and fiscally well off than the original local audiences of centuries ago, or even 1950. The other result is the recognition of the economic realities of performing an event every ten years upon which the entire economic well-being of the village is dependent. A cynic might look at Oberammergau 2010 and see a script changing not just because of demographics or new understandings of theology and life in first-century Palestine, but because American groups have demanded changes and since Americans make up the majority of the audience the village places not biting the hand that feeds them over allegiance to a medieval vow. Again, that is a cynical view, but all reports and reviews, including in Shapiro's book about the 2000 production show the village and especially Huber and Stückl as being very concerned with and responsive to criticisms of the script, especially when coming from American sources.

This approach is simply an economic necessity in the twenty-first century. "The number of tourists in Oberammergau is significant because the passion play tends to give a significant boost to US bookings in Europe every decade."[90] In other words, the passion play is major boost not only to Oberammergau but to Germany and Europe as more Americans travel to Germany during passion play years. So not only are the villagers concerned about keeping the Americans happy and coming, so, too, is the rest of Germany, as well as Austria and the rest of the European Union. What is good for Oberammergau is good for Europe, and Americans are good for Oberammergau.

Finally, we might note that all of the reviews in the American press concerning Oberammergau, all of the books and narratives concerning the Passion play are at heart about America's relationship to the play: "But then, the American debates about Oberammergau had never really been about that distant Bavarian village; they were about the future of an increasingly diverse American nation."[91] The same cultural forces driving Oberammergau to change are also the same cultural forces dividing and driving debate in the United States. Americans can go to Oberammergau for nostalgic purposes, as noted above—to feel like they are in a Christian nation presenting the Christian story. As Oberammergau shifts, so too does the United States. In that sense, the debates in the United States about Oberammergau are simply a reflection of the tensions concerning representation and religion in America, which might also be the other reason debates about *The Passion of the Christ* referenced Oberammergau: both texts at heart concern American religious identity and the role of Christianity in a nation that mandates the separation of Church and State. The irony being that Oberammergau 2010 indicates that the Bavarian villagers are much more comfortable with complexity, religious diversity and the role of Christianity than the Americans who make up more than half their audience.

NOTES

1. Jeremy Cohen, *Christ Killers: The Jews and the Passion from the Bible to the Big Screen* (Oxford: Oxford University Press, 2007), 217.

2. Susan Spano, "In the Alps, a saving grace." *Los Angeles Times* (June 6, 2010): L4.

3. Claire Sponsler, *Ritual Imports: Performing Medieval Drama in America* (Ithaca: Cornell University Press, 2004), 128.
4. Rick Altman, *Silent Film Sound* (New York: Columbia University Press, 2004) 136.
5. See http://digital.lib.uiowa.edu/cdm/ref/collection/tc/id/40556.
6. See http://digital.lib.uiowa.edu/cdm/ref/collection/tc/id/40556.
7. Altman, *Silent Film Sound* 136–7; Rick Altman, "From Lecturer's Prop to Industrial Product: The Early History of Travel Films." *Virtual Voyages: Cinema and Travel*. Ed. Jeffrey Ruoff (Durham: Duke University Press, 2006) 70.
8. Sponsler 124.
9. Sponsler 131.
10. Altman, *Silent Film Sound* 136.
11. Sponsler 131.
12. Spear 833.
13. Helena Waddy, *Oberammergau in the Nazi Era: The Fate of a Catholic Village in Hitler's Germany* (Oxford: Oxford University Press, 2010), 25.
14. "Oberammergau's Rebuke to America." *Literary Digest* (January 5, 1924): 34.
15. Altman, "From Lecturer's Prop," 70.
16. Annette von Altenbokum, *Oberammergau: Art, Tradition, and Passion* (Munich: Prestel, 2010), 38.
17. Sonja E. Spear, "Claiming the Passion: American Fantasies of the Oberammergau Passion Play, 1923–1947." *Church History* 80.4 (December 2011): 833.
18. Spear 836.
19. Qtd. von Altenbokum 39.
20. "Oberammergau's Rebuke to America" 34.
21. Spear 835.
22. "Oberammergau's Rebuke to America" 34.
23. Spear 836.
24. A. James Rudin, "Oberammergau: A Case Study of Passion Plays." *Pondering the Passion: What's at Stake for Christians and Jews?* Ed. Philip A. Cuningham (Lanham, MD: Rowman & Littlefield, 2004), 99.
25. Rudin 100.
26. Win Fanning, "McCloy, Robertson Among Dignitaries Viewing Oberammergau Premiere." *Stars and Stripes* (May 19, 1950) http://www.stripes.com/news/mccloy-robertson-among-dignitaries-viewing-oberammergau-premiere-1.25593. Accessed June 10, 2015.
27. Fanning.
28. Fanning.
29. Elizabeth Ellem, "Pomfret, Connecticut, Earns Place on Map as America's Oberammergau." *The Milwaukee Sentinel Magazine* (December 24, 1922): 6.
30. "'The Holy Night' Solemnly Played by New England Village." *The* [Spokane, WA] *Spokesman-Review* (January 18, 1914): 9.
31. "The Holy Night" 9.
32. "The Holy Night" 9.
33. "The Holy Night" 9.
34. Cohen 229.
35. Jay Romano, "2 Passion Plays Thrive on a 'Friendly Rivalry.'" *New York Times* (March 5, 1989) http://www.nytimes/1989/03/05nyregion/union-city-journal-2-passion-plays-thrive-on-a-friendly-rivalry.html. Accessed 20 August 2013.
36. Joe Sharkey, "Jersey: Sometimes a Stage is as Good as a Pulpit." *New York*

Times (June 9, 1996) http://www.nytimes.com/1996/06/09/nyregion/jersey-sometimes-a-stage-is-as-good-as-a-pulpit.html. Accessed 20 August 2013.

37. Romano "2 Passion Plays."

38. "Amid the Everlasting Hills." *Los Angeles Times* (May 31, 1920): n.p.

39. See http://www.pantagraph.com/entertainment/angels-wanted-imperiled-passion-play-needs-a-savior/article_de694480-76cb-5873-822b-27c92da44224.html and http://www.americanpassionplay.org/about.html.

40. Lee Price, "Bloomington Center for the Performing Arts." *Tour America's History*. January 7, 2013. http://touramericashistory.blogspot.com/2013/01/bloomington-center-for-performing-arts.html. Accessed June 12, 2013.

41. Louis L. Williams, *The American Passion Play: A Study and History* (Bloomington: The American Passion Play, Inc., 1970), 22–27.

42. Williams 26–7.

43. Williams 27.

44. Williams 27.

45. Jacqulein Vaughn Lowry, *Holy City of the Wichitas* (Charleston, S.C.: Arcadia Publishing, 2009), 8, 27, 99–123.

46. See http://memory.loc.gov/diglib/legacies/loc.afc.afc-legacies.200003709/.

47. M.C. O'Bryant, "Church News: Easter play held at the 'Holy City of the Wichita Mountains.'" LDSchurchnews.com (March 26, 2010) http://www.ldschurchnewsarchive.com/articles/print/59098/Easter-play-held-at-the-Holy-City-of-the-Wichita-Mountains.html. Accessed June 12, 2013.

48. O'Bryant, "Church News."

49. See http://zionpassionplay.com/history/.

50. See http://easterpageant.org/.

51. Dorothy Chansky, "North American Passion Plays: 'The Greatest Story Ever Told' in the New Millennium." *TDR: The Drama Review* 50.4 (T192) (Winter 2006): 122.

52. Williams 372.

53. Johanna Meier, *The Black Hills Passion Play* (Charleston, S.C.: Arcadia Publishing, 2008), 7, 10.

54. Glen Jeansomne, *Gerald L.K. Smith: Minister of Hate* (New Haven: Yale University Press, 1988), 193.

55. Jill Stevenson, *Sensational Devotion: Evangelical Performance in Twenty-First Century America* (Ann Arbor: University of Michigan Press, 2013), 98.

56. Jeansomne 193.

57. Timothy M. Kovalcik, *Images of America: The Great Passion Play* (Charleston, S.C.: Arcadia, 2008), 30. For some reason, throughout the volume Kovalcik spells the German village and the Arkansas mountain "Oberramagau," despite it being spelled correctly in all of the photographs of signs, programs, etc.

58. A.J. Goldmann, "New Kind of Passion in an 'Alpine Jerusalem.'" Forward.com May 26, 2010. http://www.forward.com/articles/128345. Accessed December 12, 2010.

59. "Passion Play has opened in Virginia." (Hendersonville, N.C.) *Times-News* (July 24, 1982): 11. See also Simon J. Bronner, *Encyclopedia of American Folklife* (New York: Routledge, 2006), 325.

60. Qtd. in Kevin J. Wetmore, Jr., "It's an Oberammergau Thing: An Interview with Suzan-Lori Parks." *Suzan-Lori Parks: A Casebook*. Ed. Kevin J. Wetmore, Jr., and Alycia Smith-Howard (London: Routledge, 2007), 140.

61. For example, in 1994 she said, "Every play I write is like a religious pageant," and then describes Oberammergau (Han Ong, "Suzan-Lori Parks" in *Suzan-Lori Parks in Person: Interviews and Commentaries*, edited by Philip C. Kolin and Harvey Young

[London: Routledge, 2014]: 42) and in 1996 to Una Chaudhuri ("For Posterior's Sake" in *Suzan-Lori Parks in Person: Interviews and Commentaries*, edited by Philip C. Kolin and Harvey Young [London: Routledge, 2014]: 56.)

62. Council of Centers on Jewish-Christian Relations. *Ad Hoc Committee Report on the 2010 Oberammergau Passion Play Script*. May 14, 2010. http://www.ccjr.us/images/stories/CCJR_Oberammergau_Report_2010May14.pdf. Accessed March 23, 2014. 16.

63. Council of Centers on Jewish-Christian Relations. *Ad Hoc Committee Report on the 2010 Oberammergau Passion Play Script*, 2.

64. Council of Centers on Jewish-Christian Relations. *Ad Hoc Committee Report on the 2010 Oberammergau Passion Play Script*, 2.

65. Council of Centers on Jewish-Christian Relations. *Ad Hoc Committee Report on the 2010 Oberammergau Passion Play Script*, 15.

66. Bishops' Committee for Ecumenical and Interreligious Affairs, United States Conference of Catholic Bishops. *Criteria for the Evaluation of Dramatizations of the Passion*, 1–14. Washington, D.C.: United States Conference of Catholic Bishops, 1988. http://www.usccb.org/beliefs-and-teachings/ecumenical-and-interreligious/jewish/upload/Criteria-for-the-Evaluation-of-Dramatizations-of-the-Passion-1988.pdf.

67. Bishops' Committee for Ecumenical and Interreligious Affairs, *Criteria*.

68. Anti-Defamation League, "The Oberammergau Passion Play." n.d. http://archive.adl.org/nr/exeres/164d9601-f63f-4eea-9cc1-27a4cf18348d,db7611a2-02cd-43af-8147-649e26813571,frameless.html. Accessed June 13, 2013.

69. Anti-Defamation League, "The Oberammergau Passion Play."

70. Anti-Defamation League, "The Oberammergau Passion Play."

71. Anti-Defamation League, "American Jewish Groups: We Have Not Approved 2010 Production Of Oberammergau Passion Play." February 18, 2010. http://www.adl.org/press-center/press-releases/interfaith/american-jewish-groups-we.html#.Vl1g9HarSM8. Accessed June 13, 2013; "Despite Changes, Oberammergau Continues To Transmit Negative Stereotypes Of Jews." May 10, 2010. http://www.adl.org/press-center/press-releases/interfaith/despite-changes-oberammergau.html#.Vl1g8HarSM8. Accessed June 13, 2013.

72. Cohen 217.

73. Page R. Laws, "Witness to/for the Persecution: Of Race, Religion, Mel Gibson and Stirred-up Passions" *Arbeiten aus Anglistik und Amweikanistik* 30. 1/2 (2005): 57.

74. Robert A. Faggen, "'But Is It Art?' A Prelude to Criticism of Mel Gibson's *The Passion of the Christ.*" *After* The Passion *Is Gone: American Religious Consequences*. Eds. J. Shawn Landres and Michael Berenbaum (Lanham, MD: AltaMira, 2004) 115.

75. Marvin Perry and Frederick M. Schweitzer, "The Medieval Passion Play Revisited." *Re-Viewing* The Passion*: Mel Gibson's Film and Its Critics*. Ed. S. Brent Plate (New York: Palgrave, 2004) 6. See also Gary Gilbert, "Antisemitism without Erasure: Sacred Texts and Their Contemporary Interpretations." *After* The Passion *Is Gone: American Religious Consequences*. Eds. J. Shawn Landres and Michael Berenbaum (Lanham, MD: AltaMira, 2004) 126–131.

76. Perry and Schweitzer 9.

77. Perry and Schweitzer 11.

78. Laws, "Witness" 57. In fairness, this accusation is true for most Passion plays. To choose but one example, *The Glory of Easter* at the Crystal Cathedral in Southern California also spend 95 percent of its run time on the trial and execution of Jesus. The resurrection, which was achieved with laser beams and special effects to roll the stone away from the tomb so Jesus could emerge was literally the last five minutes of the show.

79. Laws, "Witness" 59.
80. Laws, "Witness" 59–61.
81. James Martin, S.J., "The Last Station: A Catholic Reflection on *The Passion.*" *Perspectives on* The Passion of the Christ: *Religious Thinkers and Writers Explore the Issues Raised by the Controversial Movie* (New York: Miramax Books, 2004), 95–98.
82. Stephen Prothero, "Jesus Nation, Catholic Christ." *Perspectives on* The Passion of the Christ: *Religious Thinkers and Writers Explore the Issues Raised by the Controversial Movie* (New York: Miramax Books, 2004), 274.
83. Prothero 274.
84. Elizabeth Joann Montgomery, "*Oberammergau Passion Play 2010.*" *Theatre Journal* 63.2 (May 2011): 260.
85. Montgomery 261.
86. Montgomery 262.
87. Oana Lungescu, "Bavarian Passion plays to global crowds." BBC News Europe. 31 May 2010. www.bbc.co.uk/news/10198502. Accessed April 25, 2012.
88. Lungescu, "Bavarian Passion."
89. Lungescu, "Bavarian Passion."
90. Lungescu, "Bavarian Passion."
91. Spear 862.

Part 3

Interviews

An Interview with Frederik Mayet (Actor, Christ)

David Mason

Frederik Mayet was born in Munich in 1980. Alongside Andreas Richter, he was one of two actors to play the role of Jesus in Oberammergau's 2010 Passion Play. He completed a Bachelor's degree at EBC–Munich, and now splits his time between Oberammergau and Munich. He continues to work as an actor in the Munich area, and is employed as a press liaison by the Müchner Volkstheater, where he continues to work closely with director Christian Stückl. This interview was conducted in August 2013.

* * *

I saw the Oberammergau Passion Play in August of 2010, and I thought it was really terrific. It was impressive, and it was inspiring, and it was challenging, and even at the length of six hours it passed rather easily. I didn't feel it was long at all, and that's remarkable. With how many productions have you been involved?

I have been involved with only two Passion Play productions. First, I played the disciple John in 2000, and then I played Jesus in 2010. I was born in Oberammergau, but didn't participate when I was younger because my father was studying, so we didn't live in Oberammergau.

Up until 2000, you weren't involved in the production at all?
2000 was the first time I did theatre.

That was your very first theatre experience?
Yes.

And you started as an Apostle?
Yeah. It was quite interesting, then. Christian Stückl did some auditions and saw me and said, "Hey, Frederik, don't you want to join us?" He was there

with some younger guys, like, they were seventeen and eighteen. So, we did some reading and some exercises, and so on, and then one day he came up to me and said, "Frederik, I think I want to have you as John." I was really overwhelmed.

So, that was the audition process.
Yeah, that was the audition process. He was looking for some younger actors.

Have you done any other acting, since starting with the Passion Play?
In 2005 I had a small role in the play *King David*. In 2007, I had a bigger role when Christian did Stephan Zweig's *Jeremiah*. And then we played the Festspiel.

That's the play about the Passion Play's origin.
Yes, the black plague. There I had a bigger role. After the 2010 Passion Play, we did Thomas Mann's *Joseph and His Brothers*. And this year we're doing *Moses*, by Feridun Zaimoglu and Günter Senkel. We're performing tomorrow and Thursday, Friday, and Saturday. I'm playing Aaron.

So this is happening right now?
Yes, this is happening now. After 2010, we looked at our theatre and realized we wanted to keep filling it, rather than leaving it empty for nine years. We wanted to do something for the community, so we started to bring in concerts and other plays.

That is a big theatre. It's got to be hard to fill it up with off-season shows.
We built something like a wall, so we have only two thousand seats at this time. This is also really big.

All these shows you just mentioned, the Zweig and the Mann plays, and so forth, that you are in all perform in Oberammergau?
They all take place in the Passion Play theatre.

Who's directing all of these productions?
Christian Stückl.

So you work rather closely with him on a continuous basis.
Yeah, we also work together in Munich. He is the director of the Munich Volkstheater, and I do the PR and marketing there. That's my main job.

So, your professional life now is theatre.
My whole professional life is theatre now.

Did you anticipate that before 2000?
No, never. After the Passion Play in 2000, I started studying International Business Administration, and then my first job was at Amazon here in Germany,

and I hated it and quit after a year. So, when Christian did the opening ceremony of the World Soccer Championship here in Germany, in 2006, he asked me if I wanted to help him in organizing all of it, and I said, "Of course!" I quit my job at Amazon, and then after the ceremony he said that he needed someone doing PR and marketing for the folks at the theatre here in Munich. So, all my life changed because of the Passion Play. Now I'm happy.

And you expect Stückl is going to direct the Passion Play in 2020?

Yes, definitely. I'm quite sure. For him ... he always wanted to be the Passion Play director, and as long as he can stand he wants to continue.

In America we'd probably say something like "the Passion Play is his baby."

Yes, it's his baby, of course. I'm sure he will do it in 2020. He's already talking about what to do and how to organize it. It's not official, already, because the Oberammergau city council and the mayor have to sign off. But that won't be a problem.

And the other production directors will be coming back? Designer Stefan Hageneier and Music Director Markus Zwink?

Yes, I'm quite sure. We are really lucky to have those three guys. Stefan is really well-known for stage and costume design, and Markus is really dedicated to the choir and the music, and he's a really good conductor. They are all really, really important for the Passion Play. I think they raised the bar from 1980.

I think their personal commitment to this production shows. At least, the production I saw showed clearly that the people who were involved were personally committed to it, far beyond the commitment people might give a job. The people at the helm of this production clearly have a personal love for it.

That's true for most of the people involved in the Passion Play. It's a part of the identity of Oberammergau. So, we grow up with it and it becomes our community.

You think it's much developed, artistically, from 1980. In what way is it different, specifically?

I read the text from 1970. I had it in my hand, and I was reading it. If you're not a native German speaker, I don't think you would recognize it, but it was very different. The text from 1970 would be impossible to play on the stage, anymore. It was so far from the language we speak. Too stylized, maybe. Too esoteric. And in 1970, Jesus was more God than human. That's a big difference. Back then, Jesus was saying more, "You just don't get what I'm saying, but you'll understand it later." He was already in heaven. But in 2010, he's talking to real people. He's more like a real person, fighting for something. He's closer to people. That's a big difference between 1970 and 2010.

I understood that the script from 1970 had been developed to some degree over the past three decades, but I didn't realize that it had been so drastically re-written.

That's typical for Oberammergau. The script is always changing. I think it has to. It's not that we have a text and we have played it for four hundred years, and it's always been the same. I think that's not possible. A priest can't go to church on Christmas and do the same sermon he does every year. We always have to speak differently to people. We always have to find a way to reach new visitors. So, ten years. That's a very long time. You always have to go through the text and find new words and sentences to reach people. Language changes a lot in ten years, and more in twenty and thirty years. If you read the text from 1970, it's a different language.

Older. More antique.

Yes, right.

Was the script from 2010 radically different from the script in 2000?

I would say so. Not *radically*, no, but there were changes. Christian Stückl does the changes and then we have someone from the Catholic Church, a professor, look through it to certify that there are no mistakes in it. That it's theologically correct.

Otto Huber has been involved in restructuring the script as well.

Yes, he was in charge of the prologue and the choir.

I see. Huber and Stückl had different responsibilities with regard to maintaining and changing the script.

They cooperated, but they did divide some responsibility.

The productions used to be during the day. They'd start in the morning and go only during daylight hours. Is that right?

Even as recently as 2000.

Just in 2010 you decided to shift it later, so that now part of it takes place in the evening, after dark. Does this change the production—playing after dark?

Of course. It's good to do it in the dark, because you then have the ability to focus some light, which helps with the story we tell. The story starts when it's bright, and then the darkness comes on as the story progresses, so I think artistically it's good. And for the participants it's getting more and more difficult to be part of the play for half a year. Most of the people are working and the work situation is changing in Oberammergau and nearby, and more and more people like me have to drive in. I work in Munich and others work in Munich, as well. Some others are studying, and so on and on. The idea was that we'd try to make it easier for a lot of people to take part. It's easier for someone to say to the boss, "for the next half-year I can only work a half-day" than to say, "for the next half-year I can't work at all." This was behind the shift in timing, as well. We wanted to let as many as possible be part of the Passion Play.

Let's talk, then, about playing Jesus. What's it like to be Jesus on stage?

When I heard that I had been cast as Jesus I said, "Oh, God, that's going to be difficult." I first had in mind the two people playing Jesus in 2000. I was playing a disciple, then, so I was very close to them, and I liked them both. I asked them how they handle playing this role, because everyone who comes to the Passion Play has a picture of Jesus in his mind—how he walks, how he talks—so I thought it was impossible to fulfill all these expectations. I watched a lot of movies about Jesus, like Mel Gibson's, I watched multiple times. I even watched *Jesus of Montreal*, the Pasolini movie. There are a lot of movies, actually. So, while I watched these films I noted the different ways there are to play the role. And I realized that I had to find an interpretation for myself. So, I went back to the Bible, and I read some biographies of Jesus, and I tried to find my own way. I worked with Christian Stückl on characterization, of course, in rehearsal. In the Testament, it says you have to play a human and you have to play God, somehow, and that's impossible, because you can't show God on stage, you can only show the human. So we tried to show someone who is a human, fighting for something.

Was there one book or movie or other source that was particularly useful to constructing this character?

The Pasolini movie. And there was a book written by a German professor. He teaches history here in Munich, and he wrote a book about Jesus and the historical context. This book was really interesting. He wrote about Jesus and the situation of his time. The aphorisms, you know, like "when someone forces you to walk a mile with him, then go two with him"—this professor explained that in those times the Romans could force a Jewish person to carry his bag for one mile. So this aphorism has a historical context. Two thousand years ago this saying had a significant meaning. Today, we sometimes don't understand it anymore.

It was actually rooted in the real life Jesus was living.

Exactly.

Here's an acting question: How closely did you identify with your character while you were on stage?

(Laugh.) Sometimes more, sometimes less. Depends on the situation. Sometimes I was really close, and sometimes it was more like acting. Depended on the situation, the day. I always tried to be as close on the stage as it would be, but it was really important to me to put it away, afterwards, to go, drink beer with friends, and to talk. It's a role where sometimes you have to be a little bit careful.

So from night to night the degree to which you identified with your character was different.

It could be really unhealthy.

This is not just a character. You had to handle the acting assignment with some delicacy.

Yeah, sometimes.

What did you learn from portraying Jesus on stage?

If you play this role, you get a personal view of Jesus and the Bible, because you speak the words on stage for an audience. Now, when I read from the Bible, I have a much different picture in my head than I did before taking the part. I have a much closer relationship now.

I have been told that you made a practice of riding your bicycle during intermission.

True.

This has got to be strange for some of the audience members who are out walking around and to see Jesus go riding by on a bicycle.

(Laugh.) We had a three-hour break. It depended on the day. Sometimes I just slept or ate, and sometimes I went riding the bicycle. Most people didn't really recognize me...

You weren't in costume...

No, no. Not in costume. Not allowed to take the costume out of the theatre.

But some people recognized you. How did they react to seeing you out among them on a bicycle?

Most of the people could distinguish between the role and the person. There were some situations where some people couldn't distinguish so well. There was one person who came up once, saying things like "God has a plan for you" and "He chose you for this role." Then she said, "I have a prophecy for you." She was a little bit strange.

Back in the 1800s the actors who played Jesus—even into the 1900s—were treated differently by people who came to Oberammergau. They were treated as fairly special people. Do you experience that?

Yeah, of course. It's interesting. My reputation in the village is, of course, better than before. And during the passion play, prominent people came to Oberammergau, like Chancellor Merkel, and the president of Germany, and some really important politicians and stars. We would go to lunch with them, for example, so that was interesting for me. There's a difference, though, between now and 1900. I think it was in 1980 they decided that all the main roles would be doubled, so now you have two Jesuses and two Marys and two Pilates. In former times the focus was more on one person. Now, the double casting takes attention away from individuals. I think that's quite good.

Has playing Jesus changed you?

My experience in the Passionsspiele changed me a lot. I'm more mature than I used to be. And, of course, I have a different view of Jesus and the Holy Bible.

What was the most difficult part about playing Jesus?

The crucifixion. It was hard to play the mortal agony, and then being "dead," hanging on the cross for so long.

For audiences, how much distance do you think there was between you the actor and Jesus the character?

Hm. Difficult to answer that.

Maybe easier this way: how many people who came to the play, do you think, were going to church rather than to the theatre?

Oh, that's difficult, but, maybe, fifty-fifty. I think a lot of people go there because they think it's a big event, and you have to go there. Some will say it's just theatre and I go because it's artistic, and I don't go to church, anyway. But I think about 60 percent come because it's a religious experience. Perhaps it's 70 percent. I can't say exactly. But even those that have quit the church—I heard a lot of people who said, "Oh, I was very far away from the church, but now I'm thinking about it again. I found something in the things Jesus said."

Personally, there's one element of the play that is really intriguing to me. That is the tableaus.

The *lebendige bilder*...

Yes. *This is a very strange device. It's not terribly unusual if you're a frequent theatre-goer, and you see a variety of theatre. But for a lot of people in the audience, those scenes must be very strange, I think.*

It's a really old theatre meme. It's from the baroque period, something that's survived in this form because the Passion Play is so old. In former times it was used very often in theatre. I think it's something special in Oberammergau, especially in 2010, where it was so colorful and well-designed.

I thought that Stefan's design for those tableaus was really remarkable. But you've said something about how the play changes every production, and Oberammergau is always trying to update it. Why has it held onto this very old element?

(Laugh.) I don't know. I think it has something to do with wanting to keep some of the heritage. We want to keep some of the prologue and the coir and the orchestra, because they are tradition. Some parts can't change, even for us. I think if some new director came along and said, "Oh, I don't want to have the tableaus, anymore," we would kick out the director.

Some parts just can't be changed.
That's so.

Besides only being traditional, what purpose do the tableaus serve?
They're a connection to the Old Testament. The scenes from the Old Testament link to the New Testament. As it was said for Moses, it is similar here with Jesus. For me, it's really interesting theologically to have those things, and it's something important to Christian Stückl. We have here a story, a Jewish story, and Jesus was born as a Jew, and he had a bar mitzvah when he was in the temple. So, we are closer to the Jews than most Catholics or most Christians think. That's something that Stückl wants to show in the Passion Play.

In 2020, what do you expect will be different?
Oh, that's so far away. I think we will have more changes in the text, and we will have a completely new stage and costume design. But I don't know how it will go.

Do you know if Stückl is doing any edits to the script? Is he changing or updating it?
I think he will update it. He'll re-read it, and will fill in a sentence here and there. But the story is clear. There are some scenes that could be sharpened. There was one scene, called "Bethany." It's in the first part of the play. Everyone is on stage is this scene. We thought that's a scene that could be shortened, a little bit. Perhaps bring in some new text so that it's more intense.

Are you planning to play Jesus in the next one?
I don't know. Depends. If my belly grows or I lose my hair, no chance. I had the privilege to play it once. I think it's important for the Passion Play that in 2020 there is someone new or younger to play this role. Of course, I would love to play it again. but, if not, okay. You always have to give it to the next generation, and it's ten years in between. There are many other interesting roles I would love to play. So, we'll see.

You'll certainly be in the show somewhere, maybe or maybe not as Jesus.
There were some who played it twice, so there's a chance for me, but we will see. We will know in five years.

Passion Playing
An Interview with Sarah Ruhl on the Shaping Influence of Oberammergau

Jill Stevenson

As this volume demonstrates, for centuries Oberammergau's Passionsspiele has served as a significant cultural product with wide-reaching social, political, and religious resonance. It has not only inspired devotees and scholars, but also artists, one of them being the U.S. playwright Sarah Ruhl. Ruhl is the author of several plays, among them *In the Next Room, or the vibrator play* (2010 Pulitzer Prize Finalist), *Stage Kiss, The Clean House* (2005 Pulitzer Prize Finalist; The Susan Smith Blackburn Prize, 2004), *Dead Man's Cell Phone* (Helen Hayes Award for Best New Play). Her work has been produced across the U.S. and internationally, and she has received various awards including a MacArthur Fellowship (2006), the PEN Center Award for a mid-career playwright, the Feminist Press' Forty under Forty award, and the 2010 Lilly award. Arguably, one of Ruhl's most ambitious plays is the three-act cycle Passion Play. On Tuesday, November 6, 2012, the day of the U.S. national elections, I met Ruhl at a coffeehouse in Brooklyn, New York, to discuss her play and its relationship to religious performance and the Passion Playing tradition. This essay features excerpts from that conversation.

* * *

Passion Play opens in 1575 as a Northern English village prepares to stage its annual Passion Play. Act Two is set nearly four hundred years later; it is 1934 in Oberammergau and the villagers are organizing the tercentennial production of their historic play. The play's third act revolves around another community-based production, the Black Hills Passion Play, which was staged annually in Spearfish, South Dakota, from 1939 to 2008. This final act begins in 1969, shifts to 1972 and 1984, before concluding in the present. Ruhl indicates in her "Playwright's Note" that,

> [i]deally, *Passion Play* (Parts One, Two, and Three) would be performed all together in one evening (it should run about three hours plus intermissions) or else in rotating repertory. Together, the three parts form a cycle play—alone, they do something different, but they can technically stand alone.... If the resources of one theater are too limited to produce the entire cycle, I can imagine two theaters in one city collaborating to put up the cycle together. In the original guild productions of the Passion, the carpenters in the village would handle the Crucifixion scene and the bakers would handle the Last Supper.[1]

This dramaturgically rich cycle therefore engages the history of Passion Plays not only thematically, but also structurally by offering theatre artists unique opportunities to experiment with community-based production models, models that could even emulate earlier traditions of Passion Playing.

The inspiration for *Passion Play* was, in part, Oberammergau's production; Ruhl began writing *Passion Play* after rereading a children's book in which the heroine, Betsy, visits Oberammergau. Set in the early 1900s, the story follows Betsy as she meets the actors who play Jesus and Mary in the village's Passion Play. As Ruhl explained during our conversation, the story is "very sweet ... [Betsy] is kind of undone by how actively spiritual these people were. And I was a little suspicious and thought, 'Huh. What if there was more of a disjunction?'" This prompted Ruhl to research Oberammergau and its Passion Play more thoroughly. Like many people, she was especially struck by how the village's production reflected and refracted specific political ideologies during the 1930s and 1940s: "I was fascinated by how the only two outliers were Judas and Pontius Pilate, who did not join the Nazi party. I thought, 'What is that about?' And the first to join up were Jesus and the director.... You have this kind of fantasy that the gospel would offer some moral protection in a political landscape, and then to see that it was the opposite is really disturbing."

Ruhl also visited Oberammergau while working on the play. Although most people she met maintained the "official" narrative of the play during their discussions with her, one evening Ruhl met a group of younger people who were a bit more "irreverent." It was from these Oberammergauers that she learned "some of the stories and lore about jokes that were played in the Passion. Shoving wooden testicles between the legs of old Fritz.... The reality, the need for humor that's really part of the medieval Passion plays." Carnivalesque elements like these appear throughout Ruhl's play.

Given that, in some respect, Oberammergau serves as a centerpiece for this three-act cycle—as a kind of hinge on which the play turns—I asked Ruhl more specifically about Oberammergau's Passion Play.

> *After writing all three acts did you have a different perspective on the Oberammergau play? After situating it as part of this larger Passion Play lineage, did you think about it differently?*
>
> I don't know that I thought differently about Oberammergau after writing the third act. Certainly I thought differently about the whole play once it had three parts, as opposed to being three separate plays, which was sort of the original notion; that it was more of a cycle.... Having three parts puts Oberammergau in a continuum or a context as opposed to it being wholly special. That it's in a continuum of many cultures having complicated relationships with the politics of scapegoating, starting from the Middle Ages.... We tend to always think the Holocaust narratives have a kind of exceptionalism rather than placing them in a history of pogroms and anti-Semitism and extermination and genocide. I don't really know where I really stand on that because, obviously, in a way it *was* exceptional, and in a way I feel like cultural history had to begin again at zero after the Holocaust. Everything had to start over again. And in a way that felt important to me in terms of writing another act, was not stopping there, saying culture had to reinvent itself after the Holocaust.

Ruhl wrote Part Three of *Passion Play* several years after writing Parts One and Two. As she explains in her "Playwright's Note," Arena Stage commissioned her "to write a play about America, and I figured there's nothing more American than the nexus of religion, politics, and the theater."[2]

Accordingly, Part Three represents a direct, and quite personal, response to an immediate political moment. As Ruhl explains:

> It took me a long time to write it. And it's funny, having an interview on Election Day, [since] the third part is very much about American politics.... I was so angry during the years of the Bush presidency. I mean, I was just angry all the time, about politics anyway. And about how religious feeling was being made a travesty of in this country.
>
> *Yes. And what I like about your play and several other plays that have been written in response to that period is that they don't reject the need for a conversation about religion, but instead show the need for a more sophisticated conversation, because religion and devotion are critical for so many people. And devotion, in general, is a human response.*
>
> And I think it's the lifeblood of the theatre. So to demand

a completely secular theatre is cutting off your nose to spite your face.

Ruhl's choice in Part Three to focus on the Black Hills Passion also allowed her to allude to anxieties about religious performances—especially performances produced in a commercial context—that are, in some ways, unique to U.S. culture; as Ruhl remarked during our conversation, "Yes, we're such pilgrims."

Consequently, I asked her if it was particularly challenging to write a play about religion or if, as she wrote, she worried that it might be difficult to get such a play produced.

> I didn't really think about that as I was writing it. I think because my way in was, in a way, through the theatre. I mean, the original impulse was writing a play about a guy who always has to play Pontius Pilate who wants to play the role of Jesus. So in a way the original idea was about the exigencies of casting, of being miscast. Whether your identity is determined or whether there's some flexibility.
>
> ...
>
> So I think religion and devotion are all there, but I think it's something that's really hard to write about consciously, like you can't look at it directly, you have to kind of look at it obliquely. And, I think, because I had the other way in, it was useful. I mean, I was raised Catholic; all the mythologies are there, wading around in my unconscious. But I don't know that I could sit down and write about this in a direct way.

Passion Play has received several major stagings. An early version of the play was produced in workshop in London in 2002. The play then received its world premiere at Arena Stage in Washington, D.C., in 2005, directed by Molly Smith. It was subsequently produced at the Goodman Theatre in Chicago (2007), at Yale Repertory Theatre in New Haven (2008), and by the Epic Theatre Ensemble at the Irondale Center in Brooklyn (2010). Those three productions, as well as the London workshop, were all directed by Mark Wing-Davey.

I attended the 2010 Brooklyn production and one of the features of *Passion Play* that I especially appreciated was the way in which the play itself—and Wing-Davey's choices—borrowed from the medieval religious performance tradition.

> *I was interested in the structure of your play and particularly how it uses so many medieval theatre production techniques,*

such as the lack of historical realism. I think you say in your introduction to the [published] play how "history bleeds through." I really felt that happen, especially in how the anachronisms work so well. I was particularly impressed by the Brooklyn production's use of space, the doubling, and the community theatre model.

Oh, I loved it too. I have to say, I wish it ran longer; I wish they'd bring it back. Funnily enough, I was just talking to Mark Wing-Davey because I felt like, well, I feel frustrated by the lack of ability in the American theatre to just do experiments or have a process that doesn't have an end product. We're just so mired in development, so one would think there's actually support for experiments but actually development is about streamlining products. So I was saying to Mark, couldn't we just do some experiments, have a lab where we try stuff. And so I got together with Mark and Keith Reddin, who was also involved in the [*Passion Play*] production. We were saying, "Well, how would we go about this?" And we were talking about actors who we'd invite to join. And then it seemed unfair to include some folks from *Passion Play* and not others. So I said, how about anyone who's been involved with *Passion Play* with [Wing-Davey] directing can join the company.... So we're going to issue an invitation to anyone who's been involved with *Passion Play* to do some kind of experiment. Because I also feel like Mark, in the course of that process, which was long, sort of evolved this aesthetic with a kind of loose ensemble. And then it just ends. Which is what happens, but I also feel like we had the luxury of continuing in a way that you don't usually have in the American theatre.

I just kept thinking as I was watching [the play], that the production didn't just validate the staying power of the Passion Play as a genre that still has something to say, but it also validated the medieval production model and how that [model] has so much value if, as you said, you can find venues and opportunities for it.

What it really is, is community theatre, which is a dirty word in professional theatre circles.

That's so true. And it often becomes about how community theatre has no aesthetic or artistic merit. And that's unfortunate, because aren't we always performing for communities?

Well, we aren't; that's the problem. Or you get regional

theatre, which I think started with a kind of regional model and then now has New Yorkers performing for people who don't know them. You don't have that sense of connection between the community and the art, so you have this product that's imported.... [However] I think one unique thing about the community theatre of the medieval theatre is that it's really one story, one mythos that keeps getting rearticulated. And I think that's different than inventing a new story with a new community.

Given the many different productions of Passion Play, I asked Ruhl about challenges in marketing the show. She began by describing how Arena put a big picture of Jesus on the advertising materials.

And I was like—Really?! It's not really a play about Jesus. Just take it down a notch. It's really about the theatre and religion, but it isn't a play about Jesus himself.

Yes, it's not actually a Passion Play.

It's not actually a Passion Play. And we struggled with that a lot, with how to present the play, market the play, to audiences where even the words "Passion Play" are anathema to people. The Goodman had some protests from Jewish audience members who heard they were doing a Passion Play without hearing what it was about.

I'm interested in [whether you noticed] differences in audience responses.

I feel like the Chicago audiences were a little mystified. The D.C. audiences got it. The Brooklyn audiences got it. The London audience got it. They are doing a production in Boston right now.... They said they are really trying to do a kind of community model. It's very young people and students doing it, in roving locations. That's one thing—I think the youngness of the audience in Brooklyn was great for me, because that's who I'm actually writing for and I don't see them at my work in a lot of places.

...

But I don't know culturally if the way each theatre company presented it had an effect on the audience getting it or if it was the cultural landscape. I mean, in D.C. they get politics so readily, so they really latched onto the politics. New Haven is a more intellectual audience, so they probably latched on that way. Chicago is a very Catholic audience. They were just mystified by the fish; that's all they would talk about, "What do the fish mean?"

For me, the space in which it was performed made such a difference. Yes, there are plays where if it's performed in the round or a proscenium it impacts it significantly. But [in Brooklyn], it made a difference going into a space that's a converted church, where it feels like it's a bunch of people saying, "Let's put on a play." And from the moment [Passion Play] starts it's basically, "We're putting on a play." It just gave you a playfulness, an energy, to get behind the play, that I'm not sure I would have had sitting, say, in the Goodman's space.

Yes, there was a wonderful relationship I think between the actors and the audience in Brooklyn. And in some way the subject-object thing was really broken down by the space itself. It was quite wonderful. I'd love to work at that space again.

That actor-audience relationship was very much broken down during the Brooklyn production's first preview performance when a fire alarm went off, causing the audience and actors (many in Biblical costumes) to evacuate into the chilly night air. Ruhl recounts this experience in her Appendix to the published play text:

> After some milling around on the steps of the church, when it was clear we would all be outside for a while, the actors decided to go on with the play. First, Mary 2 sang a song about a tollbooth from the middle of Part Three, where we'd stopped. I thought perhaps we'd just have the song as an interlude; but slowly the audience quieted and gathered round, and somehow one after another, the actors came up and performed their scenes with no blocking, no props, no nothing, in silent agreement.... I kept thinking one of the actors would stop, but in silent agreement, they simply kept doing the play.[3]

She and I talked a bit more about that interrupted performance.

It was like nothing I'd ever experienced. I mean, we all filed out and waited, and then at some point someone just started doing the play. And then everyone improvised and joined in. And fire trucks were coming. And Jesus is out in Brooklyn in his loincloth. It really is why I do the thing—that all of these people have that willing suspension of disbelief.

Near the end of our conversation, I remarked that *Passion Play* feels like a play that could continue, with more parts added. Although to an extent she agreed, Ruhl said she really thinks she's finally finished writing the play. However, she remains interested in engaging issues of spirituality and devotion. Inspired by a story she heard recently about a reincarnated lama in the West, she said, "My next thing is that I'm going to write about reincarnation.... I think. I think. We'll see what happens with it." And, indeed, in the fall of 2014 Lincoln Center staged the world premiere of Ruhl's *The Oldest Boy*, which explores this theme.

We concluded our conversation by returning to the issue of dramatizing religion and the inherent challenges it can present.

> It is difficult to put a concrete body on these things that are very ethereal.... Because, in a way, spirituality isn't really embodied. You can have paintings, you can have literature, you can have music that acts as a kind of sublime. But theatre is not sublime. It's bodies and time; it's a big mess; it's hard to put on; it's embarrassing; it's terribly concrete.
>
> *And I think that's one of the conflicts within Christianity. It's a story about a body so it seems that it would be a natural fit with theatre. It should work, but then it doesn't really work and is problematic.*
>
> But I think it really does work for Catholics, because the Catholic service has that kind of one-to-one relationship between the concrete and the metaphor.... And [Catholics] are comfortable with that ritual, that sense of meaning, and that we are supposed to be able to see the thing unfold. Catholics aren't as troubled by it. It's this whole pilgrim culture.

Notes

1. Sarah Ruhl, "Playwright's Note," *Passion Play* (New York: Theatre Communications Group, 2010), xi–xii.
2. *Ibid.*, xi.
3. Sarah Ruhl, "Appendix: Some Notes on Set and Costumes," *Passion Play* (New York: Theatre Communications Group, 2010), 240.

Conclusion
Forty-Second in the Twenty-First
OBERAMMERGAU 2020

As this book was going to press, halfway through the period between performances, the village of Oberammergau announced the schedule and artistic lineup for 2020. The announcement carried with it implications for continuity and also some startling (or perhaps not so startling) changes. Once again the *Passionspiele* will be performed May through October. The announcement was mostly one of continuity: "Christian Stückl has been elected by the City Council of Oberammergau to direct the Passion Play of Oberammergau. Stefan Hageneier will be again responsible for the costumes and the stage design. Markus Zwink will be again the musical director of the passion play. The young Oberammergau director Abdullah Kenan Karaca has been elected as deputy director."[1] This announcement means that Stückl will have overseen the play for the majority of his life and the majority of the lives of the majority of villagers. He has directed the play in 1990, 2000 and 2010, first taking the reins when he was twenty-six years old, twenty-eight when the play was performed. He will be fifty-eight in 2020.

Also of note was the selection of Abdullah Kenan Karaca as the deputy director, a position that had been previously held by adaptor Otto Huber. Karaca, a Muslim born of Turkish decent in Oberammergau, first performed in the 2000 production when he was eleven.[2] He is now a professional director in Munich, having studied directing in Hamburg and assisted Stückl at the Salzburg Festival.[3] Oberammergau mayor Arno Nunn remarked on how unremarkable Karaca's selection is received in Oberammergau: "Karaca is a Oberammergauer like everyone else."[4] The *Süddeutsche Zeitung*, which profiled Karaca in 2015 in an article entitled "Who Should Lead the Passion Play?" anticipating he would be the deputy director in 2020, sees a potential future director of the Passionspiele in him:

Und so wird es wahrscheinlich so sein, dass zum ersten Mal ein türkischer Muslim stellvertretender Spielleiter bei den Passionsspielen in Oberammergau wird. Mit vielleicht einer großen Zukunft dort: Stückl ist 54, Karaca 26. Und ein Theaterprofi.

[And so it will probably be that for the first time a Turkish Muslim will be the Deputy Director of the Passion Play in Oberammergau. With perhaps a big future there. Stückl is 54, Karaca 26. And a theatre professional.][5]

The implication being that Karaca is perhaps being groomed as the next director of the festival, the first director of the millennial generation in Oberammergau and the first non–Catholic (not to mention non–Christian) to perhaps oversee the production. Stückl took over the direction of the play in his mid-twenties when he was a professional director working out of Munich. It is possible that Karaca will be selected to direct the production for 2030 and beyond (there will be another production in 2034, due to the quadricentennial of the vow, and 2040). A Muslim person of Turkish descent overseeing the most famous Christian play in the world would certainly mark a significant change and reinforce many of the observations and suppositions in this volume about the direction the Passion Play took in 2010 and the direction it seems to be taking for the future.

And yet, in the midst of the announcement of this potential radical transformation, Oberammergau remains in many ways the same. The announcement of the leadership team for 2020 also demonstrated the continuity of leadership (Stückl, Hageneier and Zwink are returning) and of process: "By Ash Wednesday 2019, all participants in the play let their hair grow—and men also their beards—in accordance with a long tradition, the 'Beard and Hair Edict.'"[6] As it always has, the process of rehearsing and performing the Passion Play begins with a ceremony on Ash Wednesday (the beginning of Lent), and the men of the village who intend to perform allowing beards and hair to grow for the next fifteen months. Some parts of tradition are more sacrosanct than others, and despite the changes in the script and the promise of a new generation of leadership, the process continues as it always has: "In spring 2019, the names of the actors will be announced. In addition to the major characters of Jesus, Mary, Peter, Judas, Pontius Pilate and Caiaphas, there are 120 larger and smaller speaking parts. Altogether, more than 2.000 Oberammergau villagers will participate in the 2020 Passion Play…. Rehearsals for the 42nd Passion Play will start in autumn 2019. The first performance of the 2020 Passion Play will be in May." So even in the face of the changes noted above, the continuity of Oberammergau remains. The Passion will be performed as it always has been and the rituals will be observed.

It is important to note, however, that the rituals themselves have more to do with theatrical production and the community than with Catholicism, Christianity or religion in general. The men grow long hair and beards, and the only religious marker is that they begin to do so on Ash Wednesday.

178   Conclusion

Auditions and casting will be in the Spring of the year before the performance, allowing for over a year of rehearsals. The play follows the calendar that it has for many of the past decades, allowing the village to maximize tourist season.

The fact that the rituals that now dominate Oberammergau are communal and theatrical rather than religious in nature may be a blessing in disguise, as the religious aspect of the drama is confronted by challenging times both in Germany and or the potential American audience. As noted in chapter nine, many American Passion Plays, almost all inspired by Oberammergau in one way or another, have folded. Others have reduced the size and scope of performances. The Union City Passion Play, which at its height offered eighteen shows to audiences of upwards of a thousand at each performance now presents only five shows with an aging audience of less than six hundred. The Great Passion Play in Arkansas nearly closed in 2012 and is just barely able to remain open as of this writing. Audiences are dwindling and the average age of the audience is increasing, which implies further challenges as a greying audience is not replaced by the next generation of Passion Play-goers. Changing demographics and a slow global economic recovery will challenge Oberammergau 2020 and beyond.

At home, Germany is losing both its Catholic identity and its Catholic population. "According to its own statistics, the Catholic Church in Germany lost a greater number of faithful in 2014 than in any previous year in its recent history: 218,000 people, representing 39,000 more defections than the previous year."[7] Those numbers are continuing and there will be even fewer Catholics in Germany in 2020 and beyond. The play itself is seen as historically problematic and the younger generation has demonstrated an unwillingness to let anti–Semitism slide past in the name of tradition. In addition, the world-wide scandal plaguing the Church has seen a local instance in Oberammergau. As Sonja E. Spear cannily concludes, "the Oberammergau Passion Play has never recovered its pre-war luster; most recently, the pedophile-priest scandal has rocked the village."[8] Susan Spano further observed that the audience at Oberammergau in 2010 was "almost exclusively older than 50 and part of tour groups."[9] The problems plaguing annual Passion Plays in the United States have also begun to affect Oberammergau as well.

Lastly, as implied in Spano's observation, above, the international audiences are also older and perhaps less interested in religious drama. As noted in chapter nine, the United States is the core audience for Oberammergau now, and Christianity is in decline there as well.

A May 2015 Pew Research poll entitled "America's Changing Religious Landscape" indicated that Christianity in general, including Catholicism specifically, is in decline.[10] There are more "religiously unaffiliated" Americans (22.8 percent, the so-called "nones" for "none of the above" on surveys of religious affiliation) than Catholics (20.8 percent) and mainline Protestants (14.7 percent). There were fifty-one million adult Catholics in the United States in 2014, three million fewer than in 2007. Thirteen percent of Americans were raised Catholic but are no longer Catholic, compared with just 2 percent of Americans who are converts to Catholicism. That means for every convert to Catholicism, six Catholics leave the Church. The shrinking church is not just generational, reflecting the rise of the millennials, but also occurring at all levels: "While the drop in Christian affiliation is particularly pronounced among young adults, it is occurring among Americans of all ages."[11]

So the rituals of community and theatrical production become more importance as the "traditions" of Oberammergau grow less religious and more communal and performative in nature. The audience Oberammergau must draw in the future will be perhaps less interested in religion and more interested in communal theatre creation and identity. As noted in previous chapters, the village itself is also undergoing multiethnic and multireligious transformations, with Muslims performing in the play for the first time in 2000, and only fifteen years later a Muslim being announced as deputy director.[12] Oberammergau is also growing much more secular. As noted in chapter two, the villagers now present the play as part of Oberammergau identity, separate from a Catholic, or even Christian, identity, and the two actors playing Christ do not identify the role as an act of faith. This would seem to indicate that Oberammergau 2020 will be even more secular and even less Catholic, or at least as much as one can remove faith and religion from a play about the life, death and resurrection of Jesus Christ. The play and the players reflect the audiences as well—less religious, more secular, more interested in inclusivity, diversity and community than faith.

Otto Huber was asked in 2010 by a reporter for the BBC if Jesus could be played by one of the village's residents of Turkish descent. "Actually I feel very much like somebody who lives in a global world," he responded. "In Oberammergau, spectators come from everywhere. So why not in the casting?"[13] Such a statement would have been unthinkable even just a quarter century ago, now Abdullah Kenan Karaca is the deputy director and the possibility is held out that any of the roles could go to any of the residents that meet the requirements. Oberammergau has become far less Teutonic and far more global.

In concluding this study of the 2010 Oberammergau Passion Play and looking forward to the 2020 production, we might note, as the *Los Angeles Times* review of the 2010 production observed, "After 376 years, the Oberammergau Passion play is still a work in progress."[14] One suspects that it will still be a work in progress after 386 and even 396 years, because theatre is a living art that even when reflecting the past is still primarily about the present. Gordon R. Mork reminds us that it took more than half a century after the defeat of Hitler "for the play to be purged of its most egregious anti-Jewish elements."[15] As a work in progress, Mork asserts the continuing job of the village, of Stückl and Huber and those who succeed them, is to address and if necessary remove the elements that are problematic "while preserving that which deserves to be preserved and presenting it faithfully to the hundreds of thousands" who travel to Oberammergau every time the play is performed.[16]

This last statement is a loaded one. There are and can be genuine disagreements about what "deserves" to be preserved, as has been witnessed by the lengthy debate over the last half century on the ongoing anti–Semitic elements. There is also a good deal of weigh behind the word "faithfully," which implies both fidelity to a text and a tradition whilst also engaging the idea that presenting the Passion Play is still an act of faith. Mork is also correct in reminding us of the audience itself, the "hundreds of thousands" who attend.

Theatre is the only art named after not what the artist does, but what the people who encounter the art do. "Theatre" comes from the Greek for "the seeing place," meaning the very name of the art is derived from the act of watching, not the act of performing. A dancer dancing alone still dances, a musician playing alone still makes music, an actor without an audience is only rehearsing.

In Oberammergau, whilst the initial performances in the seventeenth century may have been only a single instance in a field outside of town for a small crowd, by the twentieth century the attendance of those hundreds of thousands is vital to the experience, not to mention the identity and the economic well-being of the village. The Oberammergau Passion Play will continue to evolve. The 2020 play will be different, while also facing its own challenges and concerns and pressure from outside groups. But every decade is another opportunity for the small alpine village to further (re)define itself in terms of its past, present and future.

NOTES

1. http://www.passionsspiele-oberammergau.de/en Posted November 13, 2015. Accessed November 22, 2015.

2. Hermann Weiss, "Vom Hauptschüler zum Shootingstar des Theaters" *Die Welt* (June 2, 2013) http://www.welt.de/regionales/muenchen/article116698676/Vom-Hauptschueler-zum-Shootingstar-des-Theaters.html. Accessed November 22, 2015.

3. Egbert Tholl, "Wer die Passionsspiele leiten soll." *Süddeutsche Zeitung* (June 12, 2015) http://www.sueddeutsche.de/bayern/profil-abdullah-karaca-1.2517950. Accessed November 22, 2015.

4. Tholl.

5. Tholl (translation mine).

6. http://www.passionsspiele-oberammergau.de/en Posted November 13, 2015. Accessed November 22, 2015.

7. Inés San Martin, "Pope Francis Tackles the 'Erosion' of Catholicism in Germany." *Crux* (November 20, 2015) https://cruxnow.com/church/2015/11/20/pope-francis-takes-on-the-erosion-of-catholicism-in-germany/. Accessed November 22, 2015.

8. Sonja E. Spear, "Claiming the Passion: American Fantasies of the Oberammergau Passion Play, 1923–1947." *Church History* 80.4 (December 2011): 861.

9. Susan Spano, "In the Alps, a saving grace." *Los Angeles Times* (June 6, 2010): L4.

10. All statistics taken from Pew Research Center, *America's Changing Religious Landscape* (May 12, 2015) http://www.pewforum.org/2015/05/12/americas-changing-religious-landscape/. Accessed November 22, 2015.

11. Pew Research Center, *America's Changing Religious Landscape*.

12. Given the overarching concern with Judaism in this volume and surrounding the Oberammergau Passion Play one might argue that the village will have truly changed when a Jewish person is in leadership or onstage. Demographics make this challenging, however, unless the village changes the rules about who may participate.

13. Oana Lungescu, "Bavarian Passion plays to global crowds." BBC News Europe. 31 May 2010. www.bbc.co.uk/news/10198502. Accessed April 25, 2012.

14. Lewis Segal, "A village's long Passion matures." *Los Angeles Times* (August 15, 2010): E7.

15. Gordon R. Mork, "'Wicked Jews' and 'Suffering Christians' in the Oberammergau Passion Play." *Representations of Jews through the Ages*. Eds. Leonard Jay Greenspoon and Bryan F. LeBeau (Omaha: Creighton University Press, 1996) 164.

16. Mork, "'Wicked Jews'" 164.

Works Cited

Abbott, S.J., Walter M. ed. *The Documents of Vatican II*. New York: Guild Press, 1966.
Altman, Rick. "From Lecturer's Prop to Industrial Product: The Early History of Travel Films." *Virtual Voyages: Cinema and Travel*. Ed. Jeffrey Ruoff. Durham: Duke University Press, 2006. 61–78.
———. *Silent Film Sound*. New York: Columbia University Press, 2004.
"Amid the Everlasting Hills." *Los Angeles Times*. May 31, 1920: n.p.
Anti-Defamation League. "American Jewish Groups: We Have Not Approved 2010 Production of Oberammergau Passion Play." February 18, 2010. http://www.adl.org/press-center/press-releases/interfaith/american-jewish-groups-we.html#.Vl1g9HarSM8. Accessed June 13, 2013.
———. "Despite Changes, Oberammergau Continues to Transmit Negative Stereotypes of Jews." May 10, 2010. http://www.adl.org/press-center/press-releases/interfaith/despite-changes-oberammergau.html#.Vl1g8HarSM8. Accessed June 13, 2013.
———. "The Oberammergau Passion Play" n.d. http://archive.adl.org/nr/exeres/164d9601-f63f-4eea-9cc1-27a4cf18348d,db7611a2-02cd-43af-8147-649e26813571,frameless.html. Accessed June 13, 2013.
Aronson-Lehavi, Sharon. "Transformations of Religious Performativity: Sacrificial Figures in Modern Experimental Theatre," *Performance and Spirituality* 3:1 (2012): 57–70.
Auslander, Philip. "'Just be your self': Logocentrism and Difference in Performance Theory," in *Acting (Re)Considered: Theories and Practices*. Ed. Phillip B. Zarrilli. New York: Routledge, 1995.
Baigell, Mathew. "Barnett Newman's Stripe Paintings and Kabbalah: A Jewish Take." *American Art* 8:2 (1994): 32–43.
Bartels, G. "Oberammergau: Der Deal mit Gott." *Der Tagesspiegel*. March 7, 2010. http://www.tagesspiegel.de/kultur/buehne-alt/oberammergau-der-deal-mit-gott/1714438.html. Accessed July 19, 2012.
Bergmann, Rolf. *Katalog der deutschsprachigen geistlichen Spiele und Marienklagen des Mittelalters*. Munich: Beck, 1986.
Bishops' Committee for Ecumenical and Interreligious Affairs, United States Conference of Catholic Bishops. *Criteria for the Evaluation of Dramatizations of the Passion*, 1–14. Washington, D.C.: United States Conference of Catholic Bishops, 1988. http://www.usccb.org/beliefs-and-teachings/ecumenical-and-interreligious/jewish/upload/Criteria-for-the-Evaluation-of-Dramatizations-of-the-Passion-1988.pdf.
Brandt, George W. and Wiebe Hogendoorn, eds. *German and Dutch Theatre, 1600–1848*. Cambridge: Cambridge University Press, 1993.

Bronner, Simon J., ed. *Encyclopedia of American Folklife*. New York: Routledge, 2006.
Bruder, Kurt A. "Monastic Blessings: Deconstructing and Reconstructing the Self," *Symbolic Interaction* 21.1 (1998): 87–116.
Buckland, A. W. "Ober Ammergau and Its People, in Connection with the Passion Play and Miracle Plays in General" ("A Paper Read Before the Bath Literary and Philosophical Association, January 12, 1872"). London: Simpkin, Marshall and Co, 1872.
Burton, Isabel. *The Passion-Play at Ober-Ammergau*. London: Hutchinson, 1900.
Butler, Judith. *Excitable Speech. A Politics of the Performative*. New York: Routledge, 1997.
_____. *Gender Trouble*. New York: Routledge, 1990.
Carlson, Marvin. *Theatre Is More Beautiful than War: German Stage Directing in the Late Twentieth Century*. Iowa City: University of Iowa Press, 2009.
Chansky, Dorothy. "North American Passion Plays: 'The Greatest Story Ever Told' in the New Millennium." *TDR: The Drama Review* 50.4 (T192) (Winter 2006): 120–141.
Chaudhuri, Una. "For Posterior's Sake" in *Suzan-Lori Parks in Person: Interviews and Commentaries*, edited by Philip C. Kolin and Harvey Young. London: Routledge, 2014. 55–57.
Chesshyre, Tom. "Oberammergau Passion Play: The Day I Met the 2010 Jesus and His Bearded Bavarian Twin." *Mail Online*. October 5, 2009. http://www.dailymail.co.uk/travel/article-1218098/Oberammergau-Passion-Play-The-day-I-met-2010-Jesus-bearded-Bavarian-twin.html. Accessed July 6, 2012.
Cohen, Jeremy. *Christ Killers: The Jews and the Passion from the Bible to the Big Screen*. Oxford: Oxford University Press, 2007.
Community of Oberammergau and J.A. Daisenberger. *The Passion Play in Oberammergau*. München: Jos. C. Huber, 1922.
Cooks Excursionist and Tourist Advertiser, 1880–1920. Thomas Cook and Co.
Council of Centers on Jewish-Christian Relations. *Ad Hoc Committee Report on the 2010 Oberammergau Passion Play Script*. May 14, 2010. http://www.ccjr.us/images/stories/CCJR_Oberammergau_Report_2010May14.pdf. Accessed March 23, 2014.
Counsell, Michael. *Every Pilgrim's Guide to Oberammergau and Its Passion Play*. Rev. ed. Norwich: Canterbury Press, 2008.
Cramer, Thomas. *Geschichte der deutschen Literatur im späten Mittelalter*. München: dtv, 1990.
Crossan, John Dominic. *Who Killed Jesus? Exploring the Roots of Anti-Semitism in the Gospel Story of the Birth of Jesus*. San Francisco: Harper, 1995.
Daisenberger, Joseph Alois. *Die Früchte der Passionsbetrachtung, vorgestellt in fünf Predigten, welche zu Oberammergau in der heiligen Fastenzeit des Passionsjahres gehalten wurden von Joseph Alois Daisenberger: Ein Gedenkbüchlein für die Darsteller und Besucher des Ammergauer Passionsspieles*. Regensburg: Manz, 1872.
"Das war die Passion." *Bayerischer Rundfunk*. November 9, 2011. http://www.br.de/themen/bayern/inhalt/kult-und-brauch/passionsspiele-2010-bilanz100.html. Accessed June 12, 2012.
de Grazia, Margreta. "Anachronism" in *Cultural Reformations: Medieval and Renaissance in Literary History*, edited by Brian Cummings and James Simpson, 13–32. Oxford, New York: Oxford University Press, 2010.
Devrient, Eduard. *Das Passionsschauspiel in Oberammergau und seine Bedeutung für die neue Zeit*. Leipzig: J.J. Weber, 1851.
Diamond, Elin. "Mimesis, Mimicry, and the 'True-Real.'" *Modern Drama* 32.1 (1989): 58–72.

Diemer, Hermine. *Oberammergau and Its Passion Play*, Munich: Card Aug. Seyfried and Co, 1900.
Dinshaw, Carolyn. "Temporalities" in *Middle English*, edited by Paul Strohm, 107–123. Oxford, New York: Oxford University Press, 2007.
Dixon, Jr., John W. *Art and the Theological Imagination*. New York: Seabury Press, 1978.
Dukore, Bernard F. *Dramatic Theory and Criticism: Greeks to Grotowski*. Boston: Heinle, 1974.ww
Eck, Diana L. *Darshan*. New York: Columbia University Press, 1998.
Ehrstine, Glenn. "Das figurierte Gedächtnis: *Figura*, Memoria und die Simultanbühne des deutschen Mittelalters" in *Text und Kultur: mittelalterliche Kultur 1150–1450*, edited by Ursula Peters, 414–437. Stuttgart, et al.: Metzler, 2001.
Ellem, Elizabeth. "Pomfret, Connecticut, Earns Place on Map as America's Oberammergau." *The Milwaukee Sentinel Magazine* (December 24, 1922): 6.
Emigh, John. *Masked Performance: The Play of Self and Other in Ritual and Theatre*. Philadelphia: University of Pennsylvania Press, 1996.
Eming, Jutta. "Simultaneität und Verdoppelung. Motivationsstrukturen im geistlichen Spiel" in *Transformationen des Religiösen. Performativität und Textualität im geistlichen Spiel*, edited by Ingrid Kasten and Erika Fischer-Lichte, 46–62. Berlin: De Gruyter, 2007.
Faggen, Robert A. "'But is it art?' A Prelude to Criticism of Mel Gibson's *The Passion of the Christ*" in *After The Passion Is Gone: American Religious Consequences*, edited by J. Shawn Landres and Michael Berenbaum. Lanham, MD: AltaMira, 2004. 115–124.
Fanning, Win. "McCloy, Robertson Among Dignitaries Viewing Oberammergau Premiere." *Stars and Stripes* (May 19, 1950). http://www.stripes.com/news/mccloy-robertson-among-dignitaries-viewing-oberammergau-premiere-1.25593. Accessed June 10, 2015.
Freise, Dorothea. *Geistliche Spiele in der Stadt des ausgehenden Mittelalters*. Göttingen: Vandenhoeck & Ruprecht, 2002.
Friedman, Saul. *The Oberammergau Passion Play: A Lance Against Civilization*. Carbondale: Southern Illinois University Press, 1984.
Garber, Zev, ed. *The Jewish Jesus: Revelation, Reflection, Reclamation*. Indianapolis: Purdue Press, 2011.
Gibson, Gail McMurray. *The Theatre of Devotion: East Anglian Drama and Society in the Late Middle Ages*. Chicago: University of Chicago Press, 1989.
Gideon, Henry. "The Music of the Passion Play at Oberammergau," *The Forum* 44, no. 6 (1910).
Gilbert, Gary. "Antisemitism without Erasure: Sacred Texts and Their Contemporary Interpretations" in *After The Passion Is Gone: American Religious Consequences*, edited by J. Shawn Landres and Michael Berenbaum. Lanham, MD: AltaMira, 2004. 125–136.
Goldman, A.J. "New Kind of Passion in an 'Alpine Jerusalem.'" Forward.com. Posted May 26, 2010. http://www.forward.com/articles/128345. Accessed December 12, 2010.
Goodburn, Raymond. *Oberammergau 2010: The Village and Its Passion Play*. Suffolk: Pilgrim Book Services, 2010.
Goodman, Susan Tumarkin, *Chagall: Love, War, and Exile*. New York: The Jewish Museum: 2013.
Haberman, David L. *Acting as a Way of Salvation: A Study of Râgânugâ Bhakti Sâdhana*. Oxford: Oxford University Press, 1988.

Hartmann, August, ed. *Das Oberammergauer Passionsspiel in seiner ältesten Gestalt.* Leipzig: Breitkopf & Härtel, 1880.

Hayman, Marina. "Christ in the Works of Two Jewish Artists: When Art in Interreligious Dialogue." *Studies in Jewish Christians Relations* 4 (2009): 1–14.

Heimburger, Don. "Behind the Passion: Backstage at Oberammergau's Forty-First Passion Play." *German Life* (February/March 2010): 20–23.

Hess, Thomas B. *Barnett Newman.* New York: The Museum of Modern Art, 1971.

Herbert, James D. *Our Distance from God: Studies in the Divine and Mundane in Western Art and Music.* Berkeley: University of California Press, 2008.

Holm, Nils G. "Sundén's Role Theory and Glossolalia." *Journal for the Scientific Study of Religion* 26.3 (1987): 383–389.

"'The Holy Night' Solemnly Played by New England Village." *The Spokesman-Review* (January 18, 1914): 9.

Howitt, Anna Mary. *An Art-Student in Munich.* London, 1853, republished London: T. de la Rue, 1879.

Huber, Otto. "Welcome to Oberammergau." *Oberammergau 2010: The Village and Its Passion Play* by Raymond Goodburn. Woodbridge: Pilgrim Book Services, 2010. 4–5.

Iser, Wolfgang. "The Reading Process: A Phenomenological Approach." *New Literary Theory* 3.2 (1972): 279–299.

Jackson, John P. [author, with photographs from Joseph Albert]. *Album of the Passion-Play at Ober-Ammergau.* Munich: Joseph Albert, 1873.

Jauss, Hans Robert. "Literary History as a Challenge to Literary Theory." *New Literary History* 2.1 (1970): 7–37.

Jeansonne, Glen. *Gerald L.K. Smith: Minister of Hate.* New Haven: Yale University Press, 1988.

Kartschoke, Erika. "Eine feine liebliche gottselige Comodie: Ehelehre in Tobias-Dramen des 16. Jahrhunderts" in *Eheglück und Liebesjoch: Bilder von Liebe, Ehe und Familie in der Literatur des 15. und 16. Jahrhunderts*, edited by Maria E. Müller, 79–103. Weinheim et al.: Beltz, 1988.

Kaufmann, Lissy. "Passionsspiele: Strafe für die Apostel." *Der Tagesspiegel.* September 17, 2010. http://www.tagesspiegel.de/weltspiegel/passionsspiele-strafe-fuer-die-apostel/1936334.html. Accessed July 20, 2012.

Kennedy, Dennis. *The Spectator and the Spectacle: Audiences in Modernity and Postmodernity.* Cambridge: Cambridge University Press, 2011.

King, Pamela M., and Asunción Salvador-Rabaza, "La Festa d'Elx. The Festival of the Assumption of the Virgin, Elche (Alicante)." *Medieval English Theatre* 8 (1986): 21–50.

Kobialka, Michal. *This Is My Body: Representational Practices in the Early Middle Ages.* Ann Arbor: University of Michigan Press, 2003.

Koch, Elke. "Endzeit als Ereignis. Zur Performativität von Drohung und Verheißung im deutschen Weltgerichtsspiel des späten Mittelalters" in *Drohung und Verheißung. Mikroprozesse in Verhältnissen von Macht und Subjekt*, edited by Evamaria Heisler, Elke Koch and Thomas Scheffer, 237–262. Freiburg et al.: Rombach 2007.

Kovalcik, Timothy M. *Images of America: The Great Passion Play.* Charleston: Arcadia, 2008.

Krauskopf, Joseph. *A Rabbi's Impression of the Oberammergau Passion Play.* Philadelphia: Edwards Stern & Co, 1901; Forgotten Books, 2008.

Kulish, Nicholas. "Church Crisis Shakes German Town Long Faithful to Tradition." *New York Times.* May 15, 2010: A4, A7.

Laws, Page R. "The Power and the Glory." *American Theatre* 17 (November 2000): 34.
_____. "Witness to/for the Persecution: Of Race, Religion, Mel Gibson and Stirred-Up Passions." *Arbeiten aus Anglistik und Amweikanistik* 30. 1/2 (2005): 53–75.
Levin, Hanoch. *The Labor of Life: Selected Plays of Hanoch Levin*. Palo Alto: Stanford University Press, 2003.
Linke, Hansjürgen. "Unstimmige Opposition. 'Geistlich' und 'weltlich' als Ordnungskategorien der mittelalterlichen Dramatik." *Leuvense Bijdragen* no. 90 (2001): 75–126.
Lowry, Jacqulein Vaughn. *Holy City of the Wichitas*. Charleston: Arcadia Publishing, 2009.
Lungescu, Oana. "Bavarian Passion Plays to Global Crowds." BBC News Europe. May 31, 2010. www.bbc.co.uk/news/10198502. Accessed April 25, 2012.
MacColl, Malcom. *The Ober-ammergau Passion Play, with Some Introductory Remarks on the Origin and Development of Miracle Plays*. 7th ed. London: Rivingtons, 1890.
Madden, C. Stuart. "The Oberammergau of California." *Catholic World* 98 (November 1913): 183–191.
Madigan, Kevin. *Medieval Christianity: A New History*. New Haven: Yale University Press, 2015.
Martin, S.J., James. "The Last Station: A Catholic Reflection on *The Passion*" in *Perspectives on* The Passion of the Christ: *Religious Thinkers and Writers Explore the Issues Raised by the Controversial Movie*. New York: Miramax Books, 2004. 95–110.
Mason, David V. *Theatre and Religion on Krishna's Stage: Performing in Vrindavan*. New York: Palgrave, 2009.
Mayakovsky, Vladimir. *The Complete Plays of Vladimir Mayakovsky*. Trans. Guy Daniels. New York: Simon & Schuster, 1971.
McAdams, Dan P. "Personal Narratives and the Life Story" in *Handbook of Personality: Theory and Research*, edited by Lawrence A. Pervin and Oliver P. John. New York: Guilford Press, 1999.
Meier, Johanna. *The Black Hills Passion Play*. Charleston: Arcadia Publishing, 2008.
Meyer, Elisabeth. "Zur Überlieferungsfunktion des Heidelberger Passionsspiels: Von einer Spielvorlage zur erbaulichen Lektüre?" *Leuvense Bijdragen* no. 90 (2001): 145–159.
Molloy, George. "The Passion Play at Ober-Ammergau in the Summer of 1871." London: Burns, Oates and Co, 1872.
Montgomery, Elizabeth Johann. "Oberammergau Passion Play 2010." *Theatre Journal* 63.2 (May 2011): 260–262.
Mork, Gordon R. "Christ's Passion on Stage-The Traditional Melodrama of Deicide." *Journal of Religion and Film* 8.1 (2004): http://www.unomaha.edu/jrf/2004 Symposium/Mork.htm.
_____. "Dramatizing the Passion from Oberammergau to Gibson." *Shofar* 23.3 (2005): 85–92.
_____. "'Wicked Jews' and 'Suffering Christians' in the Oberammergau Passion Play." *Representations of Jews through the Ages*, edited by Leonard Jay Greenspoon and Bryan F. LeBeau. Omaha: Creighton University Press, 1996. 153–170.
Muir, Lynette R. *The Biblical Drama of Medieval Europe*. Cambridge: Cambridge University Press, 1995.
Müller, Jan-Dirk. "Mittelalterliches Theater: Geistliches Spiel" in *Theater im Aufbruch. Das europäische Drama der Frühen Neuzeit*, edited by Roger Lüdecke and Virginia Richter, 19–30. Tübingen: Max Niemeyer 2008.

"Music in the Air of Europe: Tourists Swarm to the Festivals." *Life* 29, no. 3, August 1, 1960.

Nagel, Alexander, and Christopher S. Wood. *Anachronic Renaissance*. New York: Zone Books, 2010.

"Oberammergau's Rebuke to America." *Literary Digest* (January 5, 1924): 34.

O'Bryant, M.C. "Church News: Easter Play Held at the 'Holy City of the Wichita Mountains.'" LDSChurchnews.com. March 26, 2010. http://www.ldschurchnews archive.com/articles/print/59098/Easter-play-held-at-the-Holy-City-of-the-Wichita-Mountains.html. Accessed January 12, 2013.

O'Malley, John W. *What Happened at Vatican II*. Cambridge: Belknap Press, 2008.

Ong, Han. "Suzan-Lori Parks" in *Suzan-Lori Parks in Person: Interviews and Commentaries*, edited by Philip C. Kolin and Harvey Young. London: Routledge, 2014. 37–45.

O'Reilly, P.J. "At Ober-ammerga in 1890, a Reminiscence of the Passion Play." London: Catholic Truth Society, 1890.

An Oxonian. "Impressions of the Ammergau Passion-Play." London: J.T. Hayes, 1870.

"A Pantomime of the Nativity." *The Literary Digest* 47 (December 13, 1913): 1175–6.

The Passion of the Christ. Dir. Mel Gibson. Perf. Jim Caviezel, Monica Belucci. Icon Productions. 2004. Film.

"Passion Play Has Opened in Virginia." *(Hendersonville, NC) Times-News*. July 24, 1982: 11.

Passionsspiele 2010 Oberammergau. Munich: Prestel, 2010.

Passionsspiele 2010 Oberammergau Textbook. Trans. Ingrid Shafer. Oberammergau: Gemeinde Oberammergau, 2010.

Perry, Marvin, and Frederick M. Schweitzer." The Medieval Passion Play Revisited" in *Re-Viewing the Passion: Mel Gibson's Film and Its Critics*, edited by S. Brent Plate. New York: Palgrave, 2004. 1–19.

Petersen, Christoph. "Imaginierte Präsenz. Der Körper Christi und die Theatralität des geistlichen Spiels" in *Das Theater des Mittelalters und der frühen Neuzeit als Ort und Medium sozialer und symbolischer Kommunikation*, edited by Christel Meier, Heinz Meyer and Claudia Spanily, 45–61. Münster: Rhema, 2004.

Pew Research Center, *America's Changing Religious Landscape*. May 12, 2015. http://www.pewforum.org/2015/05/12/americas-changing-religious-landscape/. Accessed November 22, 2015.

Price, Lee. "Bloomington Center for the Performing Arts." *Tour America's History*. January 7, 2013. http://touramericashistory.blogspot.com/2013/01/bloomington-center-for-performing-arts.html. Accessed June 12, 2013.

Prothero, Stephen. "Jesus Nation, Catholic Christ" in *Perspectives on* The Passion of the Christ: *Religious Thinkers and Writers Explore the Issues Raised by the Controversial Movie*. New York: Miramax Books, 2004. 267–282.

Rattey, Julie L. "Behind the Scenes at the Passion Play of Oberammergau." *Catholic Digest*. January 2010. http://www.catholicdigest.com/articles/travel/no_sub_ministry/2010/05-04/behind-the-scenes-at-the-passion-play-of-oberammergau.

Rauchenegger, Benno. *Oberammergau*, Bruckmann's Illustrated Guides vol. 109. Munich: A. Bruckmann, 1900.

Röcke, Werner. "Protestantismus und 'episches Theater': Jörg Wickrams biblisches Drama *Tobias*" in *Vergessene Texte—Verstellte Blicke: Neue Perspektiven der Wickram-Forschung*, edited by Maria E. Müller and Michael Mecklenburg, 75–89. Frankfurt am Main et al.: Peter Lang, 2007.

Rogerson, Margaret, ed. *The York Mystery Plays: Performance in the City*. York: York Medieval Press, 2011.

Romano, Jay. "2 Passion Plays Thrive on a 'Friendly Rivalry.'" *New York Times*. March 5, 1989. http://www.nytimes/1989/03/05nyregion/union-city-journal-2-passion-plays-thrive-on-a-friendly-rivalry.html. Accessed August 20, 2013.
Rosenberg, Douglas. "Self Portraits (As a Jew)," *TDR* 55:3 (2011): 68–71.
Rudin, A. James. "Oberammergau: A Case Study of Passion Plays" in *Pondering the Passion: What's at Stake for Christians and Jews?* edited by Philip A. Cuningham. Lanham, MD: Rowman & Littlefield, 2004. 97–108.
Ruhl, Sarah. *Passion Play*. New York: Theatre Communications Group, 2010.
San Martín, Inés. "Pope Francis Tackles the 'Erosion' of Catholicism in Germany." *Crux*. November 20, 2015. https://cruxnow.com/church/2015/11/20/pope-francis-takes-on-the-erosion-of-catholicism-in-germany/. Accessed November 22, 2015.
Sartre, Jean-Paul. *Existentialism and Human Emotions*. Trans. Bernard Frechtman. New York: Citadel, 1987.
Schechner, Richard. *Between Theater and Anthropology*. Philadelphia: University of Pennsylvania Press, 1985.
_____. *Performance Theory*, 2nd revised ed. New York: Routledge, 2003.
Scheschkewitz, Daniel. "On Being Jesus: Interview with Frederik Mayet." *Deutsche Welle*. April 4, 2010. Accessed July 13, 2012, http://www.dw.de/dw/article/0,,539 1027,00.html.
Schmid, Rainer H. *Raum, Zeit und Publikum des geistlichen Spiels: Aussage und Absicht eines mittelalterlichen Massenmediums*. München: Tuduv Buch, 1975.
Schroeder, Joseph, and Reginald Maxse. *A Guide to Oberammergau and Its Passion Play*. [Munich: Heinrich Korff, 1910] LaVergne, TN: Kessinger, 2010.
Schulze, Ursula. *Geistliche Spiele im Mittelalter und in der Frühen Neuzeit. Von der liturgischen Feier zum Schauspiel. Eine Einführung*. Berlin: Erich Schmidt Verlag, 2012.
Segal, Lewis. "A Village's Long Passion Matures." *Los Angeles Times*. August 15, 2010: E7.
Sellar, Alexander Craig. "The Passion-Play in the Highlands of Bavaria." *Blackwood's Magazine* 107 (1870): 381–96, in 1870.
Shapiro, James. *Oberammergau: The Troubling Story of the World's Most Famous Passion Play*. New York: Vintage, 2000.
Sharkey, Joe. "Jersey: Sometimes a Stage Is as Good as a Pulpit." *New York Times*. June 9, 1996: http://www.nytimes.com/1996/06/09/nyregion/jersey-sometimes-a-stage-is-as-good-as-a-pulpit.html. Accessed 20August 2013.
Shinners, John, ed. *Medieval Popular Culture, 1000–1500: A Reader*. Peterborough, Ontario: Brookview, 2007.
Spano, Susan. "In the Alps, a Saving Grace." *Los Angeles Times*. June 6, 2010: L1, L4.
Spear, Sonja E. "Claiming the Passion: American Fantasies of the Oberammergau Passion Play, 1923–1947." *Church History* 80.4 (December 2011): 832–862.
Sponsler, Claire. *Ritual Imports: Performing Medieval Drama in America*. Ithaca: Cornell University Press, 2004.
Stahl, Neta, ed. *Jesus Among the Jews: Representation and Thought*. New York: Routledge, 2012.
Stanley, Dean. "The Ammergau Mystery, or Sacred Drama of 1860." *Macmillan's Magazine* 2 (October 1860): 463–477.
States, Bert O. *Great Reckonings in Little Rooms: On the Phenomenology of Theatre*. Berkeley: University of California Press, 1987.
Stead, William. *The Passion Play at Ober Ammergau 1900*. Third edition. London: Review of Reviews, 1900.

Stevenson, Jill. "Oberammergau's Passion Play 2010: Performance and Context." *Material Religion* 7.2 (2011) 304–307.

_____. *Sensational Devotion: Evangelical Performance in Twenty-First Century America*. Ann Arbor: University of Michigan Press, 2013.

Tanenbaum, Marc H. "Report on the 1980 Oberammergau Passion Play." August 25, 1977.

Tautphoeus, Jemima van [Baroness]. *Quits: A Novel*. London: Richard Bentley, 1857.

Thimm, Katja. "Bavarian Village Divided over Updates to World-Famous Passion Play." SpiegelOnline. May 15, 2010. http://www.spiegel.de/international/zeitgeist/modernity-vs-tradition-in-oberammergau-bavarian-village-divided-over-updates-to-world-famous-passion-play-a-694970-druck.html. Accessed June 29, 2012.

Tholl, Egbert. "Wer die Passionsspiele leiten soll." *Süddeutsche Zeitung* (June 12, 2015). http://www.sueddeutsche.de/bayern/profil-abdullah-karaca-1.2517950. Accessed November 22, 2015.

Thomas of Celano. *The First Life of St Francis of Assisi*. Trans. Christopher Stace. London: Triangle, 2000.

Trojanow, Ilija. *Oberammergau: Richard F. Burton: A Glance at the Passion Play*. Züruch: Arche Literatur Verlag, 2010.

[Tuckett, Elizabeth]. *Zigzagging Amongst Dolomites*. London: Longmans, Green, Reader & Dyer, 1871.

von Altenbockum, Annette. *Oberammergau: Art, Tradition, and Passion*. Munich: Prestel, 2010.

Waddy, Helena. *Oberammergau in the Nazi Era: The Fate of a Catholic Village in Hitler's Germany*. Oxford: Oxford University Press, 2010.

Weiss, Hermann. "Vom Hauptschüler zum Shootingstar des Theaters." *Die Welt*. June 2, 2013: http://www.welt.de/regionales/muenchen/article116698676/Vom-Hauptschueler-zum-Shootingstar-des-Theaters.html. Accessed November 22, 2015.

Wetmore, Jr., Kevin J. "It's an Oberammergau Thing: An Interview with Suzan-Lori Parks" in *Suzan-Lori Parks: A Casebook*, edited by Kevin J. Wetmore, Jr., and Alycia Smith-Howard. London: Routledge, 2007. 124–140.

Wickham, Glynne. *The Medieval Theatre*. Cambridge: Cambridge University Press, 1987.

Willett, John. *Brecht in Context: Comparative Approaches*. London: Methuen, 1984.

Williams, Louis L. *The American Passion Play: A Study and History*. Bloomington, IL: The American Passion Play, Inc., 1970.

Wilson, Robert. *14 Stations*. Munich: Prestel Publications, 2000.

Wright, Amber Michelle. "Review: The Oberammergau Passion Play 2010." *Ecumenica* 4.1 (2011): 107–108.

About the Contributors

Sharon **Aronson-Lehavi** is a tenured senior lecturer in the Department of Theatre Studies, Faculty of the Arts, Tel Aviv University, and a member of the Israel Young Academy of Sciences. She is the author of *Street Scenes: Late Medieval Acting and Performance* (2011) and *Gender and Feminism in Modern Theatre* (2013; in Hebrew); and coeditor of *Performance Studies in Motion* (2014).

Joshua **Edelman** teaches theatre and performance at Manchester Metropolitan University, having formerly taught at Birkbeck, University of London and the Royal Central School of Speech and Drama. He writes on the intersections between theatre sociology, religious practice, and political struggles in the contemporary West. He is the coeditor of *Performing Religion in Public* (2013), and his articles have appeared in *Performance Research*, *Nordic Theatre Studies* and *Liturgy*.

Glenn **Ehrstine** is an associate professor of German at the University of Iowa. Alongside various essays on Minnesang, Protestant polemics, and carnival plays, he is the author of *Theater, Culture, and Community in Reformation Bern, 1523–1555* (2002) and he has also coedited two essay volumes, including *Power and Violence in Medieval and Early Modern Theater* (2014).

Jutta **Eming** is a professor of medieval German literature at the Institute for German and Netherlandic Philology, Freie Universität, Berlin. Her research interests include romances from the high to the late middle ages, genre theory and gender, emotionality, performativity, and premodern drama. She holds a project in the Freie Universität's special research center Episteme in Motion on "The Marvelous as a Configuration of Knowledge in Medieval Literature."

David **Mason** is an associate professor and chair of theatre at Rhodes College. He is the author of *Theatre and Religion on Krishna's Stage* (2009) and *Brigham Young: Sovereign in America* (2014). He has published articles on the intersection of theatre and religion in *Theatre Research International*, *New Literary History*, the *Journal of Dramatic Theory and Criticism*, and other journals.

Jill **Stevenson** is an associate professor of theatre arts at Marymount Manhattan College. She is the author of *Performance, Cognitive Theory, and Devotional Culture* (2010) and *Sensational Devotion* (2013), and coeditor of the collection *Thresholds* *of Medieval Visual Culture* (2012). She has also published essays and reviews in various journals and edited volumes.

Kevin J. **Wetmore**, Jr., is a professor and chair of theatre arts at Loyola Marymount University where he teaches a variety of topics, including theatre and theology, Catholic theatre, Asian and African theatre, and horror cinema. He is the author, co-author and/or editor of over a dozen books including *Catholic Theatre and Drama* (2010), *Modern Asian Theatre and Performance, 1900–2000* (2014) and *Shakespeare and Youth Culture* (with Jennifer Hulbert and Robert York, 2006).

Index

Adolph, Jörg 24, 25, 53, 54, 55, 57, 63
The American Passion Play 141–142
American Theatre (magazine) 34
Anselm 123
Anti-Defamation League (ADL) 36, 40, 46, 47, 88, 146, 147, 148
anti-Semitism 1, 3, 9, 13, 34, 35, 36, 39, 40, 41, 47, 49, 56, 59, 67, 75, 76, 82, 130, 135, 145, 146, 147, 178
Aristotle 108, 110
Artaud, Antonin 109
Assumption of the Virgin (Elche, Spain) 16
Auschwitz 100

Benedict XVI 33, 40, 48, 148
Bernstein, Philip 39
Biblical Stories 61
Black Hills Passion Play 97, 143, 145, 168, 171
Brecht, Bertolt 19, 58, 63, 94, 108
Burton, Isabella 77, 80

Chagall, Marc 56, 59; *White Crucifixion* 59; *Yellow Crucifixion* 59
Corpus Christi Plays 94, 121, 122
Council of Centers on Jewish-Christian Relations (CCJR) 41, 42, 146
Criteria for the Evaluation of Dramatizations of the Passion 147

Daisenberger, Father Alois 3, 16, 20, 21, 42, 126; *Früchte der Passionsbetrachtung* 20

Edison, Thomas 12, 131, 132, 134
Edison Manufacturing Company 12
Ettal Monastery 1, 16, 20, 23, 28, 48

Fluger, Tobias 28
14 Stations 62
Francis of Assisi 123
Freier, Korbinian 25, 29, 30
Friedman, Saul 37–38, 39
Früchte der Passionsbetrachtung 20

Gibson, Mel 13, 37, 131, 149–151, 156, 164; *The Passion of the Christ* 13, 37, 131, 149–151, 153, 156
Goffman, Erving 111, 112, 120
The Great Passion Play 143–144, 178
Die Große Passion 24, 53, 88

Hageneier, Stefan 162, 166, 176, 177
haggadah 45
Heidelberg Passion Play 8, 11, 12, 88–105
Hitler, Adolf 2, 7, 34, 39, 76, 97, 101, 107, 135, 136, 148, 180
Hochhuth, Rolf 36; *Der Stellvertreter* (The Deputy) 36
The Holy Night 137–139
Huber, Otto 3, 7, 21, 33, 40, 41, 46, 53–54, 55, 56, 57, 63, 88, 90, 105, 153, 163, 176, 179, 180

Jesus of Montreal 164
John XXIII 36
Joseph and His Brothers 161
Judas 24, 40, 44–45, 76, 121, 169, 177

Karaca, Abdullah Kenan 176–177, 179
Kempe, Margery 93, 124
Krauskopf, Rabbi Joseph 35, 38–39, 75, 76, 86
Krishna 12, 114–118, 119, 124, 125, 127

Lang, Anton 21, 79, 80, 133–136
Lang, Raymond 40
Lebedene Bilder see *Tableau vivant*
Levin, Hanoch 56, 60; *The Torments of Job* 60
Lewis, John J. 132, 133
Ludwig II 33, 68, 78

MacColl, the Rev. Malcolm 70, 72
Mair, Joseph 28
Mann, Thomas 161; *Joseph and His Brothers* 161
Mayakovsky, Vladimir 55; *Mystery Bouffe* 55

194 Index

Mayet, Frederik 9, 13, 21, 23, 24, 25–28, 41, 48, 104, 105, 109, 152, 160–167
McClay, John J. 136
Mead, George Herbert 111–112
Merkel, Angela 165
Mödl, Ludwig 42, 46
Molloy, George 74
Munich Volkstheater 56, 160, 161
Muslims 21, 27, 49, 67, 176, 177, 179
Mystery Bouffe 55

National Conference of Catholic Bishops (U.S.) 38, 146, 147; *Criteria for the Evaluation of Dramatizations of the Passion* 147
The National Pilgrimage Play 140
Nes, Adi 56, 61; *Biblical Stories* 61; *Untitled (Last Supper)* 61
Network (film) 130
Newman, Barnett 56, 59; *Stations of the Cross* 59–60
Nostra Aetate (In Our Times) 36, 40

Oberammergau Passion Play: 1860 Production 16, 68, 75, 85; 1870 Production 28, 67, 68, 78; 1880 Production 20, 71, 75, 77, 86, 132; 1890 Production 69, 74, 77, 78, 79, 86, 87, 131, 132, 134; 1900 Production 20, 30, 32, 38, 68, 71, 72, 78, 79, 80, 87, 165; 1910 Production 78; 1922 Production 2, 20, 33, 73, 133; 1930 Production 7, 24, 39, 107, 133, 134, 135, 136; 1934 Production 2, 7, 39, 91, 97, 99, 134, 135, 136, 141, 168; 1940 Production (cancelled) 2, 7, 40, 136; 1950 Production 2, 7, 12, 23, 36, 86; 1960 Production 36, 86; 1970 Production 16, 37, 162–163; 1980 Production 33, 37, 40, 46, 140, 162, 165; 1990 Production 8, 21, 27, 33, 37, 40, 176; 2000 Production 7, 22, 24, 34, 37, 40, 41, 46, 62, 90, 107, 152, 153, 160, 161, 163, 164, 176, 179; 2010 Production 4, 5, 6–13, 16, 17, 21, 22–26, 38–40, 41–48, 49, 53, 57–63, 66, 78, 79–84, 88–93, 102–104, 109, 111, 119, 120, 131, 142, 145–153, 160–167, 176, 177, 178, 179; 2020 Production 13, 146, 162, 167, 176–180
The Oberammergau Passion Play (1897 film) 12, 131–132
The Oberammergau Passion Play: Original American Version 144–145
Oberammergau: The Troubling Story of the World's Most Famous Passion Play 2, 9, 40, 67, 149
Die Oberammergauer Leidenschaft 24
O'Reilly, P.J. 74

Pacelli, Cardinal Eugenio Maria Giuseppe Giovanni *see Pius XII*
Parks, Suzan-Lori 145
Pasolini, Pier 164
Passio Nova 16

The Passion of the Christ 13, 37, 131, 149–151, 153, 156
Passion Play 8, 11, 13, 91, 96, 97–104.145, 168–175
The Passion Play (Union City, N.J.) 139–140
Passover 37, 38, 40, 42, 44, 45, 62, 150
Paul VI 36
Pius IX 33
Pius XII 33
Plato 108, 110, 125
Preisinger, Anton 136
The Prince of Peace Passion Play at the Holy City of the Wichitas 142

râs lila 12, 114–115, 116–118, 127
Ratti, Cardinal Ambrogio Damiano Achille *see Pius XI*
Ratzinger, Cardinal Joseph Alois *see Benedict XVI*
Reiser, Eva-Maria 24, 25
Richter, Andreas 21, 23, 30, 48, 109, 152, 160
Roman Catholic Church 3, 4, 5, 32, 33, 34, 36, 48–49, 68, 69, 146, 163, 178
Rosner, Father Ferdinand 3, 16, 20, 33, 86, 102, 107, 102, 120, 122, 128; *Passio Nova* 16
Ruhl, Sarah 8, 11, 12, 13, 88, 91, 96, 97–104, 143, 144, 145, 168–175; *Passion Play* 8, 11, 13, 91, 96, 97–104.145, 168–175

St. Peter and Paul Church (Oberammergau Village) 16, 33
Second Vatican Council 36, 40, 67, 82
Sellar, Alexander Craig 75, 85, 86
Senesh, Hannah 11
Shapiro, James 2, 4, 7, 9, 33, 36, 40, 67, 74, 75, 86, 92, 103, 105, 107, 121, 149, 153; *Oberammergau: The Troubling Story of the World's Most Famous Passion Play* 2, 9, 40, 67, 149
Smith, Gerald L.K. 143, 144
Stations of the Cross 59–60
Der Stellvertreter (The Deputy) 36
Stevenson, Christine Wetherhill 140
Stoddard, John L. 132, 133
Stöger, Maximillian 27
Stückl, Christian 3, 8, 21, 23, 27, 28, 41, 45, 46, 48, 53, 54, 55, 56, 62, 63, 153, 160, 162, 163, 164, 167, 176, 177, 180
Sundén, Hjalmar 112, 114

Tableau vivant 11, 12, 26, 40, 46, 57, 61, 62–63, 78, 81, 88–90, 94, 100, 102, 103, 104, 105–110, 117, 119–124, 125–126, 148, 150, 151, 166, 167
Thomas Cook (travel firm) 21, 71, 132
Thomas of Celano 123
Tillich, Paul 122–123
Torah 39, 42, 43, 59, 82, 150
The Torments of Job 60

Untitled (Last Supper) 61

Vatican II *see* Second Vatican Council
Veronica's Veil 139
"The Vow" 2, 4, 5, 13, 20, 21, 32, 49, 73, 83
Vrindavan 35. 110, 115–118, 124, 127

Weimar Republic 133, 136
Weiss, Father Othmar 3, 20, 103, 126
Weltgerichtspiel (Last Judgment Play) 93

White Crucifixion 59
Wilson, Robert 62; *14 Stations* 62
World War I 2, 33, 133, 140
World War II 2, 7, 34, 67, 131, 133, 136, 139

Yellow Crucifixion 59

The Zion Passion Play 142–143
Zwink, Anton 23
Zwink, Markus 162, 176, 177

www.ingramcontent.com/pod-product-compliance
Lightning Source LLC
Chambersburg PA
CBHW032101300426
44116CB00007B/840